CHARLIE CHAPLIN'S
ONE-MAN SHOW

BY DAN KAMIN

FOREWORD BY MARCEL MARCEAU

THE SCARECROW PRESS, INC.
METUCHEN, N.J., & LONDON 1984

Excerpts on pages 1 and 35 from Chaplin, Charles, *My Autobiography* (New York: Simon & Schuster, 1964). Reprinted with permission of The Bodley Head. Quotations are otherwise noted as they appear in the text.

Library of Congress Cataloging in Publication Data

Kamin, Dan, 1946–
   Charlie Chaplin's one-man show.

   Includes index.
   1. Chaplin, Charlie, 1889–1977.   I. Title.
PN2287.C5K34   1984   791.43'028'0924   83-20396
ISBN 0-8108-1675-X

Designed by Beth Ellis

For Hilary

Contents

Acknowledgments

Over the years so many friends, family members, students and colleagues have helped me with the development of the ideas in this book—sometimes simply by patiently listening—that I can hardly acknowledge them individually. I particularly valued conversations with Virginia Cherrill Martini, still beautiful in her seventies, and film scholar Timothy Lyons, one of the few people I have met who is as deeply involved with Chaplin as I am.

Many offered encouragement along the way, and in this regard I am particularly indebted to my publisher, Scarecrow Press, for their flexibility and courage in the production of the book.

For the illustrations so important to the book, I have received indispensable help from Blackhawk Films, Kino Films, The Pittsburgh Playhouse, and the Center for Film and Theater Research of the Wisconsin State Historical Society. To realize my very ambitious goal of illustrating the book with images that have never appeared in book form before, I was assisted by the expert talents of filmmaker Brady Lewis, photographer Walt Seng, and Laurel Entertainment.

I must also record my indebtedness to Jewel Walker, my mime teacher, whose superb lectures on Delsarte vividly demonstrated the power of Delsarte's methods.

Finally, it is with special pleasure that I thank Mr. Marcel Marceau for his enthusiasm for the book and for gracing it with a Foreword. The hours we spent together were magical. His reenactment—to the last nuance—of the ending of *City Lights* will always be a treasured memory.

Preface

The seed for this book was planted several years ago when I attended a public showing of early comedy shorts. Among them were Chaplin's *The Masquerader,* made during his first year at Keystone in 1914, and Buster Keaton's *Cops,* a 1922 film often singled out as Keaton's finest short. I thought it was unfair to juxtapose the mature Keaton with the beginning Chaplin, and was certain that the audience would respond more strongly to *Cops.*

I got a surprise. While *Cops* drew appreciative intermittent laughter from the audience (which was a good mix of adults and children), *The Masquerader* had them laughing, giggling and roaring throughout. Apparently something was operating beyond the plot and gags, which were rather primitive in this Chaplin film. I realized that the audience was responding much as an audience in 1914 must have—somehow the mere appearance of the Chaplin character was winning them over. Looking at the film more carefully, I noticed that even though he wasn't doing anything particularly ingenious, Chaplin seemed to be totally involved with what he *was* doing, and further, that his feelings at every moment were communicated to the audience with crystal clarity. A warmth came over the audience. We cared about how this fellow felt and what was happening in the film to affect him. By contrast, the Keaton film seemed much more cerebral, forcing us to be aware of the director/gag writer at work. The children particularly seemed to move in and out of Keaton's brilliant, cold comedy.

Chaplin's 1914 films—short, crude comedies made at a phenomenal rate of one per week—brought him meteoric fame. Although his later films confirmed his genius, it was the early ones that drew the public magnetically to the theatres. By the end of that first year, Essanay, his second producing company, could legitimately advertise in a trade journal that

MILLIONS ARE LAUGHING WITH

CHARLES CHAPLIN

THE WORLD'S GREATEST COMEDIAN IS NOW

WITH ESSANAY

There were other popular stars at the time but none who inspired so much outright physical imitation. Theatre owners sponsored "Chaplin contests" and the first of a long line of Chaplin imitators began to appear on the vaudeville stage and in films. Lines of chorus girls, doing the famous walk, sang "Those Charlie Chaplin Feet."

Tin Pan Alley was quick to capitalize on what Chaplin himself agreed was probably a temporary fad, and in 1915 there were more than twenty popular songs about Chaplin, with titles like "Charlie Chaplin Walk" and "Charlie Chaplin Waddle." By 1916 there was a thriving market for Chaplin novelties such as squirting rings, statuettes, and costume kits. In magazines and newspapers cartoons, jokes and poems featuring Chaplin proliferated:

> This is a very curious world,
> So many things are happ'nin';
> For all the girls
> Wear Pickford curls,
> And boys play Charlie Chaplin.*

Motion Picture Magazine (May 1916).

If one looks at the early Chaplin films in livingrooms or with small museum audiences, the "Chaplin craze" seems even more remarkable, since those films require a relatively large audience to work their peculiar spell. Isolated, one is too aware of the crudeness of acting, directing and gags. In addition, many newspaper critics saw Chaplin's character and performances as vulgar and even obscene. In spite of all this, he became by the end of 1914 the industry's most popular star.

Another phenomenon that, like his popularity, is endlessly discussed by critics and biographers is the speed with which Chaplin "discovered" his tramp character. The familiar costume and many of the mannerisms were fairly complete by the time of his second film appearance, in *Kid Auto Races at Venice*. By contrast, Harold Lloyd made several hundred short comedies before discovering and molding his "glasses" character.

Both the speed of Chaplin's development and his virtually instant popularity offer a clue to the Chaplin phenomenon which is confirmed by comparing his early appearances with later ones. It is that Chaplin's *way* of moving was complete and intact from his earliest appearances. Although he made rapid strides during his first three years in film in plot and gag construction, as well as in the development of his supporting players, his own movement qualities changed little. It was the sophistication of Chaplin's presentation-in-movement of his character that allowed him to rise above the material in his early films.

DAN KAMIN

Billboard image of Chaplin and Edna Purviance, c. 1915. Author's collection.

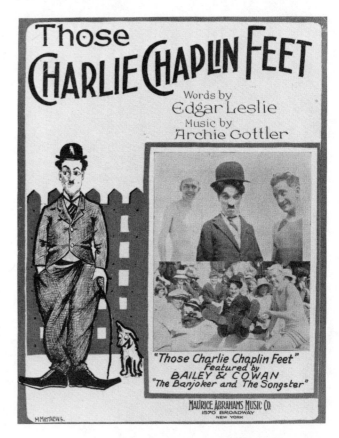

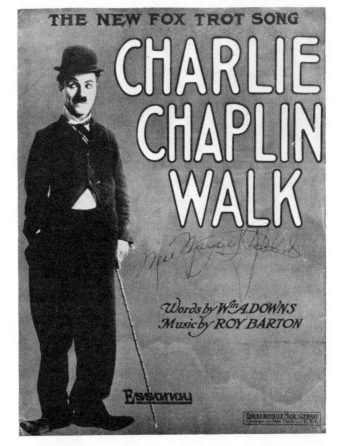

Above: Chaplin and Eric Campbell, in a theatre display poster, 1919–1923. Author's collection. *Right top and bottom:* Two exploitation songs about Chaplin from 1915–1916. In simplifying Chaplin's image for his drawing, the artist virtually eliminated Chaplin's distinctive posture and stance.

Foreword
by Marcel Marceau

Charlie Chaplin must be considered, along with Shakespeare, Goldoni and Molière, one of the creators of pure theater. What can I add, even with my experience as a mime, to what hundreds of critics and essayists have already beautifully expressed about Chaplin's work and his philosophies?

I still remember my own childhood and how he changed my life and contributed to make me what I am today. If Chaplin enthralled millions of people the world over who laughed and cried at his pantomimes, it is because there was a secret to his art . . . a special chemistry he revealed to humanity which made him one of the supreme artists of this world.

My friend Dan Kamin is a professional mime, whom I have known for years. While I was touring the United States he came to see me in my dressing room after one of my performances, with a manuscript entitled "Charlie Chaplin's One-Man Show." So many important books have been written about this great artist who inspired not only my work, but also the work of thousands of other artists of the twentieth century, that I was curious to find out if anything new could be said.

I began reading the manuscript and as I discovered Kamin's personal approach and analysis of Chaplin's professional craftsmanship, my interest grew. Instead of trying to sentimentalize or get metaphysical about Chaplin's life, Kamin thoroughly analyzes Chaplin's technique and reveals to us the art of a man who, solely through the mastery of his body, could dramatically convey all aspects of our lives. Like an historian, Dan Kamin examines all aspects of Chaplin's actions. He enlarges Chaplin's work as if using a magnifying glass, and we learn how this great artist adapted his style of English Music Hall pantomime to cinematography. We learn that Chaplin began his career as a young boy, playing a cat in "Cinderella"; we witness his love for Dickens' characters; we follow his adaptation to visual, musical slapstick, and his rise to silent comedy and drama. He discovered how to adapt theater pantomime to film techniques—this was part of his genius. Thus, we are exposed to Chaplin's magic, to his presence, identity and magnetic attraction which led millions of people to identify with the little Tramp. We follow Chaplin's career as a dancer, acrobat, actor and mime through the continuous growth of his creativity. Through Kamin's book we learn details about Chaplin's choice of costumes as well as his physical postures. We see him juggling with or without props, and confronting dramatic and comic situations with all the mystery and grace of a silent mime.

Dan Kamin draws a portrait of the great actor in both silent and speaking roles. After all, Charlie Chaplin's silent Tramp and the speaking actor were the same man. Even in a speaking role, Charlie Chaplin remained a mime actor. No one had ever played in pantomime drama like him. Chaplin remains the "supermarionette" actor who suspends his body as if hanging in space even when his feet touch the ground. He is always pulled by invisible strings and through this artifice he fills our hearts and eyes with the greatest admiration. All our weaknesses and heroic dreams are exposed to us in silence.

This is the essence of the art of mime.

Chaplin was simultaneously similar to and different from other comic actors of his time, such as Keaton, Langdon, Laurel and Hardy and Harold Lloyd. Their visual appearances and their characters are altogether different despite the fact that they came from the same stage training, but they all embody the last decades of the Victorian Era and even in the beginning of the Industrial Age, their art looks contemporary. Within the art of Chaplin and Keaton, and even in that of Laurel and Hardy, the Theater of the Absurd is foretold. They blossomed through the winds of our disturbed and violent world. This is why they remain timeless.

When I was asked to write this Foreword, I felt a little embarrassed . . . how was I even to begin to draw a picture of him? My love for Chaplin started when, as a kid, I saw him in *City Lights*. Afterwards I took my father's bowler hat and with ink, I drew a Charlie-Chaplin moustache under my nose. I created my first children's mime theater in the thirties, fifteen years before entering the mime class of the man who was to become my theater mime master—Etienne Decroux.

I have always approached Chaplin's work with eagerness and gravity which grew through the evolution of my own career as a mime. I felt the density of his art which reveals the essence of people and their behavior . . . the imperfect pupils of God. Mime, inspired by the sacred, therefore becomes sublime. Chaplin's work arouses compassion, admiration, pity and adulation. From master to slave; vanquished or victorious, he emerges unharmed from all cinematographic beatings and wars, projecting his tragicomic tales in the limelight of our lives.

Chaplin moved in all directions, from circus mime gags to metaphysical and melodramatic attitudes. He could express, through silence, humanity's eternal vulnerability. Yes, life is ephemeral, but art is everlasting.

When I created my mime character, Bip, in 1947, I realized the difference which exists between theater mime technique belonging to the stage and mime technique which has to be adapted to films. In stage mime, illusions create reality; in films, reality creates illusions. In the theater, Bip fights on the battlefield of life, surrounded by invisible forces. He takes on their volume, weight and size while leaning against invisible mantelpieces, going through invisible doors, and struggling against winds, seas and mountains.

Whether as a tightrope walker or a flying angel, in his films Chaplin is constantly fighting, like Don Quixote, against windmills. This artist reveals his genius in a real world. Here are the props and all the characters. It is in the street—whether in London or New York—that Chaplin fights for life. Hired for a job or fired a little later on, he remains the eternal Tramp, in search of a place where he can live with dignity. In a wealthy society, among miserable immigrants, factory workers, or gold-rush prospectors, Chaplin touched all subjects from pastoral comedy to street drama. He shows us love stories, city battles and other such Molièresque situations which will be eternal examples of the odysseys of men on our earth. Charlie Chaplin creates all those adventures in an industrial world with the most poetic and pathetic power film technique can reveal.

In theatrical mime art, time and space are the leading keys which open doors to artistry. Therefore the technique has to adapt itself to those conditions. In classical dance, the dancer glides through the air, freeing his body from weight. In mime, attitude is a counterpoint to action. The artist is constantly in search of gravity—defining an action with only the body under the lights, surrounded by the emptiness of the stage. Time is always compressed with an elliptic sense of drama. If Charlie Chaplin walks on an endless road, the mime walks in place, giving the illusion of continuous movement while re-creating elements, animals, objects, people, and so forth. Yet, we mimes have something in common with Chaplin; Bip, like Charlie the Tramp, is a soldier, a street musician, a tailor . . . and therefore follows the same rules of the eternal underdog, fighting in a rough world. Chaplin is the real master, being the first to make this universal theme vivid to us with his legendary art.

Compared to films, theater pantomime glows through the economy of its means. Films create a realistic wonder where the imagination of the public is raised by the wonderful medium which allows the artist to display his talent. In the theater, mime illusions enhance the imagination of the spectator, who fills in the cinematic details in his own mind. For example, in *The Pilgrim* Charlie mimes David and Goliath with two or three gestures in the middle of a longer story, it is only an interlude. In the theater Bip plays David and Goliath in four minutes and it is complete unto itself. In a sense I agree with Chaplin's implication that in films, art exists to hide artifice. Can we not conclude that in pantomime, artifice is to be shown? Therefore the mimed actions have to look real in a film. We need to see the child, the young man, the mature man, and the old man until his death. In theater the mime actor, without any change of costume or makeup will mime an elliptic time where we see the actor grow, blossom and fade in front of an audience. Therefore we wonder how Chaplin's pantomimes would have evolved if films never came into existence. This leaves the door open to speculation. But the "ifs" do not change the reality of history. It is wonderful to witness Chaplin's genius.

In the movie world his silent outcry is part of each of us. He has become as indispensable to us as Mozart, Bach, Michelangelo and Da Vinci. Chaplin was the whole Commedia dell'arte in one man. For a long time we shall see him running in front of mirrors which reproduce him infinitely in *The Circus* . . . we shall laugh at his gags in front of the statue in *City Lights* . . . we shall hold our breath before his boxing scenes . . . we shall be astonished to see him running away from cops with such grace and dexterity . . . we shall watch in wonderment as he changes himself into a lamp when pursued by cops tracking him down. No one in our lifetime will ever forget Chaplin's last look at the flower girl in *City Lights*. His eyes and tragic smile embrace all humanity and raise in our hearts deep compassion. Chaplin remains a mythic poet, an angel, a seeing brother, a mime character representing the essence of humanity. Through the artifice of a supreme style, his creativity evolved and showed him at his best. Through Dan Kamin's *Charlie Chaplin's One-Man Show* we are able to live through Chaplin's odyssey.

Only a mime practitioner could approach the subject of mime technique as it occurs in films. In all Chaplin's films silent actresses and actors surround him gracefully and we admire their talent and their reactions to Chaplin's actions. They are wonderful partners but Charlie Chaplin remains the leading hero in the center. And from there the great star he was will shine forever.

Best,
Marcel Marceau
'83

Iris In: Introduction

These days no one writes a book on Charlie Chaplin without asking at the outset, "why *another* book on Chaplin?"

My answer is simple. I wrote this because it's the book I've always wanted to *read* on Chaplin.

There are many excellent books about Chaplin, ranging from scholarly biographies (Theodore Huff, John McCabe) to sympathetic or hostile recollections by family members and associates (Charles Chaplin, Jr., Lita Grey Chaplin, Max Eastman). Analytical and interpretive volumes range from simple picture books with plot descriptions and other data, to Freudian interpretations of the man and his work (Parker Tyler), to attempts to place him in a mythologic context (Robert Payne). Often the books present Chaplin as a figure isolated from his own film contemporaries. Books about other comedians invariably draw parallels and comparisons with Chaplin, but many books on Chaplin (including his own 1964 *My Autobiography*) don't even mention the work of others. These books often treat the films as monuments and seek their philosophical, sociological or moral meanings.

What do I have to add to this vast and varied body of literature on Chaplin? My contribution is in my approach. As a professional mime performer, I am fascinated with Chaplin as a craftsman. Chaplin's films are *the* most beautiful and powerful manifestations of the art I have ever seen. In this book I will explore the mechanics of Chaplin's films—how he achieves the extraordinary effects which make his films at once funny and compelling. A glance at the literature on Chaplin demonstrates that, for most authors, the task of writing about Chaplin is more a mission than a commission. His work grips, obsesses, and stimulates poetic flights in his commentators, most of whom believe they have found the key to the essential Chaplin.

To examine movement is not easy. Anyone can observe it, but discussing it intelligibly is another matter altogether. Due to my own training I am familiar with various systems for analyzing move-ment. To these I have added large doses of personal opinion and insight, based upon both my performing experience and my years of watching, enjoying, and studying the Chaplin films.

One of the impressive things about the films is the extent to which they are solo creations. As actor, director, producer, writer and composer, Chaplin created arguably the most thoroughly personal works in the history of this most corporate art.

The greatest of Chaplin's skills is unquestionably his mime ability. Mime . . .

> *was Chaplin's supreme gift. No amount of intelligence, perception, emotion and ideas could have taken its place, for without the ability to translate them into gesture and movement, the 'Little Fellow' would have remained a dead letter, a character Chaplin might have dreamed about but never have realized.* [1]

Part One of this book, "The Mime," deals squarely with demystifying Chaplin's way of moving. To do this I detail his background training, his actual movement on the screen, and his ways of adapting his stage-movement style to the film medium.

Part Two, "One-Man Show," examines three aspects of Chaplin's films that emanate directly from his unique physical style. In Chapter 5 "The Magician," I discuss Chaplin's magical transformation gags. Critics have been applauding and discussing these gags since the beginning of Chaplin's career. I isolate eight major variations on the gag in the hope of providing new insights into Chaplin's comic development. In Chapter 6, "The Juggler," I deal with Chaplin's principles of characterization. Finally, in Chapter 7, "The Dancer," I explore, more deeply than has yet been done, the nature and implications of the dance-like qualities of Chaplin's films.

In Parts One and Two I treat Chaplin's career thematically rather than taking a film-by-film, chronological approach. This serves my purposes for eval-

Part One
The Mime

"... I was a pantomimist, and in that medium I was unique and, without false modesty, a master."

Charles Chaplin

1
The Boy Professional

Like all proud parents, Chaplin's mother and father liked to show off their child. But unlike most parents, they were seasoned stage performers. Charlie was born in 1889 in London. His parents appeared as singers in operettas as well as in music halls; impersonations of popular theatrical figures were part of their acts. Chaplin's mother, Hannah, was also a dancer. On Chaplin's testimony, she was a master mime, his first and best teacher. His father, Charles, was a popular singer in music halls of the 1880s and composed many of his own songs. His increasing alcoholism prematurely ended his life at age thirty-seven.

By the time Chaplin was two or three years old he was being pulled out of bed at night to entertain theatrical friends of the family with recitations, imitation, and dancing. His parents separated around that time and Hannah continued her stage career until Chaplin was five. When her voice failed her on stage, young Charles was pushed on in her stead and made a great success with a popular ballad, "Jack Jones," encoring with dance and imitation. It was his first and her last solo stage appearance. She worked for a time in a dance company, then quit the theatre altogether to eke out a living as a seamstress. Until her mental breakdown when Chaplin was twelve, she kept up her tutelage. They would sit by the window for hours, Hannah imitating and making astute observations about passersby. In addition to instilling her habits of observation, she taught Chaplin basic dancing and music hall comedy material and encouraged his budding talents and skills.

Chaplin began putting these skills to good use at an early age by dancing to barrel organs outside public houses (pubs), and becoming a school celebrity during one of his infrequent periods of atten-

dance by going from class to class reciting a humorous monologue, "Miss Priscilla's Cat."

At age nine, with the approval of his parents, Chaplin joined the Eight Lancashire Lads, a clog dancing act. He toured with them for a year and a half on a grueling schedule of rehearsing and performing two or three shows a day. During the Christmas season of 1900 the troupe appeared in the pantomime *Cinderella* at the London Hippodrome. Chaplin played a cat, and displayed the common touch that was prominent in his later work. He walked up to a dog and sniffed its behind! Inspired by the laughter, he looked at the audience and winked (his costume had an eye-wink device), repeated his sniffs, and for a finale walked to the front of the stage and lifted his leg, dog-style. The manager was justifiably fearful of his theatre's being closed down, and made sure there were no repetitions. Charlie continued in the role without this improvisation for another three months.

During his period with the Lancashire Lads, Chaplin began having the problems with words which were to plague him throughout his professional career. He prevailed upon the manager of the troupe to let him try a solo turn, an impersonation of the popular actor Bransby Williams, who portrayed various characters out of Dickens. Chaplin's voice was apparently too weak to put this over, and the act was not well-received.

However, being a legitimate member of "the profession" gave Chaplin access to the world of the music hall and theatre, and took advantage of it. He continually added to his repertoire of impressions and imitations of the acts and actors who struck his fancy. Prophetically, he and another boy in the troupe dreamed of a comedy tramp act, to be called the Millionaire Tramps. (A recent documentary film on Chaplin's life and art was called *The Gentleman Tramp*.)

Following a two-year period in school, Chaplin "graduated" to roles on the legitimate stage. His producer/director in several productions, H. A. Saintsbury, taught him much about stagecraft during those years. Rehearsing with Chaplin, Saintsbury patiently taught him the rudiments of "straight" acting, as practiced in 1903. Since most of Chaplin's films contain strong elements of sentimental Victorian melodrama, we can assume that this training was thorough. Saintsbury was a perfectionist in technique and timing; he toned down Chaplin's tendency to mug and introduced him to the actor's craft.

Chaplin played stage roles for two years, notably a long provincial run as the page boy in William Gillette's *Sherlock Holmes*. By now a respected professional, he often entertained other actors with his impersonations, continuing the habit begun almost in infancy. Much of the material he later included in films originated or was practiced in this way.

Following a brief period "between engagements," Chaplin worked with a music hall revue, *Casey's Circus*. This burlesque revue featured a troupe of boys doing take-offs on famous people of the day. Charlie's subject was "Doctor" Walford Bodie, a patent medicine quack. Hoping to be rediscovered by a manager and returned to theatre work, he developed what he considered to be an accurate and dramatic impersonation of the "doctor," even while he was being rehearsed in a conventional burlesque version. He later described the opening night:

> Once in the glare of the footlights, I dropped into the part, determined to play it, play it well, and hold the audience. . . I advanced slowly, impressively, feeling the gaze of the crowd, and, with a carefully studied gesture, hung my cane-I held it by the wrong end! Instead of hanging on my arm, as I expected it, it clattered on the stage. Startled, I stooped to pick it up, and my high silk hat fell from my head. I grasped it, put it on quickly, and, paper wadding falling out, I found my whole head buried in its black depths.
>
> A great burst of laughter came from the audience. When, pushing the hat back, I went desperately on with my serious lines, the crowd roared, held its sides, shrieked with mirth till it gasped. The more serious I was, the funnier it struck the audience. I came off at last, pursued by howls of laughter and wild applause, which called me back again. I had made the hit of the evening.

This account is from *Charlie Chaplin's Own Story*, a 1916 autobiography which is blatantly fictitious. Its ghost writer probably based it on interviews made with Chaplin during the incredibly busy and fertile period toward the end of 1915, and Chaplin had it withdrawn soon after publication. Indeed, the account seems too pat, Chaplin carefully establishing his serious intent to better set up the "accidental" comedy of errors. In fact, the routine seems like many of his film sequences, particularly the "absent-minded husband" opening of *The Idle Class* (1921). Regardless, it captures the flavor of his peculiar combination of seriousness and broad slapstick, a combination which seemed to be a forte with English clowns and with Chaplin's next mentor, Fred Karno, in particular. Karno reigned for many years as the undisputed king of music hall comedy. He had as many as thirty companies simultaneously touring England, Europe, and America.

While Karno exploited the juggling and song-and-dance burlesques that were music hall staples, the real brilliance of the former circus acrobat lay in his largely wordless slapstick sketches. Often set to music, these sketches spotlighted troupes trained to incredible precision. As Chaplin later stated:

> . . . each man working for Karno had to have perfect timing and had to know the peculiarities of everyone else in the cast so that we could, collectively, achieve a cast tempo. . . . It took about a year for an actor to get the repertoire of a dozen shows down pat. Karno required us to know a number of parts so that the players could be interchanged. When one left the company it was like taking a screw or a pin out of a very delicate piece of machinery.[1]

In his later writing Chaplin ignores the creative contributions of his collaborators and colleagues. But he speaks proudly of his days with Fred Karno.

After his fourteen-month run with *Casey's Circus* ended, Chaplin followed his brother Sydney into the Karno troupe. He was eighteen and remained with Karno until entering films at age twenty-four. Evidently he had decided to give up his legitimate theatrical aspirations. Indeed, to work with Karno was a considerable step up. Chaplin made the most of the opportunity and became one of Karno's featured comedians.

Karno's "factory" of comedy more than matched Saintsbury's perfectionism in acting and stage technique. To his already impressive physical skills

Chaplin now added the Karno brand of acrobatics. From Karno's leading players he learned many of the quirky mannerisms that were to make his film appearances so distinctive. For example, from Fred Kitchen he learned the trick of tossing a cigarette behind him and kicking it backward. He also learned an array of kicks and falls from Kitchen, and his tramp character walk may well have been close to Kitchen's splay-foot shuffle. Perhaps even more important was Karno's insistence on long rehearsals to attain his characteristic troupe timing and precision, which later became Chaplin's working method in film.

Though at first skeptical of Chaplin's youth and shyness, Karno recognized his mime talent. Chaplin's first significant role was in a sketch called *The Football March,* playing opposite of one of Karno's chief comedians, Harry Weldon. Chaplin's role was to attempt to bribe goalkeeper Weldon into throwing the game. His later description of the scene has the same feeling as his description of his "Dr." Bodie impersonation. With his back to the audience, he established tension, breaking it by turning around to reveal a highly reddened nose; he tripped over a dumbbell and entangled his cane with an upright punching bag: trying to release the cane he was smacked by the bag; trying to hit the bag back he was hit by his cane; suddenly his pants dropped, and looking for the button, he reached down and discarded something, saying, "Those confounded rabbits."

Weldon, waiting in the wings for his entrance cue, was puzzled by all the laughter in a role which previously had functioned only to set off his own performance. Chaplin dragged him into the flow of improvisation, saying, "Quick! I'm undone! A pin!"

The next part Chaplin played was to become his signature role in the Karno company. "The Inebriated Swell" in *Mumming Birds,* Karno's most famous sketch. *Mumming Birds* treated the audience to a show-within-the-show; a succession of beautifully bad variety acts presented behind a false proscenium. Watching the acts from an onstage box was Chaplin, in what was undoubtedly the prototype for his many drunk acts in films. Chaplin's contribution to this already classic routine was to make more physically expressive the drunk's actions and reactions within the box and to bring to it his unique concentration. Stan Laurel, a member of the Karno company at that time, says of his performance:

He even made those of us in the cast break up time after time . . . he had those eyes that absolutely forced you to look at them. He had the damnedest way of looking at an audience. He had the damnedest way of looking at you, on stage . . . they're very dark, the deepest kind of blue, and intense, just like him. And they can dominate anyone they look at. That's a part of the secret of his great success—eyes that make you believe in him whatever he does.[2]

Charlie's performance began as he was ushered to his box, located downstage left. Obviously drunk, he smiled, bowed, and took off his right glove. He tipped the girl, and took off his right glove again—this time an imaginary right glove, showing in mime the absent-mindedness and distorted perceptions of the drunk. He then tried to light a cigarette by pressing it against an electric bulb, thus introducing one of the most pervasive gag devices of his films, treating one object as if it is another. A boy in the box downstage right, opposite Chaplin, held a lit match out to him. Leaning toward it, Chaplin fell out of his box. Such misjudgment of distance was also to become characteristic of his filmic drunk acts.

At that point the curtain on the stage-within-the-stage opened and a variety show began. Charlie chased an awful singer offstage, groaned at a ham actor doing a recitation of "The Trail of the Yukon," imagined a soubrette was singing "You Naughty, Naughty Man" directly to him, and finally challenged and defeated "Marconi Ali, The Terrible Turk, The Greatest Wrestler Ever to Appear Before the British Public." Chaplin defeated the scrawny Ali simply by tickling him to the mat. Given prize money and congratulations, Charlie was asked if there was anything else he would like. "Yes, bring on the girls!" The sketch then ended in a melee of food-throwing, yelling, clothes-ripping, and general uproar.

Chaplin's great success in this role prompted Karno to offer him the important Harry Weldon role in a London production of *The Football Match.* Faced with a role that depended on dialogue, Chaplin's voice, like his mother's, failed. He suffered an attack of laryngitis during rehearsals and, after two unsuccessful performances, was put back in *Mumming Birds.*

Another important and seminal role was *Jimmy the Fearless,* the story of a boy whose parents scolded him and sent him to bed as punishment for coming home late. He dreamed himself into a series of heroic adventures, the last of which was saving his parents from being evicted, only to have the dream turn into the harsh reality of being beaten with a belt by his father. This transition from a romantic or heroic dream into gritty reality was to become a feature of many Chaplin films including; *His Prehistoric Past* (1914), *The Bank* (1915), *Shoulder Arms* (1918), *Sunnyside* (1919), *The Idle Class* (1921), *The Kid* (1921), *The Gold Rush* (1925), *Modern Times* (1936), and *Limelight* (1952).

Doughboy Charlie wakes from his dream of conquest to find himself still in boot camp. *Shoulder Arms.*

After four years in the company, Chaplin was sent to be the leading comedian in one of Karno's American touring troupes. Though the sketch chosen for their debut, *The Wow Wows*, was too verbal for American tastes, Chaplin transcended his material and received excellent notices. But he and the company both scored a much greater success by pre-

senting *Mumming Birds,* slightly revised and retitled *A Night in an English Music Hall.* A reviewer accurately assessed Chaplin's qualities during this tour, in 1911:

> The art of pantomime is recognized in theatredom as one of the most difficult known to the profession. It means that the actor must make known his intentions solely by signs and his general actions. . . . Seated in one of the music boxes is a decidedly hilarious person who evidently is suffering from too many exciting libations and consequently he insists on participating in each act in a manner that is so funny that the audience out front can't help laughing enthusiastically. He scarcely says more than three words during the entire course of the act, yet so funny are his actions that he proves himself one of the best pantomime artists ever seen here.[3]

After a summer in England, Chaplin returned to America for a 1912–13 tour. He had managed to make *The Wow Wows* into a serviceable show, though *A Night in an English Music Hall* remained his great success. Mack Sennett, who had seen Chaplin during the first tour and been struck with his easy, graceful style of movement, was now in a position to offer Chaplin work in his recently formed Keystone Film Company. The rest, as they say, is history.

Notes

[1]Cited in McCabe, John, *Charlie Chaplin* (New York: Doubleday & Co., Inc., 1978), pp. 28–29.

[2]McCabe, *Ibid.,* p. 34.

[3]"Pantomime Star at the Majestic," unsigned article in *The Butte Inter Mountain,* April 18, 1911; reprinted in Chaplin's, *My Life in Pictures* (N.Y.: Grosset & Dunlap, Inc., 1975), p. 66.

2

The Mime on Screen

By the time Chaplin entered the film world at age twenty-four, he was a thoroughly seasoned professional with fifteen full years of hard experience (two years in a dancing company, four on the legitimate stage, and nine as a music hall comedian)—seven of them with Britain's foremost pantomime company. All this experience and training was topped by his recognized genius in pantomime. Unfortunately the development of Chaplin's art can never be traced from its embryonic state because a few photos and contemporary reviews are all that remain of direct source material. The many recollections published later by those who were associated with Chaplin are often contradictory and probably contain strong doses of hindsight wisdom. Regrettably, Chaplin himself was one of the main contributors to the maze of legends and contradictions that followed him throughout his life. Whether the pain he felt as a result of his being on his own at such an early age compelled him to distort his history is a matter for speculation. Certainly Chaplin's profession was his main source of stability throughout his life. Whatever the factual reality of his personal life, however, we may be sure that his emotional reality was distilled into the films.

The only concrete and thorough evidence available begins with the films. From 1914, preserved on film is Chaplin's development of his already formidable skills. He is the first, and arguably the only, mime of genius in history whose work has been so preserved.

One of the difficulties of watching films from a past era is in distinguishing what is intended to be stylized playing and parody from the mannerisms and movements characteristic of "real" people of the period. From century to century, and even from decade to decade, fashions in movement change as do fashions in clothing. Films reflect these changes at the same time that they stylize and exaggerate them.

For a contemporary audience, films from the mid-teens inevitably have a certain quaintness. This quaintness is sometimes intriguing and sometimes maddeningly boring. Although the comedies tend to hold up better than the serious films, it is often difficult—particularly with Sennett films—to know what was intended to be funny.

But even in 1914, Chaplin's performances were seen as strange and striking. The words "peculiar," "eccentric," and "quaint" kept popping up in reviews. The Karno quality of serious, sober attention in the midst of violent slapstick was recognized by perceptive critics, as was Chaplin's investigation of the comic possibilities of virtually all his action on the screen:

> His odd little tricks of manner and his refusal to do the most simple things in an ordinary way are essential features of his method, which thus far has defied successful imitation.[1]

> Chaplin possesses that indefinable something which makes you laugh heartily and without restraint at what in others would be commonplace actions.[2]

To begin to understand "that indefinable something" which put Chaplin so quickly at the head of his profession, one must examine his medium of communication—his body.

Chaplin was a very small man, about 5'4". In his own description, "my head's too big for my body, my arms are too short for my body, and my hands are to small for my arms."[3] In *The Pilgrim*, made when Chaplin was 34, a wanted poster describes convict Charlie thus:

> *May be disguised. 30 to 35 years of age. About five feet four inches in height. Weight about 125 pounds. Pale face. Black bushy hair sometimes parted in the middle. Small black moustache. Blue eyes. Small hands, large feet. Extremely nervous. Walks with feet turned out.*

Nevertheless, possibly influenced by Chaplin's grace of movement, Somerset Maugham described him as having "a neat figure, admirably proportioned; his hands and feet are well-shaped and small."[4] Max Eastman rhapsodized about:

> *. . . the trim grace and veritable perfection of his build and carriage, which is that of the prince of tumblers, tap dancers, tightrope walkers—the prince of agility and poise—harmonize with the classic perfection of his head to make a unitary impression of great beauty. He seems to possess, above all, complete and exquisite integration.*[5]

Photos of Chaplin out of his tramp costume, or occasionally wearing bathing suits in such films as *The Cure* and *The Adventurer* show him to be in excellent physical condition. He appears to have not an ounce of fat on him, and at the same time he has none of the muscle-bound look of the physical culturist, like his friend Douglas Fairbanks. Buster Keaton, possibly from his more strenuous brand of acrobatic comedy, had a much harder musculature than Chaplin. Chaplin's development seems admirably suited to move his small frame, while at the same time preserving maximum flexibility.

Considering Chaplin's body section by section reveals aspects of his physical technique of communication.

There is a striking contrast between the way Chaplin holds his head and Keaton's head position: Keaton often thrusts his head forward of his body, reinforcing his frequent attitude of puzzlement, his straining to see and figure out the world, comically expressed by his endless mechanical devices and ruses to adapt to it. Chaplin, on the other hand, positions his head directly and squarely above his trunk. (His shock of hair extending in back makes his head appear to be centered even when it is slightly forward.) This implies a certain self-contain-

ment, aptly reinforced by his quaint ways. Comically, this is also expressed by Chaplin's consistent attempts to change the world to adapt to himself, as by pulling someone toward him with his cane. Dramatically, it is expressed by his "outsider" status.

Chaplin was hired by Sennett to replace Ford Sterling, then the reigning comic "heavy" (villain) at the studio. Mimicking some of Sterling's gestures, Chaplin, during this early period, occasionally thrusts his head forward to indicate aggression, strikingly altering his character. He soon abandons the head-far-forward position, and in fact increases his use of its opposite: the head pulled backward over the trunk, to indicate prideful elegance, in comic contrast to his seedy appearance, or disdain, as when he impersonates royalty.

Another important aspect of Chaplin's use of his head is in his presentation of his face to the camera, most blatantly when he smiles and laughs, often covering his mouth with his hand. These conspiratorial laughs are powerful invitations for the audience to share his point of view in a scene—in fact, we *must* share his point of view to delight in his violence and comeuppance to his enemies. These laughs are either hidden from or disapproved by the other characters in the scene. They are aimed directly at the audience.

The joke is on the diners, the laugh is for us. *The Rink*.

The laughs also invite the audience's collaboration in Charlie's flirtations. Scenes of his slinging his leg onto a girl's lap or pulling her knees to him with his cane seem bold even today. As reviews from the period show, the effect in 1914 was shocking and, in the eyes of many, obscene. It is interesting to note that as Chaplin's sex life became the subject of tabloid headlines, his screen character became less aggressive in making advances towards the women in the films.

Looking at the camera. *A Dog's Life.*

Charlie bows to us after saving the day. *The Pawnshop.*

More subtle than his laughs and coy smiles are his glances. In the early films Chaplin rarely plays a scene without glancing at the camera. In some instances his eyes are not focused on the camera lens, but his face is presented to the audience, in effect inviting them to look into his eyes and increasing their vicarious participation in his emotions. The importance of this device in Chaplin's work can hardly be overestimated. Scenes are consistently set up so that the audience can watch the actions between the characters and at the same time engage in a continuous one-to-one "dialogue" with Chaplin.

His acting thus takes on a presentational, highly stylized quality, a self-consciousness (or audience consciousness) that reaches an exuberant comic peak in the series of films Chaplin made for the Mutual company in 1916–1917. In these films the dialogue with the audience frequently becomes more important than the action with the other characters. In *The Pawnshop* and *The Cure* climactic scenes which have become melodramatic are disrupted when Charlie turns to us with a decorative bow. While the presentational mode was toned down in the more "realistic" features, Chaplin's playing style remains stylized throughout his career.

Nor was he unique in addressing the audience directly. A standard carryover from the stage to early comic films was the "take" directed toward the camera. Chaplin's leading lady from 1915 to 1923, Edna Purviance, directs many "distressed heroine" glances at the camera. Fatty Arbuckle would even direct the camera to tilt upward if he was changing his pants—a playful acknowledgement of the reality of the medium. Both Oliver Hardy and James Findlayson made elaborate use of direct camera stares. The main difference in Chaplin's use of the device is its subtlety and frequency. It becomes so much a part of his screen movement that it is hardly noticeable. Yet the fact is, viewers *never* lose the feeling of his awareness of them. Even when he is involved in outrageous comic blunders he never appears simply stupid, since on one level he shares the audience's participation and enjoyment from an observer's point of view.

Because of his unique playing style, the Chaplin character is able to unify many characteristics and roles, thus standing out from the other Keystone comics, whose portrayals are based primarily on a single amplified characteristic, such as "fat," "dumb," or "pompous."

Chaplin's tramp makeup serves to reinforce his unique style. His wearing of clown-white, in effect, sets him apart from other players whose faces appear gray by comparison. His eyebrows are drawn higher and heavier than his natural brows, and his eyes are heavily outlined in black. The "toothbrush" moustache adds a simple, distinctive spot to his face and serves also to highlight the shape of his nose and alter the shape of his upper lip. His lips are darkened, and the whole is set off by his mop of dark, curly, tousled hair, topped by his too small derby (which recapitulates the shape of his too-small moustache).

One has only to look at a picture of Chaplin out of makeup to see how much of a construction is his screen self. The difference in appearance is startling. Even photos that show Chaplin in costume minus his moustache seem strange, and one has to search for the tramp image. Most intriguingly, photos of Chaplin in full costume and makeup which catch him between the scenes or behind the camera directing also seem unlike the familiar figure. The tramp is created only when Chaplin consciously engages the camera in his unique "dialogue."

On the other hand, in a rehearsal film of the scene in *City Lights* in which Chaplin studies the statue of a nude woman while pretending to look at a smaller statue of a man on horseback, Chaplin wears a pullover sweater and slacks, and his hair is gray. It is most disconcerting to see the tramp emerge from this sporty-looking gentleman, but there he is. Interestingly, photos of Chaplin out of makeup generally show him presenting his forehead—his intellect—to the camera.

If Chaplin's use of his head and face invites an intimate collaboration in his emotional life, his use of his trunk engages immediate trust, sympathy, and empathy, and communicates the essence of his relationship to other characters.

Charlie Chaplin in *Easy Street*.

Chaplin, 1921. Collection of Jewel and Marge Walker.

A posed shot from *The Cure* with Chaplin and Edna Purviance. Note heavy makeup.

Framing his trunk. *The Pilgrim*.

As the center for the vital life functions of breathing, circulation, and digestion, the trunk is, next to the head, the body's most vulnerable area. But unlike the head, the trunk is not protected entirely by bone, thereby making man vulnerable to physical attack. In the social/emotional life, this is symbolized in the presentation of the trunk to others. For example, if someone crosses his or her arms when speaking, there is a sense (conscious or unconscious) that they are not being "open." Like the handshake, the open trunk indicates a nothing-to-hide, defenseless attitude.

Chaplin consistently presents his trunk frontally and openly in his films. He accentuates its openness in several ways. First, he never crosses his arms, though occasionally he frames his trunk by placing one hand on his chin, the other supporting the elbow of the first, making an "L" shape. Second, his coat is too tight, making his trunk appear to be proportionally smaller than his lower body, which is clothed in baggy pants. More importantly, this has the effect of clearly outlining the shape of his trunk so one is immediately aware of any postural change. Third, when Chaplin puts his hands on his hips, he puts them high up on his sides rather than at the waistline, or, for rear shots, on his mid-back, with

Helen Keller visits the set of *Sunnyside*. Chaplin's posture and expression are unlike his Tramp character, except for his direct gaze at the camera. Photo courtesy American Foundation for the Blind.

fingers pointing downward. In this way he again brings attention to his trunk.

Chaplin himself analyzes the rationale behind appearing small:

> Everyone knows that the little fellow in trouble always gets the sympathy of the mob. . . . I always accentuate my helplessness by drawing my shoulders in, dropping my lip pathetically and looking frightened. It is all part of the art of pantomime, of course.[6]

The combination of a small, helpless, open presentation of his trunk invites both sympathy and trust, which, taken together with the head movements further induces vicarious participation in Charlie's adventures.

Chaplin makes full use of the clearly defined shape of his trunk to communicate a wide array of emotions and attitudes: He elevates his upper chest to indicate pride or cockiness; he draws his shoulders downward and backward to indicate helplessness and vulnerability (his head moves somewhat foreward when he does this); he pulls his shoulders upward and inward to indicate childlike coyness (this sometimes functions to soften his "outrageous" flirtations with women or, occasionally, men); he folds his trunk downward in the middle to indicate depression; he presses it forward to indicate a false front of confidence (literally deflated in *Shoulder Arms* when, bravely volunteering for a dangerous mission, he is told, "You may never return!").

In short, through his trunk position and presentation, Chaplin gives an intimate sense of how he feels at every moment, something rare during a period when comic gestures were so stylized and exaggerated as to seem hopelessly hammy and unreal, such as Ford Sterling's indication of rage by jumping up and down in place. Although Chaplin's playing is stylized, it is based so firmly on accurate physical equivalents of emotional states, and played with such conviction, that it is read clearly by the audience, who become almost subliminally identified with his character.

The pelvis is the sex and power center of the body, the meeting place of the most powerful muscles and bones, as well as the physical center of gravity. Chaplin often tilts his pelvis backward—that is, he curves the lower part of his spine to make a "swayback." This serves several expressive functions: It reinforces trunk and head positions suggesting cockiness and pride; it suggests the studied ele-

gance of a ballet dancer's stance; and it also suggests a small child trying to appear strong by drawing his pelvis back and locking his knees.

This tilted-back pelvis also de-emphasizes the genitals. This makes Charlie's flirtations more childlike, therefore less sexual and "safer" in his early films. In effect, he holds back so that his advances are not seen as gross and vulgar. On the other hand, the pulled-back pelvis is a common position for women in our culture, indicating sexual allure, and

Charlie's stance. *The Rink.*

its assumption by Chaplin is an example of his flirting with the audience and its perception of appropriate roles. Thus, he can suggest a man, a child, or a woman, and he can flirt with both sexes.

Seen from the rear, the tilted-back pelvis draws attention to Chaplin's posterior, a prime comic object in his films. Part of the comedy results from his tender treatment of it, rubbing it after particularly hard falls. In his autobiography Chaplin quotes an early, perceptive admirer:

> What I like about your comedy is your knowledge of fundamentals—you know that the most undignified part of a man's anatomy is his arse, and your comedies prove it. When you kick a portly gentleman there, you strip him of all his dignity. Even the impressiveness of a Presidential inauguration would collapse if you came up behind the President and kicked him in the rear. There's no doubt about it: the arse is the seat of self-consciousness.[7]

This might be amplified by adding that since the "arse" is also the location of the function of elimination, the least-dignified aspect of life, it can be used in the same sense as thumbing one's nose. Chaplin does this eloquently in the massage wrestling scene from *The Cure* as well as in the sly opening scene of *City Lights,* where he sits squarely on the nose of a newly dedicated city monument.

The tilted-back pelvis also reinforces the fastidious element in the tramp. Against this fastidiousness Chaplin is able to joke boldly about sexual and scatological subjects which in other hands would seem gross and obscene—for instance, his numerous jokes of mistaking water or another liquid for urine (*Easy Street, The Cure, A Dog's Life*) or, even more boldly, getting "real" urine on his hands (*The Kid, The Great Dictator*). In *Modern Times* Charlie is tying his shoe when the prison attendant slops some beans on his plate. When he gets up and sees what is on the plate, he immediately looks up at the sky, suggesting that this stuff might have fallen from passing birds (a wonderful commentary on institutional food).

In motion, however, Chaplin's pelvis usually returns to a more structurally sound position under his trunk in order to accomplish his many falls, kicks, and other violent actions without injury. Here Chaplin's gracefulness comes to the fore, with its elements of dance, acrobatics, and gymnastics. Chaplin's body balance was matched by his increasing ability to express the content of a scene with inspired flights of choreographic comedy.

The extensions of the trunk—the arms—further communicate emotions by reaching out to embrace or reject. Chaplin's use of his arms contributes to his predominantly emotional style of playing. The positioning of his hands high on his hips is, in effect, a caress of his trunk. Further, his arm gestures often occur at chest level, linking them with emotional

Referring to himself. *Modern Times.*

expression, as opposed to head-level (mental) gestures or pelvis-level (physical/sexual) ones. Chaplin minimizes the appearance of strength in his arms by drawing his shoulders in and back as previously discussed, and de-emphasizes the hands—the "mental" part of the arms—by using them as extensions of his forearms. Seldom is he seen bending his hands at the wrists.

It is possible to divide the hands into physical (the heel of the hand, where the arm bones come through), emotional (the soft upper palm, which caresses), and mental (the fingers, with their capacity for fine, precise movements and discrimination) regions.* It is in his use of his hands that the extraordinary emotional quality of Chaplin's performances can be most clearly seen. For he almost always touches people and objects with the center, emotional part of his hands. His fingers are most often used as a single unit, linking them to the emotional palms; the heels are in turn linked to the emotional forearms. Taken together, these movement habits combine to give his touching a strong sensual quality, as if he is caressing everything he comes into contact with. Too-long sleeves often cover the heels of his hands, further accentuating the emotional and sensual touching.

Chaplin's caressing touch enhances the sentimental and romantic themes in his films as well as the transformation gags in which he handles one object as if it were another. By contrast, Keaton's performances are dominantly physical and intellectual, so it is not surprising to find strong antiromantic elements in his films.

A concrete example of Chaplin's use of his hands may be found in his most romantic film, *City Lights.* During scenes in a blind girl's apartment, Charlie refers to himself several times by straightening his fingers and patting his chest with his upper palm, at the same time nodding his head. Bringing his palm to his heart this way gives a much more sincere, emotional quality to the gesture than, for instance, if he pointed to himself with his thumb.

Another of Chaplin's most distinguishing characteristics is his stance. The splaying of his feet suggests ballet, comically exaggerated and contradicted by oversized shoes and baggy pants. The shoes make it necessary for Chaplin to walk by lifting his feet straight off the ground and then moving

*Dividing the body into mental, emotional and physical regions is a notion used in modern actor training. It is derived from the work of the nineteenth-century teacher and theorist François Delsarte. A good work on Delsarte's system is *Every Little Movement,* by Ted Shawn (N.Y.: Dance Horizons, Inc., 1963).

them forward, thereby presenting the inside of his leg to the viewer. Note again that this indicates openness and defenselessness. Like the hand, the foot is presented emotionally; the soft inner arch facing the camera, rather that the "intellectual" toes or the "physical" heels.

Taken as a whole while standing still, Chaplin's body frequently resembles that of a ballet dancer. The head is held upright, the trunk is elevated, the pelvis is pulled backward, and the feet are splayed. The differences illuminate Chaplin's character. Unlike a ballet dancer, who accentuates his form by wearing tights, Charlie wears baggy pants—his clothes *aspire* to elegance (they represent formal wear) but are in fact shabby. Instead of the gestures at head level typical of ballet, Chaplin's gestures are at chest level, frequently seeming to caress his own body or objects. Thus, he gives the impression of someone who aspires to upper-class appearance and balletic elegance, while in fact he is earthbound, both physically and emotionally.

Imitators of Charlie Chaplin often make the mistake of allowing the splay feet to suggest a side-to-side duck waddle or clowny movement in their version of his walk. The fact is that Chaplin's walk is remarkably stable. Given the posture he has established, he walks as efficiently as possible. Side-to-side-tilts are usually at hip rather than shoulder level. If shoulder movements, exceptionally high or low steps, or side-to-side swaying at the shoulder level are used, it is to communicate a specific feeling. For instance, after a particularly triumphant defeat of an adversary, Charlie will sometimes use a side-to-side swagger, suggesting a sailor. In later films, when pathos predominates, Chaplin sometimes adds a slight limp to his walk. But the "basic" walk—if one can be isolated—involves a sense, reinforced by his clothing, of weight in the legs and feet . . . a solidity and stillness at the center of gravity in the pelvis. The centering of trunk and head squarely over the bottom half of the body is an unusual position in a culture whose people often bend slightly forward at the waist as they walk. The result of this posture and walk is the impression of a highly idiosyncratic, emotional, independent individual.

An initial fascination with Chaplin can be increased by looking at still photographs. But even in the films, he seems carefully "composed" into a series of still poses. There is a peculiar quality of immobility to his movement. This results in part from the self-consciousness of his style, expressed both by presentational positioning to the camera and by the selectivity of the movements. Sometimes

Fooling the audience. Charlie as a tree, standing on a tree stump, center. *Shoulder Arms.*

this capacity to be still is used as a gag, as in *The Adventurer* and *The Vagabond* when Charlie stops a full run to "freeze" with his face to a wall, becoming invisible to his pursuers. An ingenious variation of this is the scene in *Shoulder Arms* where Charlie, in a tree costume, fools the other characters as well as the audience several times by freezing and "becoming" the tree. The combination of movement and stillness also gives Charlie a puppet-like quality. Again, this sometimes becomes a joke in itself, as when he pretends to be a mechanical fun house figure to elude police in *The Circus*.

But the main effect of this stillness-in-motion is to impose a geometrical precision on Chaplin's performances which is completely consistent with his presentational style, as for example in his frequent gesture of shrugging his shoulders with his arms extended straight out to the side, or lifting his hat straight up off his head or kicking someone so that his leg in a piston motion, extends parallel to the ground. In his famous corner skip, Charlie halts his forward momentum by extending one leg sideways and skipping with the other, then abruptly turns ninety degrees to round the corner. Chaplin himself was fully aware of this characteristic of his movement: "in pantomime the technique of movement is so mechanical."[8]

This mechanical quality, far from dehumanizing him, provides Chaplin's movement with an underlying structure which does two things: It leads to the numerous gags in which a person is made to seem like a thing, the culmination of which occurs in *Modern Times;* and it creates a contrasting background for his very organic, flowing movements at times of strong feeling. The precision of his movements also enables him to direct attention to subtle changes of posture or facial expression which would hardly be noticeable in a more "naturalistic" performer, and imparts to moments of sadness or tenderness a startling intensity.

His puppetlike qualities are further reinforced by his costume and makeup. The distinctive, dark shape of the costume and the strongly patterned face make him a human caricature. Part of his initial impact was certainly the uniqueness and power of his outline on the screen, which was quickly translated into toys, statuettes, and newspaper cartoons. Stills of Chaplin from even his earliest films reveal the magnetic power of his silhouette to draw attention away from the other characters, whose bodies are more conventionally clothed. In the case of those clowns who wore exaggerated makeup and costumes, like Chester Conklin or Mack Swain, the very absurdity of their exaggeration compels disbelief, even more so because often they are acting in realistic settings such as parks or streets. Chaplin's costume manages to strike a middle ground, suggesting clownish exaggeration with an unusual combination of ill-fitting but realistic-looking clothing.

Fortunately, Chaplin's appearance and movement were complemented by the film technology of the period. The high-contrast images produced by early film stock made Chaplin's makeup look relatively natural. In later years, even while he altered the appearance of the other players in his films to be more in keeping with the times, Chaplin's makeup and costume appeared increasingly artificial, partially due to technical improvements in film stock which clearly show how unnaturally white his face is and how unreal his eyebrows look. On the other hand, contrast Eric Campbell, the heavy of the Mutual films, with Harry Myers, who plays the millionaire in *City Lights;* it is the difference between a cartoon and a characterization. Groucho Marx, whose performances are always on a tongue-in-cheek level, can get away with blatantly artificial makeup more easily than Chaplin, whose performances demand that the audience see him as a three-dimensional character. Chaplin strikes a delicate balance between clown and person.

At least as important as the high-contrast qualities of early film to Chaplin's work was its speeded-up, "jerky" quality. While serious dramas were at a disadvantage because of this (at least from a modern perspective), comedy filmmakers were quick to capitalize on the possibilities for faster-than-life motions. Sennett particularly became a master at this, and his trademark became the comedy chase scene.

But while Sennett was the master of group motion in chases, Chaplin proved the master of solo movement. His mechanical, precise motions seem even more so when seen faster than life; the relative stillness and economy of his motions make the 1914 tramp clear and distinctive while those around him seem frenzied and unfocused. The rootedness and heaviness of his posture frequently make him a kind of eye in a storm of violent action, even if he has created the storm himself!

As he grew more mature and independent as a filmmaker, Chaplin was to learn to direct other characters in such a way that their performances thoroughly complement his own to the extent that other characters become almost extensions of him. But in the Keystones, the audience is left with the effect of a troupe of stars who are doing their best to be funny as individuals. While occasionally there is skillful acrobatic ensemble work, Chaplin, at this early stage, stands apart because of his skill as a mime rather than because a background has been carefully constructed to spotlight his character.

Chaplin's mime skills show very overtly in his manipulations of the audience's sense of his size, weight, and posture.

The clearest examples of size manipulation are in the Mutuals. In all but the solo *One A.M.,* gigantic Eric Campbell is Charlie's antagonist. However, the physical relationship between the two varies dramatically. In *Easy Street* Charlie as a policeman is terrorized by Campbell as the king tough of a slum neighborhood. Their physical relationship is the rock against the feather. Massive, immovable, seemingly indestructible, Campbell doesn't even blink at Charlie's hardest blows with a night stick; Charlie eludes him only with quicksilver movements and ruses. On the other hand, in *The Adventurer* they trade blow for blow throughout the film. Campbell here is one up on Chaplin because of a class difference rather than a size difference. While Campbell is obviously a larger, stronger man than Chaplin in terms of bulk, his relative clumsiness combined with their equalized size here give Chaplin the decided advantage.

Chaplin accomplishes the size transformations in several ways. Primary among these is the sense of emotional relationship. In *Easy Street* Chaplin is terrified of Campbell, while in *The Adventurer* Campbell is outraged at Chaplin's presence at a society party, and Charlie merely deals tit-for-tat with Campbell's abuses. There is no physical intimidation.

Among the rest of the Mutuals, size difference is minimized in *The Rink, The Count, The Pawnshop,* and *The Cure,* and becomes a major factor in *The Vagabond, Easy Street,* and *The Immigrant.* In these latter films, Chaplin exaggerates the tramp's pathetic outsider qualities through his own smallness, as described earlier. For example, an early scene in *Easy Street* finds Charlie trying to decide whether to apply for a policeman's job. He musters up his courage, expands his chest, and pulls his shoulders back, but his stride into the police station becomes wavery midway—highlighting the moment that his fear overcomes his courage. Throughout these latter films Charlie's insecurity and physical frailty are only occasionally overcome by bursts of courage. On the other side of the spectrum, in the first set of films Charlie is presented as a plucky character whose energy, vitality, and confidence in his impersonations simply sweep along the other characters in the films. He affects them more than they affect him.

Complementing these size changes is Chaplin's manipulation of his weight. By and large in the films he appears light when he is victimized, heavy when he becomes the aggressor. At times this takes on the power of illusion. In *The Cure* Charlie feels intimidated by masseur Henry Bergman, a man shorter but stouter than he. Charlie stands casually as Bergman comes to look him over, which Bergman accomplishes by turning him from back to front as if Charlie is a piece of cardboard. He then sits Charlie down and pushes him to a reclining position with what looks like a flick of his hand; Charlie's knees remain up as he goes over backward, suggesting both his lightness and his lack of compliance in the movement. This sets us up for a brief "fear" scene as Charlie watches Bergman maul a victim, and finally for the confrontation between the two in which the massage turns into a wrestling match. Naturally, Charlie defeats Bergman with superior agility and the aid of a hot radiator.

The wrestling scene offers a fine opportunity to see Chaplin's physical techniques, since he wears a bathing suit throughout. He makes the most of his visibility with several effective postural changes. In his "tough-guy" wrestler pose with spine curved in a semi-circle and arms held threateningly outstretched, a spinal undulation brings his pelvis back and into the radiator and causes him to instantly jump away, arching his entire back and rubbing his behind. He then resumes his original "tough-guy" position, ending finally with a "cock-of-the-walk" posture after he has vanquished Bergman and an-

other attendant. He struts around in triumph, his pelvis pulled back, his head and upper chest elevated, and his elbows out as he pumps his knees up and down.

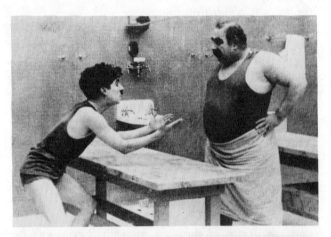

Top: A massage becomes a wrestling match. Charlie and Henry Bergman in *The Cure.*
Center: Charlie twitches his posterior at Bergman.
Bottom: Charlie struts in triumph.

Edna's doughnut is heavier than Charlie expected. *The Pawn-shop.*

Chaplin's manipulation of his body's size and weight is extended to his handling of objects. In *His Musical Career* (1914) Chaplin is Mack Swain's assistant piano mover (Swain was to later replace Eric Campbell after Campbell's death in 1917). Of course, puny Charlie does all the heavy work while boss Swain merely gives orders and relaxes. Chaplin's simulation of weight in the prop piano is effective, as is his inability to unbend after carrying the piano. In *The Pawnshop* Charlie adds weight to a doughnut Edna has baked. While the prop doughnut is heavy enough to break a plate, Charlie's exaggeration of that weight is deft. He takes it in his left hand, which immediately pulls his entire arm straight downward. The weight further translates into his trunk, which sags sideways and pulls him off balance. He then lifts it by bending his arm at the elbow, handling it like a dumbbell. This image is reinforced with a couple of upward "presses," and finally Charlie tosses it onto a plate, which shatters. Sense of weight is again used to comic effect in *The Pilgrim* (1923) when Charlie as a bogus minister compares the collection boxes which have been circulated on opposite sides of the congregation. As a final example, in *Behind the Screen* Charlie lifts not only a prop piano, but eleven bentwood chairs, in a startling image which makes him look like a human porcupine.

On a sloping surface, one's own body weight becomes a formidable force, and Chaplin explores the comic possibilities in the dining scene in *The Immigrant,* and both the comic and thrill possibilities in the cabin-on-the-cliff scene in *The Gold Rush.* The tilting set in *The Immigrant* stimulates a comedy of slipping and sliding of people and plates of food, whereas in *The Gold Rush* it sets up a delicate examination of equilibrium and balance. In that film, when Charlie and Mack Swain stand at opposite sides of the cabin it balances, but when they both go to the same side it begins sliding over the cliff. Note that here their weight is presumably equal.

But in *The Immigrant* Charlie also boldly fakes the rocking movement simply by tilting the camera back and forth and coordinating to the camera tilts his own side-to-side body glides. He accomplishes this by extending one leg sideways in the direction of the tilt, while the other shuffles in the same direction. The artifice is made rather transparent by the fact that Charlie is the only one who reacts to the motion of the "boat". Everyone else remains stock still.

Clearly, the skills to manipulate one's body as well as objects in this fashion indicates a high order

Chaplin and Mack Swain in the tilting cabin of *The Gold Rush.*

of what might be called "pure" mime skills. On a concrete level these skills are demonstrated in scenes in which Charlie uses imaginary props. The removal of an imaginary glove in Karno's sketch *Mumming Birds* is probably only one of many such tricks Chaplin learned from his mentor, and which recur throughout the films. Other examples are: eating an imaginary meal for Paulette Goddard in *Modern Times*; showing an invisible brood of children by indicating their heights in *The Pawnshop* and *A Dog's Life*; indicating a shapely woman by tracing her outlines in *Modern Times* and *The Great Dictator*; performing the invisible flea act in *Limelight*; and playing both David-and-Goliath and the narrator during the sermon in *The Pilgrim*.

But going beyond a general description of these and other Chaplin scenes is difficult. To describe movement in words is like trying to describe music in words. One can throw a limited spotlight onto one small aspect at a time, but the impact of the whole can only be experienced directly. While some of the aforementioned scenes sound like clichés, particularly describing the shape of a beautiful woman with the familiar double S-curve made with the hands, Chaplin's handling is so original that one watches without the cliché ever coming to mind. The difference lies in the subtle shadings of mime technique, the rhythms and shapes in space of Chaplin's performances.

On the evidence of numerous accounts, Chaplin's social relationships, particularly at parties, consisted, to a great measure, of performing. Late in life he said, "It was always hard for me to make friends. I was shy and inarticulate. Doug Fairbanks was my only real friend, and I was a showpiece for him at parties."[9] These performances took the form of outright imitations of celebrities like Eleanora Duse, Jimmy Walker, or Howard Hawks in revealing situations; or of impromptu pantomime illustrations of stories he was telling, such as of being on a fishing trip, discussing slavery or the Crucifixion. He would switch from role to role, portraying objects and animals as well as characters.

Chaplin also had more polished party turns. Wedging his cane against the floor, he would walk up a wall or he would portray both the bullfighter and the bull in a comic story of the bullring. For one charity performance he did a dance with invisible balloons. Another piece had him as an art connoisseur in a museum, studying a wall of paintings. The first one is about three feet off the ground and they get progressively higher, with Chaplin seeming to become taller as he strains to see them.

Minister Charlie and his dubious congregation.

David . . .

. . . and Goliath. *The Pilgrim*

Max Eastman introduced Chaplin to elaborate party games of impromptu speechmaking (by drawing subjects and characters to present them out of a hat) and charades, including an elaborate drama game in which pairs of people would hastily create a one-act play. The David-and-Goliath sermon which is the high point of *The Pilgrim* came from one of these sessions.

Regrettably these flights of impromptu invention were never recorded—there are occasional glimpses in newsreel footage, but it may be assumed that the best of them found their way into the films.

These performances served Chaplin as methods both for gathering material and testing it on audiences (one writer describes Chaplin going into the "waiter dance" from *Modern Times* while out to dinner with Paulette Goddard). They are also interesting in that they are close to current stage practice in contemporary mime, with its conventions of imaginary props and one person portraying an array of characters. As will be explored later, this kind of mime format underlies all of Chaplin's work.

Still, solo invisible-prop mime at a party or onstage is very different from filmed mime. Although Chaplin's stage mime background dominates his films, it is his ability to conceive scenes and direct them specifically for the film medium that gives the films lasting value. The filmed record of a great clown is merely a document, and seldom stands on its own merits as a film (usually the humor of the original will be lost). So the final area in this examination of the role of mime in Chaplin's work is his adaptation to the film medium.

Notes

[1]Cited by McDonald, Conway, Ricci, *The Films of Charlie Chaplin, op cit.*

Charlie pantomimes an eagle to show French girl Edna that he is an American soldier. *Shoulder Arms.*

[2]*Ibid.*, p. 119.

[3]Chaplin, cited by McCabe, *op. cit.*, pp. 235–6.

[4]Maugham, Somerset, cited by Cotes, Peter and Niklaus, Thelma, *The Little Fellow*, (New York: The Citadel Press, 1965), p. 11.

[5]Eastman, Max, *Great Companions* (New York: Farrar, Straus and Cudahy, 1959), p. 213.

[6]Chaplin, "What People Laugh At," *American Magazine*, (Nov. 1918), cited by McCaffrey, Donald in *Focus on Chaplin* (Englewood Cliffs, N.J.: Prentice-Hall, Inc., 1971), p. 51.

[7]Chaplin, *My Autobiography* (New York: Simon & Schuster, 1964), p. 217. Reprinted with permission of The Bodley Head.

[8]*Ibid.*, p. 217. Reprinted with permission of The Bodley Head.

[9]Cited by Candice Bergen "I Thought They Might Hiss," *Life*, April 21, 1972, p. 90.

3

The Mime Behind the Screen

"... My technique is the outcome of thinking for myself ... it is not borrowed from what others are doing."

Charles Chaplin

Although Chaplin denied credit to many of his film collaborators, he wrote of Mack Sennett with the same respect and gratitude he always gave to Fred Karno, his stage mentor. And with good reason, for the Keystone film world Chaplin entered in 1913 was to provide him with the foundation for all his later work. But first he needed to master the elements of that world—and the film medium—to suit his own emerging purposes.

Chaplin and others have recorded his bewilderment at the technology of filmmaking when he arrived at Keystone. Used to the straightforward rehearsal-performance routines of his stage years, he couldn't at first grasp the role of editing in the film process, which made it possible (and practical) to shoot scenes out of sequence. Evidentally he learned quickly, for he was both directing and writing his own films within a few months. By the end of his year at Keystone, his films were technically equal or superior to the other work being done there at the time; within two more years Chaplin would utilize the medium with far more sophistication than Sennett ever attained.

Chaplin recognized that his training gave him a distinct advantage over the other Keystone players. The intimate, natural style of pantomime acting he had mastered on stage was far more effective on the screen than the crude sign-language pointing and gesticulating of the Keystone troupe.

Although his physical skills and gifts were highly evolved at the beginning of his screen career, his skills as a director were not. But by a curious matching of stage technique to film technology, he found the medium compatible. High-contrast film stock, film silence, and speeded-up action all enhanced

the effectiveness of his performances.

The screen world was even more silent than the stage world of Fred Karno, where Chaplin played essentially wordless parts in sketches which featured music, singing, and dialogue. In the complete silence of film, Chaplin blossomed. It is to his great credit that in his mature silent films sound is never missed.

A special bonus Chaplin got from the silence was the unreality it imposed on the silent screen world, an unreality further stressed by the faster-than-life action. A convention of Sennett's film world was that no one could be injured, despite falls from rooftops, plunges from cliffs, or assaults with knives, guns and pitchforks. Bodies in the Keystone films were treated as objects—flying objects as often as not. Since Chaplin's stage work was strongly acrobatic, this was a natural transition for him to make. "The Little Limey," as he was at first disparagingly called on the Keystone lot, earned the company's respect by demonstrating his sophisticated techniques for falling without injury.

Since contemporary filmmakers have tended to misuse the device of speeded-up action, it is hard for a modern viewer to appreciate its place in Chaplin's art. The most common mistake made by modern filmmakers is to use undercranking* for a nostalgic or cutely comic effect, suggesting only the poorest and most clichéd qualities of silent comedies. Woody Allen used it with some success in *Sleeper*,

_____

*The term undercranking dates from the days of hand-cranked cameras; by cranking the film through the camera at a slower speed than it was later to be projected, the result was faster-than-life action. Chaplin's films are often shown at twice the speed of the real-life action.

his most visual comedy; scenes of slipping on a giant banana peel or reeling drunkenly after being awakened from suspended animation are well enough conceived and executed to justify the device. But in his *Love and Death,* undercranking becomes a facile evasion in a primarily verbal film, covering up uninspired visual gags.

Undercranking works for Chaplin in several respects. It serves, as has been mentioned, to underscore the mechanical precision in his own movement. For Chaplin, as well as for other slapstick comedians, it also serves to make the knockabout comedy—essentially a comedy of force and pain—less "real", and hence comfortably removed from life. No one ever seems to get hurt in these films, though exaggerated comic expression of pain and discomfort accompany the falls, blows, and burns which the comics sustain. Fast motion enhances not only Chaplin's acrobatic tumbles but also his balletic qualities and physical resilience. Part of Chaplin's resistance to making sound films must surely have been that the slowing down of his motion would make him appear more sluggish (aside from the fact that he was in his forties, no longer the lithe acrobat of the Mutuals made fifteen years earlier). Chaplin solved this problem in part by building into his sound films opportunities for undercranked scenes, which had music and effects added later.

In his silent films Chaplin sets a pace and varies the undercranking subtly from scene to scene. In general, however, in films made before *The Great Dictator* (1940) he moves at faster-than-life speed.

In contrast, for Keaton the sense of mass and gravity (the realness) of large objects was critical. Keaton wanted the audience to know the heaviness of the trains in *The General,* or the building front which falls on him in *Steamboat Bill, Jr.* To enhance appreciation of the very real danger in his films, Keaton preferred to have his films shot and projected at the same speed.

Despite Chaplin's frequent use of the device, seldom is the audience really aware of it as such, and then only in specific scenes. For example, it is used to exaggerate Charlie's grace on roller skates in *The Rink* and *Modern Times,* to help the revolving door gags in *The Cure,* including the effect of falling-up-the-stairs from the momentum built from the spin. Otherwise, it is used as an accent.

Other forms of trick photography such as slowed motion, objects appearing and disappearing or changing, people seeming to float, fly, and change size have been used since the turn of the century. The early pioneer of this work, Georges Méliès, was in fact a stage magician who saw film as an extension of his illusionary art.

Even into the twenties trick photography was often used in comic films. The films of Larry Semon, for example, are filled with animated objects and other "impossible" gags. Keaton stated that Semon's comedies probably got more laughs from audiences than anyone's, but they were eminently forgettable. Today they are hardly watchable. Perhaps because today's audiences are more "filmwise," perhaps because of the use of that kind of humor in animated films, the tricks in Semon and Sennett films have no more intrinsic interest.

The major silent-film comedians seldom used trick photography. Keaton and Lloyd understood no less than Chaplin that the audiences must believe in the reality of their performances. Thus, all developed a taste for sustained long shots to show that they were doing their own feats. When Chaplin falls backward off a ten-foot ladder in *The Pawnshop* there are no convenient cutaways to close-ups which would allow him to fake the fall. The audience clearly sees him land, spring up, and check his watch. For Keaton and Lloyd the sustained long shot became even more critical since they specialized in "thrill" comedies, doing dangerous stunts themselves. Although he doesn't usually employ thrill comedy, a similar integrity in Chaplin's films shows that his incredibly precise and subtle performances are accomplished in sustained action, rather than easily constructed in editing.

A backwards fall. *The Pawnshop.*

Chaplin occasionally used special effects, but like Keaton, who used trick photography in *The Playhouse* and *Sherlock, Jr.*, he found ingenious ways to disguise the effect through the physical skill of his performance. For instance, in *Pay Day* (1922) Charlie, as a bricklayer, is thrown bricks from below, which he catches in the crook of his leg, on the back of his heel, etc. Of course this is a film reversal of the real action of removing bricks from the wall, placing them on his leg, and letting them drop. But much easier said than done! Chaplin had to conceive his movement so that the reversed film did not make the trick obvious (the way Sennett would employ this device would be to show someone "diving" backward from a swimming pool to a diving board). A casual viewer of *Pay Day* will be impressed by this as yet another of Chaplin's skills and be unaware of the film trickery.

Another example of the same trick occurs during the balloon dance in *The Great Dictator*. The dictator "jumps" from a static standing position to the top of his desk. Here attention is drawn to the effect, but it is so skillfully executed that one can't be sure whether it is reversed action of Chaplin jumping down or whether he is being lifted by some sort of hoist.

Chaplin uses the effect a third time in *The Bond*, showing ribbons winding around himself and Edna. Here no attempt is made to disguise the effect, but the entire short propaganda film is more highly stylized than usual, with stark black background and crescent moon—a stage set in contrast to Chaplin's usual gritty street scenes.

A different kind of film trickery is used in the teetering cabin scene in *The Gold Rush*. A miniature cabin (and a miniature Charlie hanging out of it) is intercut with interior shots of Charlie and Mack Swain inside. Here the effectiveness of the acting, the desperate struggle of Charlie and Mack to get out of the cabin through the door at the uptilted side, the cleverness of the gags, and the exterior shots balance into a unique Chaplin version of the thrill comic climaxes of his two competitors, Keaton and Lloyd. Even though dangerous stunts are not actually being performed, the rhythm of the editing combines the elements into a satisfying climax.

Frequently cited criticism of Chaplin the director/producer are: the shoddiness of his sets; the "staginess" of his framing (compounded by the usually static camera); the length of time he gives to individual shots in the films (sometimes one shot will run several minutes); and the gaps in continuity in his editing. All of these "flaws," seen in relation to the importance of mime in Chaplin's films, becomes understandable (though not always justifiable). For Chaplin, his own movement on the screen is the core of interest. "I am the unusual and I do not need camera angles."[1] Such an attitude was understandably infuriating to those critics attuned to cinema technique as almost an end in itself. It was also frustrating to many of Chaplin's assistant directors on the set. During the 1960s particularly, Chaplin's critical reputation was low in contrast to the then recently rediscovered cinematic silent masterpieces of Keaton.

Miniature cabin, puppet Charlie. *The Gold Rush*

Chaplin genuinely felt that if his own performance was up to snuff, other details of the film became unimportant. Robert Parrish, who played the bratty newsboy in *City Lights,* visited the studio while Chaplin was viewing rushes (prints developed just after shooting a scene for review purposes) from *Monsieur Verdoux.* One of a number of repetitions of a scene caught an electrician in the shot. The very fact that Parrish noticed the electrician was proof to Chaplin that his performance hadn't worked; if it had, the viewer wouldn't notice the superfluous details.

Repeated viewings of the films reveal a richness of character types and minor gags occurring in the backgrounds, but it is difficult to take one's eyes off Chaplin even for a moment. Most of the ensemble serves to enhance his own performance. Some gags are lost unless seen on a large screen, such as a side shot of the assembly line in *Modern Times* which shows about ten workers behind Charlie doing operations on the metal nut plate.

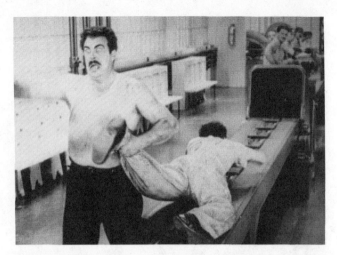

Charlie on the assembly line in *Modern Times*. Note workers in background.

Repeated viewings of the films also reveal glaring gaps in the editing continuity. In *The Vagabond,* for example, Charlie is being chased around and through a bar; he loses his hat in one exterior shot, and it reappears as he runs through the bar's interior.

Since the films center so much on Charlie's body, cuts from long to mid-long shots or close-ups frequently find Charlie in new positions. Although in the early years these gaps can be partially explained by the incredible speed with which the films were made, the fact is that they occur throughout Chaplin's career. Even in the famous ending of *City Lights,* which alternates between close-ups of Charlie's face shot over the shoulder of Virginia Cherrill, and close-ups of her face shot over Charlie's shoulder, the position of Charlie's hand, holding a rose, changes—his forefinger is in his mouth in his close-ups, but his whole hand is at shoulder level in hers. Nevertheless James Agee eulogized this scene as "the greatest piece of acting and the highest moment in movies."

Similar continuity gaps occur in lighting and in the look of costume or hair. One is forced to conclude that Chaplin didn't care about these lapses. After all, many second-rate Hollywood productions have *perfect* continuity, and he wasn't competing with *them*. Most likely he simply recognized that the power of his films lay in his own performances, so that these aspects of the filmmaker's craft could be defiantly overlooked. Although the films of Keaton and Lloyd do not contain such continuity flaws, it is also true that both are "team men" to a much greater extent than Chaplin, both in production and acting. They allow the other players

distinctive roles. Not until *The Great Dictator,* with its brilliant caricature of Mussolini by Jack Oakie, does Chaplin allow other actors to have major comic scenes in their own right.

It is impossible to assess Chaplin the director without considering Chaplin the mime performer. The end product of the conception and direction of a Chaplin film is the performance, and in this respect Chaplin's directing is most effective. Midway through his Essanay series of films (1915) Chaplin developed a sense of framing and cutting (editing) that reinforced his character's movements. Because his movement style expressively incorporates every part of his body, he developed a marked preference for the stagelike full-figure framing, occasionally pulling the camera back to reveal movements over a large area for ensemble groupings, or moving closer for scenes involving eating and other small movements. Facial close-ups are extremely rare in his work, since it has been his preference (and ability) to express emotions on a larger physical scale.

It is important to realize that despite their "staginess," Chaplin's films could not effectively be reproduced on stage. The full figure on screen might be fifteen feet high, making possible a subtlety in performance which would be lost on the stage. In the long shots, due partially to his unique makeup, Chaplin's face is clearly visible (similar to the effect clown-white makeup has of amplifying facial expressions on stage). So, by and large, Chaplin could dispense with close-ups, saving them for moments of high intensity such as the ending in *City Lights.*

By the time of the Mutuals, Chaplin had a firm grasp on directing technique. He had not only grown as a mime, polishing characterization, gag structure, and performance rhythm, but as a director. He consistently found the best framing, angle, and distance from the camera to present his performance. In *Easy Street,* for example, he sits on a backless chair and tumbles over backward. Shot from full front, his upper body disappears as he falls. Any other angle would have reduced the surprise and impact of the gag.

By examining one of the Mutual films in detail, we can see Chaplin's development both as mime performer and director after only three years in film.

Note

[1] Cited by Theodore Huff, *Charlie Chaplin* (New York: Arno Press & The New York Times, 1972), p. 297.

4

One A.M.

One A.M., Chaplin's fourth film in his series for Mutual, is unique in several respects. It is his only solo film—except for a brief appearance by Albert Austin as a cab driver, Chaplin sustains the entire twenty minutes himself, substituting inanimate props for human characters. This represented for Chaplin a departure from traditional stage and film experience. Except for his burlesque turns with the *Casey Circus* troupe years before, Chaplin's stage work had been i ensembles. And although many of his routines in films have the appearance of solo performances, most involve other characters, even if only to play minor roles, as in *The Pawnshop* where a bewildered and finally enraged Albert Austin watches Charlie dissect his alarm clock.

The plot of *One A.M.* is simple. Charlie arrives home and goes to bed. But the simplest actions—opening the door, lighting a cigarette, going upstairs—become extremely complicated because Charlie is roaring drunk. *One A.M.* is Chaplin's most thorough exploration of the altered awareness of the drunk.

Upon its initial release Chaplin is reported to have said, "one more film like that and it will be goodbye Charlie."[1] In his last book, however, Chaplin evidently looks back on the film with some pride, calling it "a pure exercise in mime and technical virtuosity, with no plot or secondary characters."[2]

Although *One A.M.* does not hold up as well as some of the other Mutuals, it offers a fine opportunity to examine Chaplin's movement and directing technique away from the emotionally involving plots and characters of the tramp films of this period.

One A.M. begins with Charlie's arrival in a cab. He has great difficulty opening the door. He reaches through the window for the outer handle, but it is located at the front of the door out of reach. He sticks his head out the window and sees the handle and again reaches, but this time the window frame blocks his arm. After trying unsuccessfully a third time, he slaps the window frame. He sticks his head out again, looking downward where he thought the handle would be. Chaplin thus introduces two characteristics of his drunken state: his reliance on habitual behavior instead of immediate perception; and his persistence and repetition of this behavior after it has proven ineffective. The repetition also serves to clarify the character's actions and intentions and, with slight variations, becomes a running gag on the man's ineffectiveness.

Now comes the film's first title: "They should build these handles nearer the door." There are a total of nine such titles in *One A.M.*, and they serve to clarify the actions with humorous verbal comment, as well as to cover awkward cuts in the action. When serving the latter function they, like the film's occasional close-ups, seem superfluous.

Charlie emerges from the cab, his arm through the door frame to turn the handle. Forgetting that his arm is hooked around the frame, he tries to reach into his pocket for the cab fare. When he notices, he kicks the door away in such a manner that it returns to hook his arm as he transfers his handkerchief into his right hand. Charlie wipes his mouth (demonstrating clearly what object he is holding) and tries to put the handkerchief into his pants pocket, but succeeds only in pushing it downward against the door which is still between his arm and body.

Charlie's lack of awareness is complemented and compounded by a "tortured logic" gag. Dropping his handkerchief, he looks downward through the door window, and reaches through it for the handkerchief. This time the lower window frame blocks him. Straightening up, he pushes the door away and dives toward the handkerchief, and is again caught at the waist by the returning door. This is really exactly the same sequence as the previous one of reaching into his pants pocket, but on a larger scale—his waist, rather than his elbow, is caught by the frame. The sequence is brought to a close by Charlie repeating the push of the door, this time grabbing the handkerchief just before the returning door knocks him back into the cab.

terns of movement are also highlighted by the length of the individual shots. The action described thus far has been accomplished with only six separate shots. For each of them the camera frames the action widely so that camera movement is minimal and subtle.

Chaplin's eyes waver and are unfocused as part of the drunk characterization. His facial expressions are restrained, suggesting an attempt to maintain control and dignity.

Climbing into the house through the window, Charlie offers another example of tortured logic. Inside the house he discovers his key in his vest pocket, so he returns (through the window) to the

Charlie then stands, trying to decipher the cab meter as Albert Austin waits. The numbers on the meter shift as Charlie studies them, finally stopping at 0000. Charlie merely drops some ashes from his cigarette (which he has held throughout these scenes and will hold through most of the film) into Austin's hand, and wanders toward his front door. Although the audience sees the numbers moving, it is presumed that this is to be interpreted as the drunk's distorted perception, a device which occurs in several other places in the film.

The trip to the front door enables Chaplin to show his drunk's swaying movement; he walks a kind of S-curve to the door, finds it locked, and turns toward the camera and walks to the front of the porch to check his pockets for the key, reinforcing this with a title, "Where's my key?", and revolves back toward the door to check under the welcome mat. Revolving again toward the camera, he returns to the front of the porch to check his pockets.

All these turns and S-curves impose a formality to the drunk's pattern of movement that somewhat belies his drunkenness throughout the film. The pat-

outside to open the door. This kind of gag would become central in the work of Laurel and Hardy ten years later.

The drunk's already impaired sense of balance is further tested by a small rug as he enters the house. With the aid of concealed wires, the rug slides as Charlie steps on it. After a series of slides and revolves on the rug, Charlie finally releases the doorknob he has been holding and falls, propelling the rug into the house. Another title, "I must have a skate on!" covers a slight change of rug position to prepare for Charlie to rise, walk forward, and take a rather spectacular fall on the rug, both legs flying upward as he lands on his rear end. Close examination reveals Chaplin's technique for falling without injury. As one leg flies into the air, the other cushions the fall, often aided by one arm, and then immediately flies up to join the first leg. With undercranking, the subterfuge is undetectable.

Falling is a main motif in *One A.M.*—more so than in any other Chaplin film. He falls no less than twenty-six times during the twenty-minute film. Undoubtedly this is the "technical virtuosity" Chaplin

When Charlie takes his flying fall on the rug he lands between two stuffed animals. After he enacts (largely with his legs) his fear of these animals, it dawns on him that maybe they aren't alive. Warily, he nudges the bobcat with his foot and pats it on the snout. Next comes a brilliant touch. Standing with hands in pockets, confident now that the cats are unreal, he kicks one on the rump, which causes it to whirl and "bite" him on the ankle. This makes the viewer share the drunk's perception that the animal is alive.

After repeating the above gag with variations, Charlie moves toward a round table in the center of the living room to get a drink. His staggering walk and focus on the liquor bottle serve to distract us from the fact that his right hand is attaching his cape to the table. This prepares another sustained sequence. Charlie, glass in hand, walks around the table toward the liquor decanter; but since his cape is caught the table top revolves with him and the decanter stays out of reach. This prompts another title, "That's the fastest round of drinks I ever saw." After circling the table several times in both directions, Charlie notices that his cape is caught. Smiling toward the camera, he drops the cape from his shoulders. Then comes another brilliant variation. Looking at the decanter to distract us from his careful placement of his foot into his cape, he begins circling the table again, this time his foot drags his cape which turns the table with him. After two quick revolutions he falls and the table (in the same shot) revolves exactly 180 degrees, bringing the decanter right to him. "What detained you?"

refers to and it is impressive. Each fall is slightly different from the others, and they climax in an amazing series of falls down the staircase. But Chaplin's facility with falling leads him somewhat astray, and the variations on this theme become wearing. Chaplin uses falls with far greater effectiveness in other films. Of the Mutual group, *The Cure* in particular shows a sparing use of falls, each one a further progression in the story. In that film, falls become insults, outrages, and comeuppances; Charlie steps into the "health spring," falls on Eric Campbell's gouty foot, and so on. Without other characters to play against, Chaplin's inspiration runs dry, and the falls in *One A.M.* lose meaning and impact with repetition despite their variety and technical perfection.

Chaplin uses his mechanical movement technique to advantage during his falls. When his legs come down, they lever his trunk upward into a sitting position, which serves to distance his portrayal from a "genuine" limp and sloppy drunk. His perceptions may be distorted, but he remains lithe and energetic.

The table routine demonstrates Chaplin's great ability to make highly choreographed material appear spontaneous. His concentration on his apparent task is so intense that we never notice the preparatory movements of attaching his cape to the table or catching his foot carefully in his cape. Both the ingenuity of the gags and his execution of them make the actions appear to just happen, though repeated viewing makes clear the care that is taken to vary the action and position it for maximum visibility.

Now that he is within reach of the decanter, Chaplin introduces another motif suggesting his drunken state. He braces a hand on the table to rise, suggesting the need for stability. From this point on in the film he uses the table, bannisters, and walls repeatedly for support and guidance.

Charlie next tries to pour himself a drink and light a cigarette. Unable to squirt seltzer properly into a small wineglass, he squirts it instead into an open

work cannister and onto his feet; lighting his perpetual cigarette, he confusedly holds the burning match and shakes out the cigarette as if *it* is a match, tossing it away. The match momentarily burns his fingers. Retrieving his cigarette from the floor, he makes several attempts to toss it into the cuspidor (after the third attempt, a title appears: "This *has* been done!"). Elaborately positioning himself above the cuspidor, steadying one hand with the other, he drops it in the manner of a tightrope walker pleased with having completed a difficult and dangerous feat.

Although this sequence uses small objects, it is done entirely in long shot, Chaplin communicating by glances and repetition so clearly that the viewer knows what the objects are even without being able to see them well.

A closer shot follows, framing Charlie from the waist up. He takes another cigarette, lights a match, looks at the match and shakes it out. He is puzzled because he can't get a draw on his unlit cigarette (the action of inhaling necessitates a closer shot).

Walking back toward the front door, taking a slide on the rug in stride, Charlie tries to hang his cape on the coatrack. But the peg is slanting downward (another drunken fantasy image?). Charlie holds onto the cape with both hands, his arms enlarging the movement of the cape sliding off the peg. Walking with his cape back into the living room he slides on the rug and falls, moves to the center of the room and "hangs" the cape where he assumes the rack to be, though of course it merely drops to the floor. Chaplin used this gag in many earlier films; it was one of his holdovers from the stage.

Diving toward the table, Charlie finally gets his drink, tilting his hat back and gargling in a characteristically idiosyncratic gesture. Getting up off his knees after having his drink, Charlie walks behind the table, checking his vest pockets for matches. Seeing a stuffed ostrich, he flips his top hat onto its head with a flourish. Following yet another skirmish with the stuffed bobcat, Charlie falls in front of the stairway on the left side of the living room (there are two, parallel stairways, one on each side). A close-up is followed by a title, "Good night!"

Holding his arms outstretched like a tightrope walker, his right hand delicately touching the bannister, Charlie ascends. As he gets higher he falters, stepping backward as if magnetically drawn. After a series of forward and backward steps, he is finally overpowered and descends backward down the stairs, moving smoothly toward the table for another drink. Ironically, the motion of tilting the glass back-

ward to his mouth causes him to fall backward (holding onto the glass and decanter as he goes). After putting the decanter and glass on the floor, he checks his nose for injury (he also does this after several of the other falls). Rising, he tries unsuccessfully to strike another match. Turning back to the stairs, he climbs all the way up by hanging onto the bannister with both arms, but is knocked down by the huge pendulum along the upstairs balcony wall. He falls in a spectacular somersault, sliding feet first on his stomach down the stairs, and turning upward as he reaches the bottom.

Walking across to the other staircase, he ascends smoothly but walks quickly back down when he sees the pendulum again. Fortifying himself with another drink and checking his vest pockets, he discovers (as another title informs) that he has "no more matches." Charlie spies a chandelier and attempts to light his cigarette on one of its globes (a gag used in *Mumming Birds* years before). To reach the chandelier he crawls onto the table and continues crawling in place on the table top, since it revolves under him. Accelerating, he crawls and finally gets up and walks faster and faster in place, arms outstretched for balance. A waist-up shot from below reinforces the image of the determined Charlie staring at the light and getting nowhere fast. Finally Charlie loses his balance and falls off the table, revolving on the floor. His cigarette is coming apart at the seams.

Charlie makes another attempt on the left staircase. He reaches the top, staggers and falls, rolling himself up in the carpet on the way down. (This reveals the thick foam pads on the steps which makes such stunting possible.) At the bottom, Charlie's head and arms emerge, and he pours himself another drink from the conveniently placed decanter on the floor.

Choosing a new approach, Charlie climbs the coatrack, swaying at the top as he would do two films later on a ladder in *The Pawnshop*. As he walks to the door, he gets hit again by the pendulum (which crosses both upstairs doors in its swing). On his way down the right staircase he dislodges from the corner a stuffed bear, which falls down with him, scaring him into a quick trip upstairs via the coatrack. After another couple of blows from the pendulum, Charlie finally manages to crawl through the upstairs door.

The entire staircase sequence is a triumph of theme and variation, and along the way Chaplin manages to recapitulate most of the other routines in the film with rugs, stuffed animals, table, drinks, and cigarettes. Despite occasional awkward cuts, the framing and length of major individual shots are flawless. All the ascents and descents on the staircase, for instance, are done in sustained single shots, showing the overall pattern of the movement as well as demonstrating that the sequence is really being executed by Chaplin on the set, rather than constructed in the editing process. One gets the impression, in fact, that most of the cuts throughout *One A.M.* serve to reposition angles and props for the master long shots, and that if he could have, Chaplin would have used even longer sustained takes (as Hitchcock painstakingly accomplished in 1948 in *Rope*, which gives the illusion of a single take lasting 81 minutes). Camera movement throughout the film is minimal and subtle, and camera placement highlights the wide-ranging and often complex action. Although some cuts are poorly matched in terms of editing continuity, each reveals appropriate placement for clear communication of Chaplin's intention. In the cigarette and drinking scenes, for example, the viewer can dispense with details because Chaplin's actions and reactions are being portrayed through the movements of his entire body. He is a master at enlarging and clarifying the subtlest, most intimate actions.

Once upstairs, a brief walk through a room filled with more stuffed animals and mounted animal heads brings Charlie into his bedroom for the climax of the film—his struggle with the Murphy wall bed. Although this sequence is as long and intricate as the preceding stairs sequence, it uses only eight shots, as compared with sixteen for the stairs sequence.

1. In the bedroom, Charlie lights his cigarette, puts his hat on the floor, and drops the match into the hat. He looks around.

TITLE: "Where's the bed?"

2. Charlie looks behind a drape, finally seeing the switch panel on the back wall. He presses

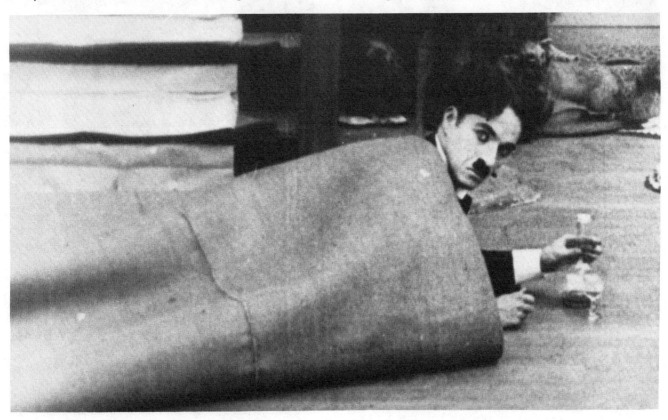

a switch and the bed revolves out from the side wall, sweeping him along with it for six complete revolutions, whereupon it throws him onto the floor. He pushes the switch to stop the bed. Trying again, the bed sweeps him with it in the opposite direction for three more revolutions before he manages to get to the switch.

3. A waist-up close-up of Charlie studying the bed as he leans against the back wall.

4. Charlie steps out to drop more ashes into his hat, walks in front of the bed and again presses the switch. The bed abruptly descends to the floor, trapping Charlie underneath (he grasps at a support under the bed to cushion this fall). Emerging from the tail of the bed, Charlie sits down and notices that his hat is trapped under the back leg of the bed (dropping his ashes brought attention to the hat position earlier). After trying unsuccessfully to lift the bed, he tries pulling the hat upward by the brim, but manages only to tear the brim from the hat. He sits back down on the bed and drops his cigarette from his mouth; stooping to pick it up, he is unaware that the bed rises into the wall. He stands and puts the cigarette back into his mouth, then sits and falls backward. Returning to the switch, he is again pushed under as the bed descends. This time he manages to raise it about thirty degrees off the floor before emerging from the end. He tries to push it down to the floor, but it bounces and hits him on the chin. He gets on the bed to bounce it down, but

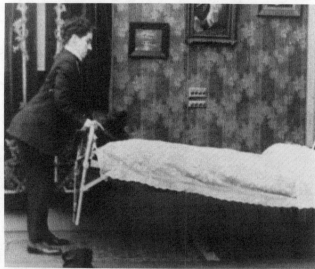

is himself bounced off. Finally, he dives onto it and is taken by it into the wall, his head and arm visible at the upper corner as he tries to get out.

5. A medium close-up showing Charlie struggling to get out.

6. The bed comes down. Charlie sits on the edge, puts the hat brim onto his head. His cigarette is in his mouth as he gets up, turning quickly to dive onto the bed as it rises. He forces it down, sits on it continuing to force the bed down. After hanging his coat over the tail of the bed he repeats the getting-up-forcing-down sequence twice and finally loses as the bed returns to the wall. As he stands facing the bed it comes out of the wall from the bottom, Charlie landing on its underside. He gets off and tries to get underneath it (on the mattress side).

Giving up, he fluffs his coat as a pillow and lies down on the underside, but the bed rises into the wall, causing Charlie to do a backward somersault onto the floor. He gets up, walks to the bed, gestures "forget it" and lies down on the floor, whereupon the bed falls down rightside up over him.

7. Charlie emerges from the tail and looks back over the bed.

8. Crawling from under the tail, Charlie warily grips the bed rail as he rises, leaps onto the bed and falls with the mattress through the frame, which rises into the wall. Rising again, Charlie doesn't notice the frame has descended, and trips over it as he walks forward. Gathering up his coat and the remains of his hat, he walks away, defeated.

Going into the bathroom for a drink of water, Charlie ends up soaking himself in the shower. He finally climbs into the tub, covers himself with the bath mat, drapes his coat over the end of the tub and rests his head on it. He indicates, by a sudden downward tilt of his head, that he has fallen asleep. The End.

The bed sequence demonstrates both the strength and weakness of *One A.M.* On the one hand, it is an example of Chaplin's ability to milk a single situation or prop for gags, and to invest the gags with a resonance beyond their humor. On the other hand, the bed is one of Chaplin's rare trick props. Although the audience is perhaps meant to presume that the bed, like the taxi meter and pendulum, is a delusion of the drunk, these props impair the usual integrity of Chaplin's gags. Normally he makes the viewer see ordinary props in a new way through skillful movement, as he did with the stuffed animals and table earlier in the film. Impossible gags and trick props proliferated through the silent era and beyond, but Chaplin used them very rarely after *One A.M.*, preferring to root his gags in physical reality by exaggerating natural laws.

Both the trick props and the joke titles suggest Chaplin's fear of monotony in a solo film. Although later films have solo sections, Chaplin never repeated the experiment of *One A.M.*

Although atypical, *One A.M.* offers a rich excursion into Chaplin's film world. It spotlights two of his great strengths: fusion of conception, performance, and filming; and an ability to create sustained comedy material from simple actions and to spin seemingly endless variations from each prop and situation.

For a modern viewer, *One A.M.*, as well as other Chaplin films made before 1917, may offer some difficulties. Among these are poor print quality and tampered-with editing and titles. Since Chaplin's estate does not control the copyright on pre-1918 films, well-preserved, clean, exact prints of many of the early films are not available. Their very popularity encouraged illegal duplication for the black market, and their ownership changed many times over the years, resulting in varying degrees of poor preservation and tampering to modernize them.

Another difficulty for TV-weaned viewers is Chaplin's uncompromising physical style of acting. Some gags will be missed despite the clarity of Chaplin's presentation. In addition, audiences are now unfamiliar with silent film conventions such as speeded-up action. Since the silent film era has been distilled to the work of a few filmmakers and stars, most people will not appreciate Chaplin's achievement in the context of what others were doing at that time. *One A.M.*, with all its flaws, certainly holds up far better than any other comedy made during its period. Finally, when *One A.M.*

was made, Chaplin was the most popular star in the world, with his vast audience following his adventures as audiences now follow weekly situation comedies. Today audiences see Chaplin's work isolated not only from its period, but from the rest of his work as well.

But *One A.M.* needs no apologists. It still works as entertainment and, for those who probe deeper, as a display of the clockwork mechanics of this century's great visual comedian.

Notes

[1]Huff, *op. cit.,* p. 71.

[2]Chaplin, *My Life in Pictures, op. cit.,* pp. 130–131.

Part Two
One-Man Show

"... when I see my old films ... I'm surprised to think that I did it really alone."
Charles Chaplin

5

The Magician

It doesn't matter how serious the story is—it all amounts to a bit of business or a gag. In the end, everything is a gag.[1]

Upon seeing his first Chaplin film, *The Gold Rush,* when he was nineteen, this author was struck by a magical quality in many of the visual gags and routines, particularly the "Oceana Roll," in which Chaplin impales two long rolls on forks and has them do a dance on the tabletop. The gag was at once ingenious, graceful, and—there is no other word—magical.

Dancing the "Oceana Roll." *The Gold Rush.*

There is a response people invariably have to a seemingly impossible magic trick—they laugh. There is really nothing *funny* about the trick. This kind of laughter is very different from the laugh in response to a joke—it is a laughter of delight which stems from the surprise of having one's perceptions about reality playfully contradicted.

Similar laughter of delight occurs when people see someone doing what seems impossible—juggling, banjo playing, and balancing acts. Examples from films include the dancing of Fred Astaire, the acrobatics of Buster Keaton, and the juggling of W. C. Fields.

Chaplin elicits both kinds of laughter in his most characteristic gags. Their underlying structure is a confusion of one thing with another as when he makes rolls and forks behave like legs and feet in *The Gold Rush.* These kinds of gags have been called "transformation gags," "metamorphosis gags," and "visual puns." Whatever they are called, Chaplin is unique in his ability to conceive and execute such material. While by no means his only gag format, close examination of his films reveals the frequency with which transformation gags occur, and the many variations of them that percolate through his films. Virtually all of his greatest comic sequences have at their heart a transformation gag. They are central to his achievement.

Although there are overlaps, here for the purpose of examination are the eight major variations on the gag.

(1) Object/Object

The most obvious and common transformation takes place when Charlie uses one object as if it is another. This type of transformation gag reaches an exuberant peak in the Mutual series. For example, in *The Vagabond* Charlie sets out to rescue Edna from the gypsies. Deciding that a thick branch will be a more effective weapon than his violin bow, he strides toward the encampment. But he encounters one of the ruffians midway across a bridge. Immediately Charlie turns and holds the stick over the side of the bridge as if he is fishing.

Now this ruse is not too imaginative. Since a stick with a string attached often functions as a fishing pole, the objects are too similar for the transformation to be startling. Rather it is Charlie's reflexive quickness and his sincere absorption in the act of fishing, completely fooling the gypsy, which make the sequence funny. More imaginative is Charlie's transformation of a roll of dough into a lei, and a wooden spoon into a ukelele, to give Edna a kitchen serenade in *The Pawnshop*. In another moment the dough serves as a rope to pull Charlie's rival around the neck. As far back as 1914, in *Dough and Dynamite*, Chaplin uses dough as bracelets, handcuffs, quicksand, and, of course, missiles.

A kitchen serenade. *The Pawnshop*.

From the beginning of his film career one can sense Chaplin exploring unusual ways of handling objects, though the object transformations in the early films lack finesse. In the Keystone films, for instance, Charlie is fond of blowing his nose into tablecloths and on ladies' skirts. "Mr. Chaplin is funny with a funniness which transcends his dirt and his vulgarity,"[2] read an early review. Eventually Chaplin was able to merely suggest such earthy material with transformations. Thus, in both *The Cure* and *Easy Street* Chaplin *thinks* he has been urinated upon, but the audience has clearly seen that he had inadvertently spilled water or milk on his lap and made the assumption that it was a toy dog (*The Cure*) or a baby (*Easy Street*) that wet him. We have the

pleasure of seeing his disgust without being ourselves disgusted. Contrast this approach to that taken by Max Linder, the French comedian popular in the 1910s. In *Max's Hat* (1913), Max has trouble arriving at his destination with his hat intact. After going through several hats, he finally arrives and deposits his hat, only to have a dog urinate (on screen) into it, and the host drench himself trying it on.

By the time of the Mutual series, Chaplin was greatly skilled in the treatment of such "gross" material. In *The Vagabond*, waiting for Edna to return to a painstakingly prepared breakfast, he casually mimes a routine in which he catches flies from the air with his left hand, places them into his right pocket, and crushes them with a blow from his right fist. He is about to place another fly into his pocket when Edna comes back with the well-dressed artist she met in the woods. Charlie shakes his hand and the man is disgusted to find a crushed fly in his grasp. In the same film Charlie uses a sock as a washcloth to clean Edna's face, ears, and nose. The earthy theme is ironically concluded at the end when, meeting Edna's long-lost, wealthy mother, Charlie shakes her hand and sniffs distastefully at the perfumed smell it leaves on his hand.

As these transformations define Charlie's relationship with the upper-class world of *The Vagabond*, his mock elegance in his own world is shown by his table setting for breakfast. Turning over a washtub, he spreads a checkered shirt over it for a tablecloth. Going one step further, he carefully rolls the sleeves into peaked napkins, and during the meal tucks the end of one into his shirt for a napkin-bib. This concept is reworked for the famous New Year's Eve dinner in *The Gold Rush*. In that scene Charlie tears a newspaper to simulate a lace tablecloth. The scene climaxes in the dream sequence with Charlie's transformation of rolls into feet and forks into legs for the "Oceana Roll" dance, only to wake up to the reality of having been stood up by his guests.

In the Mutual group of films *The Pawnshop* stands out in its object transformations; the film is a virtual catalogue of ways to use one thing as if it is another. The scene in which Charlie dissects an alarm clock, treating it as if it is a heart (listening with a stethoscope), a mouth (pulling a tooth with pliers), a jewel (looking at it through a jeweler's loupe which is actually a telephone mouthpiece), a can of sardines (opening it with a can opener and being repelled by the odor), and so on, has often been described and is justly famous. At the end of the sequence, with the pieces scattered on the counter,

Charlie "winds" the empty clock case with the key, which causes the pieces (via unseen magnet) to move around on the counter. This sort of impossible gag, which Chaplin experimented with extensively in *One A.M.* (the film made before *The Pawnshop*) is far more typical of lesser comedies of the teens and twenties, and Chaplin seldom ventured into this territory again. How much more inventive and satisfying when Charlie dries the dishes by passing them through a clothes wringer, passing a cup through twice, and then passing his own hands through to dry them. The wringer is later used to flatten a wad of dough for Charlie's pie-making.

Sometimes the transformations of objects make a satirical or ironic point. Charlie strides with great authority to open the combination-lock safe in *The Bank,* only to emerge carrying his janitor bucket and mop, and similarly opens the safe in *The Pawnshop* for his bag lunch. In *Work* (1915) the lady of the house immediately puts her valuables in a safe after meeting paperhangers Charlie and his boss, whereupon they collect *their* valuables and ostentatiously safety-pin them into Charlie's pocket. One of the most brilliant transformations occurs in *The Kid,* and it is set up by a funny and earthy sequence. Charlie strolls down a slum street and is doused several times with garbage thrown out of windows. Finding an abandoned kid next to some garbage cans, Charlie immediately looks up—perhaps this bit of "human garbage" was also thrown from a window.

As Chaplin took greater amounts of time to make his films, elaborately planned object transformations replaced the spontaneous ones that filled the Mutual films. In *The Kid* Charlie has rigged the infant a bottle made from a coffee pot with a nipple on the spout, and the infant lies in a makeshift hammock, with the "bottle" hanging from a string for easy access. Meanwhile Charlie is busy cutting a hole in a cane chair and placing a pan beneath it for a potty. In a later scene Charlie lies reading in bed as the now grown kid prepares breakfast. He stretches, poking a foot through a hole in the bedspread. Moving to the foot of the bed, he puts his head through the hole and rises, effortlessly and elegantly transforming the spread into a serape dressing gown. This scene is said to have taken Chaplin two weeks of shooting to perfect, a luxury he could hardly afford in the film-a-month schedule of the Mutual comedies. The loss in spontaneity that results from such carefully prepared props is usually more than compensated for by the gain in beautifully conceived and perfectly executed gags.

The last major object transformation in a Chaplin film also uses a carefully prepared and, in this case, a "fake" prop: the large, global balloon in *The Great Dictator.* The symbolic nature of the prop and the fact that the sequence is executed by the dictator give the scene an unusual quality. Rather than identifying with the character as usual, the audience is forced into an awareness of the absurdity of the character. So accurate is this image, reducing Hitler's monstrous craving for power and domination to an infantile desire for a toy that the scene invariably evokes delight and admiration for Chaplin the writer/scenarist.

(2) Setting/Setting

A transformation on a larger scale is Chaplin's turning one setting into another. The tramp costume itself provides the starting point. An ill-fitting assemblage of formal clothing, it is richly suggestive of strong contrasts—rich vs. poor, elegant vs. bedraggled—which Chaplin was to exploit so effectively as his "gentleman tramp" characterization evolved. The formal aspect of the costume is reinforced through Charlie's carefully trimmed moustache, fastidious, delicate movements, and courtly manners. But the shabbiness of the clothes and inappropriate settings for such mannered behavior contradict the bid for elegance. Thus, Charlie cleans his fingernails (*The Tramp*) or prepares a meal (*The Vagabond*) as if he is in a well-appointed mansion, while in fact he is in the rural countryside. In the rude cabin of *The Gold Rush* Charlie similarly creates mock gourmet meals for Thanksgiving and New Year feasts.

Often Charlie reveals his "true" character by act-

Thanksgiving Dinner in *The Gold Rush.* The nail becomes a wishbone.

ing as though he is in a different setting. As an escaped convict taken into a rich household in *The Adventurer,* Charlie wakes up in the morning wearing striped pajamas, and has a panic-stricken moment as he thinks he is back in his prison garb. Reaching behind him, he reinforces this impression when he touches the brass bars of the bed. In *The Pilgrim,* again as an escaped convict, Charlie is wearing stolen minister's clothing to effect his flight. But he grasps the railway ticket window bars as if back in his jail cell, and even after he realizes his error, his hands unconsciously stray back to the bars. In each of these cases one becomes aware of the transformation of settings through Charlie's eyes, by the way he moves and reacts. Both Buster Keaton and Harold Lloyd use the same idea in a way that also fools the film audience. In *Cops* Keaton seems to be saying goodbye to his girl from behind prison bars. In the next, wider shot we see that the bars are the gates of her mansion and that she is telling him to make good if he wants to win her—an ironic beginning to a film that centers around Buster's complete inability to "make good" at anything besides arousing the animosity of the entire police force. In *Safety Last,* made a year after *Cops,* Harold Lloyd appears to be in the death house, behind bars with a noose in view, prison officials and a parson standing soberly by, his girl sobbing on the other side. But the next shot reveals the group to be in a railroad station. The police officials are in fact conductors, the noose a mail carrier, the others merely waiting for the train. Harold is leaving for the big city. The difference between Lloyd's transformation and those of Chaplin and Keaton are in the relationship of the isolated gag to the rest of the film. Lloyd's sequence has nothing to do with either his character or the rest of the film (unless a point is stretched to relate the death house gag to the thrill comedy of the building climb later). Chaplin and Keaton have integrated the gag into their films' fabric of characters and plots.

But with Chaplin the transformation of settings usually does not involve audience-fooling camera shots; it is accomplished by his own movement rather than by camera movement. After playing the violin for Edna outside the gypsy wagon in *The Vagabond,* Charlie takes a series of elaborate curtain calls and bows as if he is in a concert hall. The camera is placed so that his exits and returns can occur around the side of the wagon. Interestingly, this same sequence of bows occurs in *Caught in a Cabaret,* an early Keystone, but is ineffective in the context provided in that film—Chaplin the actor

was ahead of Chaplin the scenarist. In *Pay Day,* a drunken Charlie, thinking he is on a streetcar, strap hangs from a salami in a food stall. When the owner comes to kick him out (Charlie is by this time reading a newspaper as he strap hangs), Charlie merely hands him the "fare," which neatly pays for the salami Charlie still grasps as he is pushed out of the stall. The identity of the setting as simultaneously a streetcar and a foodstall has been carefully maintained. The capper of this delightful sequence is an object transformation. Finding himself on the street with the salami, Charlie strikes a match to light it, thinking it is a cigar.

In *The Bond,* standing at the alter to be married, Charlie reflexively lifts his foot to find the bar rail. This idea is elaborated on in the remarkable church sequence in *The Pilgrim.* Convict Charlie is posing as a minister in front of the Sunday church congregation. He sees the number "12" superimposed above the church elders seated to his right, begins to light a cigarette (until he sees the shocked look on the elders' faces), leans against the lectern and, drinking a glass of water, again reflexively lifts his foot to find the bar rail. He finally takes elaborate curtain calls and bows after his sermon, so pleased with himself that he doesn't realize that no one is in fact applauding except a small boy. Chaplin's slight, subtle movements during most of the action described above serve to transform the church into settings the convict is more at home in—a saloon, a courtroom, and a theatre.

Sometimes the transformation of settings takes on a playful character. In the dressing room of *The Cure* Charlie has caused a fight between two men by throwing his shoes over his dressing-room curtains. Standing on either side of the curtains, about to fight, they see Charlie's pants come sailing over. Simultaneously they whip the curtains open to reveal Charlie, dressed in a bathing suit, in a coy "September Morn" position. He breaks his statue pose to pull the curtains closed, and the dumbfounded men pull them open again to reveal Charlie in a swashbuckling pose, cane held like a sword . . . another exit and Charlie is revealed dancing like a ballerina. Abruptly Charlie strides past the still-befuddled men into the massage room. The dressing room has become a music hall display of *tableaux vivants* ("living statue" scenes popular in the early years of the century).

Even more playful is Charlie's break from the film's action during a melodramatic moment in *The Cure* to take a very theatrical hop and bow to the camera, transforming the film "reality" into a stage

Escaped convict Charlie sees the church choir as a jury. *The Pilgrim.*

performance for the audience's benefit. He does this twice in *The Pawnshop,* once after a tightrope routine performed on a piece of rope on the floor (no other characters are present during this scene), and another time at the film's finale after he has saved the day by conking villain Campbell over the head with a rolling pin. These bows to the camera take to the extreme the many glances and smiles at the camera so central to Chaplin's presentational acting style, and they don't occur in Chaplin's work after the Mutual series. That series still remains a high point of exuberant spirits and express-train speed, carrying the viewer along and almost daring him or her not to be taken in despite the outrageous flaunting of dramatic conventions—a quality not found in later films until the Marx Brothers' manic films of the thirties.

The setting transformations discussed so far are accomplished with Charlie's movements. Sometimes, though, large groups of people become involved. After getting drunk on Charlie's liquor which has been thrown into the mineral water well, the spa residents in *The Cure* transform the place into an orgiastic dance hall. One man sits playing a lamp as if it is a clarinet, others dance or pursue women. In the restaurant scene in *Modern Times* a group of college men use the duck Charlie inadvertently tosses them as a football, which Charlie intercepts and brings to a "touchdown" by leaping onto and overturning his customer's table. Less subtle in the same film is the camera dissolve from a group of sheep to people emerging from a subway (the film's original title was *The Masses*).

Chaplin's most overt and elaborate setting transformation is of a slum street into heaven for the dream sequence of *The Kid.* Although a straightforward set redressing is done, making this more of a camera trick than is usual in Chaplin's work, the dissolve of the set around the sleeping Charlie is perfect, as were Buster Keaton's similar (but bolder) dissolves in the movie sequence of *Sherlock, Jr.* three years later. In the latter, Buster walks into the movie screen, whereupon the setting suddenly changes around him, though his body appears to be in the same place. Like Chaplin's scene, this was accomplished by measuring Buster's position in the frame, going to a new location, and resuming filming. In *The Kid* the dissolve into the dream was easier to accomplish, since Charlie is lying asleep in a doorway: the dissolve back to reality nicely matches the movement of the angel cop shaking dead angel Charlie to the movement of real cop shaking the sleeping Charlie, who is still flapping his arms.

Tightrope act on an electric cord. *The Pawnshop.*

(3) Body/Object

The violence so prevalent in Chaplin's films is considerably softened by a third type of transformation gag, the treatment of human bodies as if they are objects. Chaplin's quality of immobility leads to his comic freezes to elude pursuers, and his becoming a "thing" (e.g., a tree in *Shoulder Arms*, and a fun house mechanical figure in *The Circus*). In both *The Pawnshop* and *The Circus* he literally pulls himself upward by the seat of his pants. His treating himself as an inanimate object functions to minimize the sense of pain we assume a falling body would feel. When Charlie falls backward into a tub in *The Vagabond*, or off a park bench in *A Woman*, as in many of his falls his legs jackknife straight up as if he is a hinged toy. Bodies, after all, can feel pain, but toys cannot. This is extended to Charlie's dealings with other characters. In *Making a Living*, his

first film appearance, Charlie slaps a man's knee for emphasis as he speaks; when the man moves his leg, Charlie pulls the knee back to continue his slapping. Fallen bodies are often trod over as if they are carpets, rear ends are moved aside and then put back as Chaplin passes, or dusted like pieces of furniture.

Kicking a rear end is an obvious way of puncturing dignity, as exploited by both Sennett and Chaplin. In treating bodies as objects Chaplin found many ways to accomplish the same thing. In *The Bank* he solicitously takes a man's pulse, looks at him in a concerned way, and asks him to stick out his tongue, only to use it to moisten a stamp. In *The Cure*, a virtual ballet of careening bodies, Eric Campbell's bandaged foot becomes the sore point of the film, stepped and sat upon, caught in revolving doors, and kicked. Yet so skillfully defined is Eric's obnoxious character that we feel only delight

Lifting himself onto a curb. *The Pawnshop.*

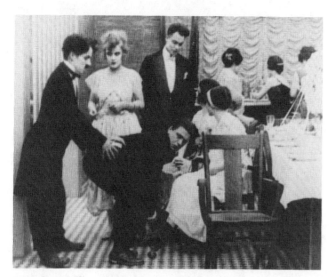

Charlie moves the man's rear end aside. *The Rink*.

at the many painful insults perpetrated by the resourceful Charlie. In this film, the very exaggeration of the foot in its huge bandage and the frequency of assaults upon it serve to make the foot a comic object and prevent the viewer from painfully identifying with Eric's plight.

Chaplin's last extended routine using the body as an object is the wonderful musical routine with Buster Keaton in *Limelight*. During this, Charlie's leg shortens as if drawn up by a string and he is forced into a lopsided walk. Because of the wideness of his pants and the camera angle, the audience cannot see his knee bend, and the illusion of the leg shortening is perfect.

A variation on the body being an object is the mechanical persistence of repetitive movements, which makes the body machinelike. Charlie often forms habits quickly. Running back and forth behind a bed to elude Eric Campbell in *Easy Street*, he becomes so comfortable with his pattern that he fails

Charlie gets some use out of affliction. *The Floorwalker*.

to notice that Eric has reversed direction and runs almost into his arms. In *The Pawnshop,* Edna consoles Charlie by patting his face. When her hand drops, Charlie simply puts it back to resume its patting. In *The Rink* Charlie sits next to a woman who is absently kicking her crossed leg. Bending to pick something up, he gets a kick in the rear, which delights him; he puts his hat in position to be "kicked" by her foot onto his head, whereupon he applauds her briefly and tips his hat by leaning backward against the wall. Repetition can aid flirtation.

It can also lead to cruel jests. In *The Floorwalker* Charlie places a stringed instrument under the shaking fingers of an old man, transforming affliction into music.

Habits persist even in sleep. In the flophouse of *The Kid* a sleeping pickpocket probes Charlie's pockets. Charlie lets him proceed. But when the man finds a dime, Charlie grabs the coin and stuffs the hand back to find more.

Repetitive movement works to Charlie's advantage in the fight scene of *City Lights.* His rhythmic repetitions so hypnotize his opponent and the referee that they begin fighting each other. (This scene is examined in detail in Chapter 7, "The Dancer.")

The climactic body-as-mechanical-object scene in Chaplin's work is the opening factory sequence of *Modern Times.* A slave to the assembly line, Charlie repeatedly tightens nuts with his two wrenches—a repetitive movement enforced by the speed of the moving belt. So programmed does he become by the machine that when he takes his breaks he still continues his jerky tightening movements. During lunch he passes his fellow worker a bowl of soup, spilling it all over as he reflexively jerks. The factory sequence contains two elaborate high points, both of which involve Charlie literally becoming part of the machinery. In the first of these Charlie is strapped to a feeding machine to eliminate the lunch hour for greater efficiency. Naturally the machine goes berserk and violates Charlie's person by spilling soup over him, spinning a corn cob in his mouth at high speed (giving the impression that his teeth are flying out as the kernels spray), pushing large metal nuts into his mouth, and so on. In the second scene Charlie, trying to keep up with a speedup on the assembly line, follows a nut-plate into the bowels of the machine and is literally "eaten" by the machine. Accompanied by music box music, he is wound among the giant cogwheels and then ejected when the machine is reversed. He emerges to plunge into a mad dance of tightening everything in sight with his wrenches and spraying

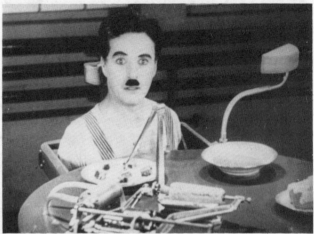

with his oilcans, as well as assorted mischief among the factory control switches. Taken as a whole, the factory scene is a most thorough working out of the theme of the body's capacity to be machinelike, as well as the psychological toll this takes when taken to extremes.

(4) Animated Objects

The complement to treating bodies as objects is treating objects as though they are alive. The first example of this type of transformation is Charlie's fight with a dressmaker's dummy in an early Keystone, *Mabel's Married Life*. A drunken Charlie returns home and accidentally brushes against the dummy as he removes his coat, causing it to sway back and forth. Not having noticed the dummy before, he is startled into believing that it is a person (the dummy wears a hat and sweatshirt like that worn by a man who recently terrorized Charlie in a bar). Charlie continues to treat the dummy as a man, even to the point of sniffing and concluding that it has been drinking. Inevitably, as Charlie pushes at the dummy, it rebounds to knock him over, ultimately winning the fight between them.

Charlie often uses his cane as an extension of his arm in the early films. Holding it upside down in *Getting Acquainted* (1914), he raises his hand to his head, which causes the cane to lift Mabel's skirt (whereupon he sternly reprimands it). A source of much comic business in the early films, the cane was used to grab people around the neck, trip them at the ankle, corkscrew them in the belly, and pull the arms and knees of pretty girls on park benches toward Charlie. In *A Night Out* Charlie tenderly puts it to bed.

In later films other objects often serve similar functions. In *The Idle Class* Charlie's golf club "accidentally" snags the clubs out of a passing golfer's bag. The arms of the tree costume in *Shoulder Arms* end in convenient knobs and pointed sticks, for wartime mayhem.

One A.M. is Chaplin's most concentrated experiment with this type of transformation gag. Almost every object in the house seems alive and malicious in the eyes of the drunken Charlie, and in some cases to the audience as well. But perhaps the most effective instance concludes an earlier film, *The Bank*. Charlie wakes up from his dream of foiling a bank robbery and winning the fair Edna to the reality of kissing his mop and caressing its "hair."

Opposite:
Into the bowels of the factory. *Modern Times.*

Opposite:
In the feeding machine. *Modern Times.*

Opposite:
Charlie reflexively twists the soup bowl while handing it to his friend. *Modern Times.*

(5) Person/Animal

A variation that Chaplin uses on rare occasions is Charlie's transformation of himself into an animal. In *Behind the Screen* Charlie picks up eleven bentwood chairs, creating a startling human porcupine image. In many films he performs movements that suggest animals—wiping his feet by shuffling in place quickly like a dog, holding his leg out to the side and shaking it, again like a dog. These animal suggestions reach their climax in *The Gold Rush* when the starving Mack Swain "sees" Charlie as a chicken in a series of nicely matched dissolves. Chaplin originally had someone else in the chicken costume but was dissatisfied with the filmed result, so he got into the costume himself for the scene. Chaplin's imitation of a chicken makes evident how many of the tramp's precise, angular movements are in fact reminiscent of a chicken. Thus, this "gag", while not often overt in the films, in fact partly underlies Chaplin's conception of the tramp character, and is a clue to the eccentricity of many of his gestures. A related motif occurs when Charlie kicks dirt backward on something, burying it like a dog.

(6) Body Part/Body Part

A transformation gag with which Chaplin often fools the audience occurs when he substitutes one body part with another. In *The Gold Rush* we see Charlie's feet sticking out from under a blanket after a night's uneasy sleep with starving cabin-mate Mack Swain. Suddenly Charlie's head pops up between the feet. In a moment it is apparent that he has merely reversed position, putting his hands into his shoes and his head at the foot of the bed to better watch Swain; but for a moment the impact is that of a hilarious image of impossible body contortion.

Usually Chaplin uses two actors for this type of gag. In *The Kid* Jackie Coogan (as the kid) is hiding under the flophouse bed to elude the proprietor. Charlie, on the bed, is trying to distract the man. Suddenly Charlie's legs lift to a high angle and Jackie springs between them. With barely a pause, Charlie lowers his legs and Jackie's head "becomes" Charlie's knees under the blanket. Charlie rubs Jackie's head to show the proprietor how sore his enlarged knees are.

In the First National series of films (1918–1923) Chaplin spins his richest variations on this gag (it

A human porcupine. *Behind the Screen.*

Charlie turning into a chicken. *The Gold Rush.*

An unusual sleeping position. *The Gold Rush.*

seldom occurs at all before this time and, even when it does, is not set up to create a strong visual illusion for the audience). Charlie's arms become those of the unconscious Albert Austin in *A Dog's Life,* a thief's arm becomes Charlie's in *The Idle Class,* and Charlie mistakes Sydney Chaplin's foot for his own in *Shoulder Arms.* Charlie stuffs his dog down his pants to sneak it into a cafe in *A Dog's Life,* resulting in a startling image as its white tail wags madly out of a hole in the pants.

One of the best workings out of the gag occurs in *The Kid.* As Charlie leans against an open window while flirting with a laughing woman, her husband's hand comes through the window to choke him, but Charlie assumes it is the woman's hand (which is resting on the window sill behind him). We share Charlie's bizarre perception as his panic mounts, of the woman choking him as she laughs hysterically.

Chaplin's last major body-part confusion scene is an elaborate one that opens *City Lights.* A new city monument (''Peace and Prosperity'') is unveiled to reveal Charlie asleep on the lap of the middle figure. By the end of this ingenious routine, Charlie has impaled his pants on a sword, sat squarely on one figure's nose, used the outstretched hand of another to rest his foot as he ties his shoe, and brought his own nose against the thumb of yet another outstretched hand, simultaneously tipping his hat to someone below and making a massive nose-thumbing (the figures are larger than life) at the entire crowd.

Right: A dog in Charlie's pants beats the drum. *A Dog's Life.*

Charlie can't understand why he has no feeling in Syd's foot. *Shoulder Arms.*

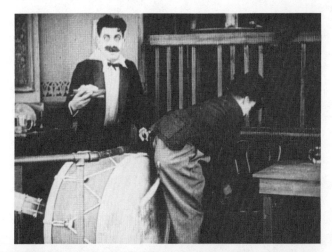

Charlie substitutes his arms for Albert Austin's. *A Dog's Life.*

A production (posed) shot not showing the exact position of Charlie and the laughing woman in *The Kid*.

Charlie inadvertently thumbs his nose at the crowd below. *City Lights*.

(7) Action/Action

One of the subtlest variations occurs when Chaplin transforms one kind of action into another. After Charlie begins using a stick as a fishing pole in *The Vagabond* he takes the object transformation one step further. He begins tugging at the "fish," looking over the side as he pulls. The gypsy obligingly looks over Charlie's shoulder, and the movement of pulling up the fish is smoothly transformed into a blow on the gypsy's head—weapon to fishing pole back to weapon. In *The Cure*, watching Henry Bergman "massage" a victim by stretching him out (Bergman pulls the victim's legs as his bare foot presses the man's chin), Charlie taps the table three times and holds up Bergman's hand as if Bergman were the victor in a wrestling match. This is taken an elaborate step further when it is Charlie's turn. Sliding from end to end of the table to elude Bergman, he finally gets on all fours, making Bergman's attempts to lay him down look exactly like a wrestling match. Finally Charlie flips off the table to face Bergman, his hands outstretched in the classic wrestler's opening position.

In *The Pawnshop* Chaplin transforms four fights with fellow employee John Rand into other activities. Fighting in the store room when boss Henry Bergman enters, they both immediately fall into working movements. With no break in the rhythm, Charlie is suddenly washing the floor (and a violin) and Rand is busy at his desk. Outside, Charlie traps Rand between the rungs of a ladder, and has a small boy hold the end so he can "shadow box" with the helpless man. When a policeman appears on the scene, Charlie's fighting movements (which have become stylized and dancelike) are completely transformed into a graceful dance, and he glides back into the pawnshop. Back in the storage room, Charlie is getting the better of Rand, holding him around the neck and punching him, leaping on him as Rand is bent helplessly backward against the desk until Edna enters from the kitchen to find Charlie writhing on the floor and cowering away from the bewildered Rand. His subterfuge earns Charlie Edna's ministrations. The final fight takes place in the kitchen where Charlie and Rand are at each other with the dough. When boss Bergman again enters they are both suddenly "helping" Edna with her pie-making, Charlie passing dough through the clothes wringer and rapidly trimming it around the pie shells.

Sometimes the transformation does not work so smoothly. Masquerading as a German officer in

Fighting until . . .

. . . the boss appears. *The Pawnshop*.

Shoulder Arms, doughboy Charlie is surprised to see his C.O. brought in as a prisoner. Their hugging reunion is transformed to abuse when the Kaiser's chauffer glances back at them. The routine is, for Chaplin, a bit forced, but works better in this context than does an earlier version in *The Floorwalker* which is not well enough motivated to justify the action at all.

As implied above, camouflage is often the purpose of the transformation of one action to another. In *The Adventurer* Charlie drops ice cream down his pants. To cover his action of shaking it out his pant leg, he rises to reach toward Edna and chuck her on the chin. In the same film, escaped convict Charlie is startled by the sound of the champagne cork being popped by butler Albert Austin. Reflexively he raises his hands, only to smooth his hair when he realizes his mistake (and follows this with a back kick to the innocent butler.)

A beautiful working out of this gag occurs in *The Gold Rush*. Black Larson and Big Jim are struggling for possession of a rifle in the small cabin, and their strength is equally matched as they flail about. Despite Charlie's attempts to find a safe place to stand, the rifle is somehow always pointing at him. The earnestness with which the men fight and Charlie's desperation to get out of the line of fire make this hilarious sequence utterly convincing, as the fighting and covering of Charlie with the gun overlap perfectly. An interesting sidelight to this routine is that a year earlier Buster Keaton had performed a very similar solo routine in *The Navigator* in which his foot becomes entangled in a rope attached to a small cannon whose fuse he has just lit. Whichever way Buster moves, the tiny cannon follows.

Charlie cowers to win Edna's sympathy. *The Pawnshop*.

Whichever way the men turn, the rifle points at Charlie. *The Gold Rush*.

Yet, perhaps the most ingenious of all Chaplin's action transformations occurs in *The Idle Class*. The rich, alcoholic husband gets a note from his wife saying, "I have found a new place to live until you stop drinking." Turning his back to the camera, he picks up her photo from the table and gazes at it longingly. His head bows, his back and shoulders begin to heave, and he seems to be crying uncontrollably—until he turns toward the camera to reveal that he has been shaking a cocktail which he nonchalantly pours and drinks. Essentially, this is a superior reworking of the opening gag from *The Immigrant* in which Charlie bends over a shipboard rail—his whole body heaving as though seasick—only to turn and reveal a fish he has just caught.

(8) Relationship/Relationship

The final kind of transformation gag—that of transforming one kind of relationship to another—is deeply intertwined with Chaplin's concept of Charlie as he relates to other characters. It will be noted that many of the transformations that involve confusing one person's body parts with another's automatically shift the relationship between the characters. Thus, sitting on a park bench in *The Idle Class*, Charlie becomes a thief in the eyes of the man next to him when the real thief picks his pocket from behind (and runs away as the man grabs Charlie). The woman Charlie is flirting with in *The Kid* seems to him to have become a violent maniac until he discovers that it is her husband in the window who has been choking him. But the arms substitution scene in *A Dog's Life* goes even further. Two thieves have stolen Charlie's money (which, ironically, he had found after the same thieves had earlier buried it after stealing it from a rich drunk). As they sit drinking in a cafe, Charlie, who is behind a curtain, knocks one of them out and slips his arms under him to substitute for the arms of the unconscious man. Gesturing to the other thief, he causes the unconscious man to seem to carry on a conversation, which ends when he knocks out the second thief with a beer bottle. So far, a straightforward body-part substitution. But then the first thief wakes up, rubbing his head. He picks up the broken beer bottle and of course assumes that he hit the other thief—naturally they both believe that. During their ensuing fight, they discover Charlie being held by the bartender, who has just seized the stolen wallet. One thief grabs the wallet, and the other reaches for

it because they no longer trust each other. So the first jerks the wallet away, allowing the bartender to grab it, which releases Charlie and gives him *his* chance to grab the wallet and run. The scene happens with breathtaking speed, but the relationships—and the viewer's clear understanding of each person's point of view—make the characters' behavior credible and natural.

The struggle for the wallet. *A Dog's Life.*

In this instance Charlie was purposely manipulating a relationship. Often, however, he accidentally causes misunderstandings to occur. In *The Cure*, throwing his shoes over the dressing room curtain, he causes the two occupants to go at each other in a cleverly designed sequence. One shoe hits Eric Campbell who, looking back and assuming it is the man sitting on the other side of the room, throws his shoe at the innocent man. Then Charlie's second shoe comes over, also hitting the other man, who of course thinks Eric has thrown *both* his shoes at him. This is too much! He throws one back and they both grab shoes, ready for battle. Each man thinks the other has thrown two shoes at him, well justifying the shift of relationship from strangers to enemies. Similar sequences occur in *The Idle Class*. Golfer John Rand hits a ball that lands near Charlie, who has none. Charlie assumes it dropped from his pants and hits it. As Rand upbraids Charlie, Mack Swain's ball lands near them, and Charlie points it out as Rand's. After Rand hits it, they stroll along like the best of friends. Rand offers Charlie a cigarette from his case. Taking the case, Charlie hands Rand a cigarette and nonchalantly pockets the case, at which point Swain catches up to them and begins beating Rand. Later, Charlie hits a ball which beans

Swain, who has been drinking from a liquor bottle. Charlie's next ball breaks the bottle, and Swain begins weeping. Walking along to get his ball, Charlie crushes Swain's hat and strides away before Swain looks up to see Rand strolling by. After a cutaway shot to Charlie we see Swain again pummeling the prone Rand.

Charlie tries to charm Mack Swain. Note his face is directed more at camera than at Swain. *The Gold Rush*.

The Idle Class is particularly rich in its manipulation of mistaken identity. Early in the film Charlie longingly looks at Edna as she rides past him on a horse. He has a daydream of rescuing her when her horse gets out of control and then marrying her. After waking from this fantasy, he sees a horse standing nearby with a woman lying on the ground. When he rushes over and tries to lift her, she proves to be ugly, so he merely replaces her on the ground with a look of distaste. (An earlier version of this gag occurs in *The Adventurer* when Charlie chooses to rescue Edna from drowning instead of her mother.) The climax of the film (and its relationship transformations throughout) comes during a masquerade ball scene, where Charlie and his millionaire counterpart are confused by nearly everyone. After a poignant scene between Edna (who is married to millionaire Charlie) and the tramp, Mack Swain, who turns out to be Edna's father, introduces Charlie as Edna's husband. Charlie protests, "She is not really my wife" and Swain is outraged.

A running theme in Chaplin's films is Charlie's ability to perform any job with extraordinary skill. Thus, he becomes a super violinist, cop, roller skater, bricklayer, soldier, father, singing waiter, etc. In addition he can easily masquerade as any character.

Many of the early films cast Charlie in imposter roles; he impersonates royalty, rich men, women, and so on. Although he is labled "the tramp," in fact he is an unemployed vagrant in only a handful of films. Usually he is gainfully employed, and in a few instances, even married. This variety and flexibility in roles within a single film leads to bold transformations of his character which alters his relationship to others. In *Police*, for example, Charlie has entered Edna's house to rob it, but she captures him. By the time the police arrive, however, he has so charmed her that she introduces him as her husband, whereupon he immediately masquerades as her husband, flexing his knees and taking command of the situation. The role switch becomes another kind of camouflage. In *The Adventurer*, finally collared by the police after a long chase, he introduces his captor to Edna, and vice versa, repeating the introduction until the cop lets go of him to shake Edna's hand, whereupon he, of course, escapes.

Relationship transformation allows Chaplin to get away with seemingly homosexual behavior. Facing his double in *The Floorwalker* as though looking in a mirror, he suddenly plants a kiss on the man's nose. Watching Eric the bully roll up his sleeve for the knockout punch in *Easy Street*, Charlie kisses his hand. He plants another kiss on Eric after trapping him in double doors in *The Adventurer*. Even more explicitly, in both *The Cure* and *A Dog's Life* Charlie misinterprets the actions of other men as flirtations and responds by coyly flirting back. Yet the amazing thing is that because of Charlie's fluid role changes (as well as the other transformations that permeate his work) these gags never suggest that he is either homosexual or doing "homosexual baiting" jokes, as sometimes occurred in other silent comedies; he is simply responding to the situation, shifting roles, and using his kisses and flirtations as a child might try to charm his way with winsomeness.

The film that weaves the most elaborate fabric of role switches is *City Lights*. Charlie's millionaire friend knows him only when the friend is drunk, a blind girl thinks he is a millionaire, the police think him a thief, and a boxer thinks he is a homosexual.

City Lights in fact contains more homosexual joking than any other Chaplin film. A critical scene at the beginning of the film sets it all up. While sneaking glances at a large nude statue in a window, Charlie pretends to study a small statue of a horseman. This brilliant scene contains many elements. As Charlie backs away from the window like an art connoisseur, a sidewalk elevator descends, rising just as he steps onto it. Discovering his danger, he

Charlie sneaking a glance at the nude. *City Lights*.

Apparent millionaire Charlie about to push a bum away from the cigar he saw first. *City Lights*.

reprimands the worker coming up on it, until the man emerges fully to reveal that he stands about a foot and a half taller than Charlie. But the thematic importance of the scene is how effortlessly it establishes Charlie's heterosexuality through his fascination with the female nude statue. For the rest of the film Charlie's sexuality will be questioned. In scenes with the millionaire and the boxer, Charlie pats, rubs, kisses, and flirts. But ultimately this sexual "unmanliness" is translated in the film to unworthiness—Charlie questioning his worthiness to be loved by the blind girl through his struggle to provide for her, knowing all the while that his masquerade as a rich man must end, and he will stand revealed—as he does at the end—stripped of disguises and pretenses. Without sexuality and without money, is he worthy of love?

One other gag from *City Lights* serves to show how sophisticated Chaplin had become in his manipulation of the audience's sense of the film characters' perceptions of each other. Given a Rolls Royce by his millionaire friend and wearing his borrowed evening clothes, Charlie is locked out of the house when the millionaire sobers up in the morning. A man strolls by smoking a cigar. Immediately Charlie hops into the car and follows him. When the man throws the cigar onto the sidewalk, Charlie stops and rushes to push away another tramp reaching for it. Charlie picks up the cigar and rides away, leaving the baffled, outraged bum to stare at this spectacle of the rich robbing the poor. Since the audience knows the truth underlying the appearances, they can appreciate each character's point of view and marvel at the brilliance and resonance of the gag. The typical audience response to

this gag is to laugh and then laugh again as it "sinks in." The cigar gag appears in a different context at the end of *The Gold Rush*. After striking gold, newly rich prospectors Charlie and Mack Swain are sailing home "on the good ship success"; they stroll along in fur coat finery, and Charlie reflexively picks up a cigar butt from the deck. Mack scolds him and offers a cigar from a fancy cigar case. While this again stresses the incongruity between appearance and reality, the gag is a minor one in *The Gold Rush*.

Having examined eight major variations Chaplin weaves on the gag of transformation, it seems worth going into a little more detail about the magical nature of these transformations in the film medium.

Magic in real life is a blatant contradiction of commonsense reality. The magician manipulates the audience's habits of perception, particularly the sense of constancy of objects. For instance, suppose a magician closes a hand over a coin. It is assumed that the coin is in the hand although it cannot be seen, for the same reason that it can be assumed that the roof is not about to cave in—it is convenient to make that assumption. But this is a mental short cut and can lead one up a blind alley if the magician was clever enough to have only *apparently* put the coin in the hand, or to have removed it without the audience's knowledge. When the magician opens the empty hand, the audience comes smack up against a contradiction of their assumption, and of the very law of constancy. In a playful way, the magician undermines the reality people live in.

Early films worked on the level of magic tricks. The illusion of a moving image on a flat surface was itself enough for the first film audience. Pioneers like stage magician Méliès sought to go further and pre-

New millionaire Charlie forgets that he no longer has to pick up cigar butts from the ground. *The Gold Rush.*

sent impossible images within the film, to do things that could never be accomplished on stage. But soon film, like theatre, became primarily a vehicle for stories. The medium established conventions of "reality" in its own terms, and audiences comfortably sat back to become involved with the characters and with the stories, just as they would in watching a play or reading a book. The audience "suspension of disbelief" was achieved.

By the time Chaplin entered films, the editing, close-ups, time lapses, and other conventions of films were accepted as universal traditions. Mack Sennett exploited Méliès-type trick photography against this context of film "reality" for his particular brand of knockabout comedy. But in his own

films, Chaplin soon began pursuing a different vein of trickery which made only occasional and subtle use of the broad Sennett techniques. Increasingly, he substituted his various forms of transformation gags for the impossible film gags favored by Sennett and Méliès.

An impossible film gag or magician's trick leaves the audience ultimately unsatisfied—there is a cheat involved, a secret technique. Chaplin discovered, as Keaton and Lloyd did after him, that by presenting himself so that his skill was shown clearly apart from film trickery, the audience got the pleasure of magical surprises without the cheat. The trickery was transparent. This is one of the qualities that makes Chaplin's films interesting and involving even after repeated viewings. Knowing the effect beforehand allows the audience to appreciate Chaplin's great skill at setting up the gag. Indeed, in his best films the setups contain such good gags themselves that they dovetail with the "payoff" gag sequences. In his execution of the gags Chaplin often achieves such a merging of conception, choreography, and characterization that repeated viewings are virtually necessary to appreciate all the nuances and levels—a first viewing sometimes merely establishes the magic-trick level.

Like magic tricks, many of the transformation gags involve deception. On occasion the audience is fooled, as when Charlie successfully masquerades as a tree in *Shoulder Arms.* More often, however, it is the characters in the film or Charlie himself who get fooled.

Sometimes Chaplin plays the trickster without transformations. This kind of gag has Charlie trick-

A Chaplin gag setup: In another moment the flypaper will be pushed by the child onto Sydney's face. Note that Chaplin's position enables him to do the actual movement. *The Pilgrim.*

The child distracts Charlie, who doesn't notice that the cake he is icing has been covered by a bowler hat (by the child, of course). *The Pilgrim.*

Chaplin as trickster: He twists his ear, and smoke comes out of his mouth. *Modern Times*.

ing the other characters with magical ploys. As his pockets are being emptied by a thief in *Police*, he simultaneously picks the thief's pocket. As his shrewish wife takes the money hidden in his hat-band (*Pay Day*), he retrieves some from her purse and slips it back into the hatband. He manages to grab a meal of fruit as the butler throws him out of the mansion in *City Lights*, and he gets an after-dinner cigar as the policeman who has him collared calls for the paddy wagon in *Modern Times*. When the cop whips his cigar away, Charlie grasps the puffs of smoke with his hand, and taps the top of his hat, "causing" more smoke to emerge from his mouth, just as in *The Great Dictator* where he pours water into his ear and simultaneously squirts it from his mouth. Like the transformations, these ruses delight by their plausibility (the other characters seem to be really fooled) and by their sheer beauty of design and execution. The trickster gag structure in

such streetwise ruses and playful flourishes is a central aspect of the Charlie character.

But all the skills themselves are merely a bonus. Ultimately the transformations and related gags and idiosyncratic gestures fuse with the comic and dramatic content of the films, as has been indicated through many examples. They define Charlie's character and his relationships with other characters. This fusion can be appreciated by contrasting transformation gags in Chaplin's films with those used by Harold Lloyd. Lloyd began his career as a Chaplin imitator (a common practice during the late teens), and his feature films of the twenties owe far more to Chaplin than has generally been realized. Lloyd borrowed from Chaplin much more than Keaton, who found his own distinctive gag structures and rhythms. But, like the example described earlier of the railroad station/death house from *Safety Last*, Lloyd's gags often come across as ruses by the director or writer rather than the character. Although they are sometimes very ingenious, the audience never feels they really have much to do with Lloyd's character, which in fact has dated badly from a modern audience's point of view. To motivate his climb up a building in *Safety Last,* for example, Lloyd's character must anger a policeman. But Lloyd sets this up with a rather gratuitous act of cruelty towards the cop, which lends his character little audience sympathy. With Chaplin, on the other hand, it is rarely possible to make a distinction between conception and performance. The transformations stem directly and effortlessly from the core of the character, and seem inseparable from him.

The transformation gags have their opposite in Chaplin's films. The man who is the master of reality and perception, transforming the world according to his immediate needs, often has great trouble using things in ordinary ways. *One A.M.* offers the most complete study in the lack of common sense, which is one reason it is exceptional in Chaplin's work. Overall, there are fewer transformations in it than in other Chaplin films of the period (except for treating inanimate objects as though they are alive, a gag that doesn't occur much in other films).

When Chaplin plays the drunk, which he does many times, he uses a gag structure of absent-mindedness. Rather than fooling others with his ruses and transformations, the drunken Charlie fools himself. Thus, lighting a cigarette in *One A.M.,* he keeps the match and discards the cigarette, or forgets to light it and can't understand why he can't draw smoke. The drunk act also allows the usually graceful Charlie to misperceive distance, as by hanging his coat on thin air, thinking the coatrack is right next to him.*

The cumulative effect of all the transformations and related structures that permeate Chaplin's films is of an unstable, fluid world, and at its center a character amazingly adept at assuming many roles

and performing a seemingly endless array of skills. The Mutual films contain the densest concentration of transformations, the world of objects and characters being in constant flux around the dancing figure of Charlie.

The examples discussed in this chapter are chosen from among hundreds. Naturally, Chaplin often repeated and developed his gags, but to his great credit he managed to find new twists and contexts for the gags and skills. His unusual movement skills, such as roller skating and violin playing, each appear in only two films. No doubt he felt the need to create new material since even his earliest films have remained in constant circulation.

Chaplin exploited different types of transformation gags at different times in his career, notably object/object and action/action transformations during the Mutual period, and body part/body part transformations during the First National period. What emerges as a striking fact is that transformation gags abruptly cease to fill the films beginning with *The Great Dictator,* as if Chaplin found them incompatible with the dialogue comedy in his later films. While their absence gives fuel to theories about his ''decline,'' the very suddenness of their disappearance implies that he had in some way outgrown them.

But up until that time, Chaplin is a magician of comedy. He manipulates reality to his audience's and his own great delight.

Notes

[1]Chaplin, *My Life in Pictures,* op. cit.

[2]*Photoplay,* October 1915.

---

*It is interesting that although in real life Chaplin had little taste for liquor (his father died an alcoholic), he found in it such a rich source of humor. Invariably when he plays a rich man he is drunk, and although the tramp seldom has the means to buy liquor, he sneaks it cleverly at every opportunity. A glance at the films of Keaton and Lloyd reveals the comparative importance of liquor in Chaplin's work, as his great contemporaries seldom used it. This is ironic, since in real life Keaton was an alcoholic. In *Limelight* drunkenness is treated as a serious problem, intertwined with Calvero's (Chaplin's character) professional and personal fate—Chaplin's first serious treatment of a theme that was obviously a preoccupation.

6
The Juggler

"We look . . . for some little incident, some vignette that fixes the other characters. The audience must never be in any doubt about them. We have to fix them on sight. Nobody cares about their troubles. They stay the same. You know them every time they appear . . . He's the one we develop."[1]

The characters at Keystone—the people who inhabited those abused, flying bodies—provided Chaplin with a base for his own film world. This chapter explores the nature of the characterizations as well as Chaplin's juggling of them for his own purposes.

This is an elusive area to pursue, because basically the actors at Keystone do not portray characters at all, but rather *types* which are composed of a few emphasized characteristics. Their reactions to events serve mainly to advance the plot, and are rooted more in convention than in emotional reality. Feelings such as jealousy, rage, cruelty, cowardice, and bravado alternate with bewildering frequency in a single performance.

Chaplin was able to take from these primitive conceptions the seeds to populate his own film world in order to transform Sennett's world to a world somehow still vital to a modern viewer. There are problems in the transformation related to the Sennett source. In a world of violent slapstick one humanizes the characters at one's own risk, for if the audience sees a character as too "real," and that character seems hurt by the action (either physically or emotionally), the distance necessary for comedy vanishes. In his own characterization Chaplin introduces dissonant notes when he is hurt in *The Tramp* and *The Adventurer*. Watching these scenes rather jars the viewer, even though at the same time he or she may admire Chaplin's dramatic acting skill. Another problem of departing from character types is simple consistency, as Chaplin's tendency was to mix types (cartoons) with caricatures (drawings) and

characterizations (portraits). This can be examined by isolating the various roles in Sennett's films and tracing their development in Chaplin's work.

Heavies

Sennett hired Chaplin to replace his head comedian Ford Sterling. Sterling played the heavy, generally in a "Dutch" (comic German immigrant) makeup familiar to audiences through vaudeville performers such as Weber and Fields. Although Sterling apparently used a Dutch dialect when he played his scenes, naturally this was lost on the film audience, so he found a physical equivalent, in what soon became a signal movement for Sennett comedy. Excited or angry, he stands in one place and jumps, his knees and feet splayed to the sides, legs remaining bent as he reaches the top of the jump (usually he doesn't actually elevate his body with this movement).

The term "heavy" must be qualified in its Keystone sense. Since most of the characters share the same cardboard quality, no particular moral judgments are made and the male characters simply take advantage of everyone in sight. Thus, Sterling gives essentially the same performance whether he portrays a flirtatious rogue, a married man, or the chief of the Keystone Kops.

Stating in his autobiography that when he arrived at Keystone almost everyone on the lot imitated Sterling, Chaplin implies that in his own performances, he did not. That isn't quite true. He often adopted the aggressive head-forward posture and facial expressions affected by Sterling, occasionally even imitating Sterling's hop in place. Soon, however, he replaced these with his own distinctive gestural trademarks. As a Keystone comedian Chaplin fit right into the character mold, adding a casualness to his cruelty that somewhat undercuts it—flicking cigarette ashes into a woman's open hand, sticking knives into posteriors, and pushing people into lakes.

At Keystone, the guiding rule was to get quickly to the larger actions of fights and chases, and the motivations for these actions were flimsy as often as not. Chaplin recognized and fought against this anti-character trend at Keystone. But there was no revolution with Chaplin's original Keystone films. More than he admitted, Chaplin found the Keystone flexibility about motivation congenial, and his tramp would always embody some of the flexible characteristics of the Sennett heavy—in particular, the streak of casual cruelty. What changed more was his vision of his relation to other characters. Chaplin learned to make his own actions seem justified and motivated, by, for example, his need for food or shelter, or to protect himself from powerful enemies with streetwise ruses. Thus, the same violent actions

that seemed gratuitous in Chaplin's early films became admirable in later ones.

Many of the crasser elements of the Keystone heavies—jealousy, bullying, and cowardice in particular—were given to other characters in later Chaplin films. Often the heavies in Chaplin's later work—the orphan officials and doctor in *The Kid,* or the circus owner/ringmaster in *The Circus*—are just as cardboard as their Keystone predecessors. If anything, they are even more limited by being better focused; the doctor is simply callous, the orphan official simply pompous, and so on.

At Mutual Chaplin added an important dimension to the heavy roles; the element of power. At Keystone no character was made to seem really powerful or threatening; they were comic heavies, with the many scrambling, frantic clowns placing an often desperate emphasis on the comedy. Chaplin was able to embody a genuine sense of power and threat when he discovered Eric Campbell and featured him in eleven of the twelve Mutuals.

Campbell had been a Gilbert and Sullivan actor, as he clearly demonstrated by the ease with which he assumed melodramatic postures. A large, barrel-chested man, he had a penchant for standing rather balletically on his toes with one foot extended. Campbell's contribution to the success of the Mutu-

Eric Campbell. *Behind the Screen.*

als cannot be overlooked. His performances are gems of comic exaggeration, with enough menace in his movements and facial expressions that cause one to believe that the bully of *Easy Street* or the waiter in *The Immigrant* could easily harm Charlie. They are kept on a comic level, particularly by his ludicrous tapering bottom half (the opposite of Charlie's physique) and his exaggerated makeups. Campbell's large, powerful gestures and glowering looks at Charlie perfectly counterpoint Chaplin's quicksilver, light movements. With Campbell as a foil, Chaplin was able to explore not only chase and fight scenes, but also a particularly rich vein of insult humor which climaxes in the Chaplin-Campbell scenes of *The Cure*. These scenes are "justified" by Chaplin's manipulation of their role relationship. Eric is invariably in a higher social class, a "have" to Charlie's "have-not" by virtue of being either rich, Charlie's employer, or simply physically powerful and brutal. Against Campbell's boiling antagonism or outraged dignity, Chaplin was able to spin exhilarating triumphs.

With the First National series of films the heavies become a little "heavier" and more realistic. The thieves in *A Dog's Life, The Pilgrim,* and *The Kid* seem like hardened professional criminals. By contrast, when Eric Campbell plays a thief in *The Pawnshop* he melodramatically strokes his moustache and scowls. Charlie insultingly plays with him until the final moment, when he foils Campbell's robbery attempt with a blow from a rolling pin.

Part of the change resulted from Chaplin's growth as a storyteller. Stealing is a central theme in *A Dog's Life,* for example. The film begins with Charlie as a thief, stealing his breakfast from a hot dog vendor (but stopped by a cop before he eats it). But Charlie's theft is justified in the context of the film. He is hungry. The scene, not at all played for sympathy, is a lively parody of the desperation of Charlie's position. Getting his hot dog, he reaches back under the fence for the mustard brush; discovered by the cop, he leads him a merry chase, the cop laboriously circling the fence while Charlie simply rolls back and forth under it, managing in the process to untie the cop's shoelace and stick a pin into his rear end. A similar scene later shows Charlie stealing buns from a lunch wagon, he and brother Sydney playing a catch-me-if-you-can game as Charlie stuffs innumerable pastries in his mouth the moment Sydney's eyes are off him. These two scenes by themselves would put Charlie in a role similar to that of his Keystone rogue, except for several elements; the gritty looking slum environment, the hunger, and,

most importantly, the fact that in between the scenes is a third scene in which Charlie, again in a rhythmically fascinating sequence, tries and fails to get a job from the local employment office. Charlie steals because he is unable to find work in his environment, not because he is a true thief.

This moral dimension is highlighted by the contrast of Charlie with the two real thieves of the film. After pulling a drunken millionaire into an alley, they emerge to find cops in pursuit. One of the thieves buries their loot—a wallet full of cash—in Charlie's vacant lot. Except for the sudden pull of the millionaire into the alley, nothing about the theft is comic. The design of the scene emphasizes the clear motivation of all five participants. The crooks duck into an alley, out of sight of the camera, as the millionaire rounds a corner and staggers toward the camera down the sidewalk. He is pulled in (leaving the actual mugging to the viewer's imagination). The thieves emerge with the wallet, one facing the camera and the other opposite, and they simultaneously see two cops (the viewer sees only the one in the background). Cops and crooks cross each other in opposite directions, one cop-and-crook pair running out of frame in the foreground while the second cop appears from the foreground and chases the second crook out of the upper right frame. Immediately after they vanish, the millionaire staggers out of the alley, rubbing his head. As well as being an ingeniously designed pattern of movement, the scene, shot in one sustained long shot, leaves no time for comic posturing; the thieves *are* the action of stealing and fleeing.

Later, in the Green Lantern Cafe, one of the thieves wants to dance with cafe-singer Edna. He is quite brutal about pulling her to him. There is none of the comic exaggeration Eric brought to such scenes, wiggling his eyebrows or making kissing motions with his fingers to his lips. This man seems to have more than flirtation on his mind. When Edna resists she is promptly fired by her boss—evidently her job entails more than singing.

When Charlie created the misunderstanding between two men in the dressing room of *The Cure* it was gratuitous. When he does the same thing with these thieves in the arm-substitution scene of *A Dog's Life* it is not only a satisfying reversal, but further depicts the thieves' inner world—they quickly go from being comrades ("thick as thieves") to enemies. And this time they are not holding shoes or Sennett bricks, but a broken bottle. When they catch up with Charlie in the lunch wagon they fire at him with guns. The softening of this scene by Char-

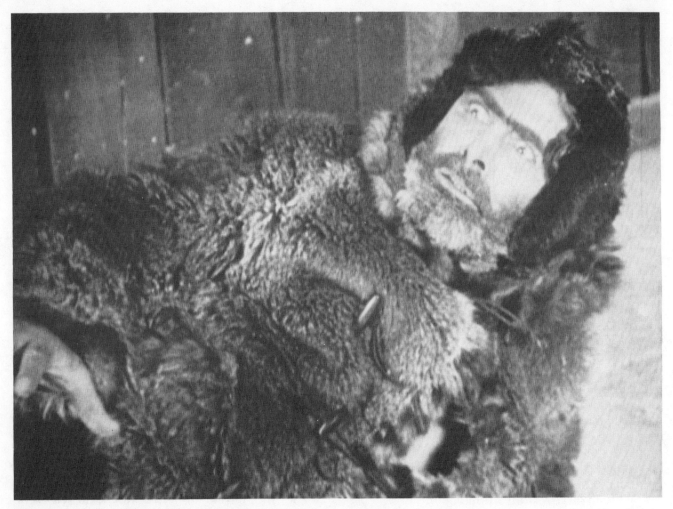

Tom Murray as Black Larson. *The Gold Rush*.

lie's transformation of the wagon into a shooting gallery—his and Sydney's heads popping up in turn—doesn't alter the serious danger element. Eric had never fired a gun at Charlie in the Mutuals, and the cops who did were easily outwitted. The violence and danger are concluded when the thieves viciously choke Charlie, letting go only when police arrive (allowing Charlie to get out of the wagon with a graceful backward somersault).

It is only one short step from these thieves to Chaplin's ultimate heavy—Black Larson in *The Gold Rush*. As indicated by his name, Black Larson is villainy and treachery personified. Wanted for murder, he cold-bloodedly murders two policemen and leaves Charlie and Mack Swain to starve.

Black Larson is no caricature. A powerful-looking man with a full, natural beard and moustache, he goes about his business efficiently. Even the thieves of *A Dog's Life* retained some comic exaggeration in their movements, makeup, and Albert Austin's

droopy moustache. Black Larson is played perfectly straight, not even scowling as he commits his murders. His only deviation, in fact, from his cold, expressionless demeanor occurs after Big Jim has wrested a gun from him. He crouches, panting . . . his mouth slightly open in a cold, wary rage. Once Larson has served his purpose in the film he is eliminated by a massive act of nature: "The North. A law unto itself." Larson is caught on a collapsing cliff and plunges to his death.

The progression from type to archetype is neither linear nor absolute in Chaplin's films. Throughout his career, types and caricatures drawn from Keystone models, his stage experience, and his memories of Victorian "straight" heavies continue to populate the films. After *The Gold Rush* Chaplin made *The Circus*. In this film the ringmaster is an important character whose insensitive actions motivate the other character's reactions. At the film's opening he cruelly throws the pretty equestrian—his stepdaughter—to the ground because she failed to execute a trick properly. She thus has a complex double relationship with him, as both stepdaughter and employee. Unfortunately, the ringmaster is a shallow cliché, simply hard and cruel down to his handlebar moustache and whip. He is neither evil, like Black Larson, nor comic, like Mack Swain and Eric Campbell. His performance is a period piece, one of the few in Chaplin's later films, and members of a modern audience feel uncomfortable in their reaction. Laughing at a character whose performance is clearly intended to be serious creates a distance unusual in a Chaplin film. In contrast, though they are cut from the same cloth as the ringmaster, the orphan officials and doctor in *The Kid* work much

better, for two reasons: they seem to belong in the Dickensian atmosphere of *The Kid*'s slum setting; and their callousness is effectively played against the "real" serious situation of the kid's illness, with brilliant comic reactions from Chaplin as well as poignant dramatic ones. The comedy underscores their pomposity; the drama, their power. By contrast, the scenes between the circus owner and Charlie are flat and uninspired.

On the other hand, the *comic* heavies in Chaplin's films, derived directly from Keystone, are refreshingly well drawn. Two of the best characters in this vein are played by Chuck Reisner, who also worked as assistant director to Chaplin. In *The Kid* Reisner plays a bully, brother to a boy the kid has

Chuck Reisner, Edna and Charlie in *The Kid*.

bested in a fight. Reisner portrays the ultimate brute, with cauliflower ears, ridiculously padded shoulders, and apelike walk. He is like a dumber version of Eric's bully portrayal in *Easy Street,* even to the point of bending lampposts and smashing brick walls with his blows as he tries to hit Charlie. And like Eric in *Easy Street,* he has a religious revelation that temporarily reforms him. As he is about to smash Charlie, Edna comes to him and quotes a line of scripture, "Turn the other cheek," and the brute does. Taking advantage of the opportunity, Charlie promptly conks him with a brick and keeps conking him as the stunned Reisner staggers after the departing Charlie.

In *The Pilgrim* Reisner plays a different type of comic heavy. As Charlie's former cellmate, he immediately sizes up the situation when he sees Charlie as a bogus minister, and determines to loot Edna's family, who are putting Charlie up for the night. Here Reisner is the ultimate sneak, picking pockets and ruthlessly out for whatever he can get. However, Charlie outwits him at every turn in a scene of delightfully conceived one-upmanship in the presence of the unknowing family group. After Reisner secures one of the men's wallets, Charlie picks it from Reisner's pocket and returns it to the owner's pocket. When Reisner gets it again, Charlie performs a mock magic trick, flourishing a handkerchief at both men and producing the wallet he has "mysteriously" transferred into Reisner's pocket. As usual in Chaplin films, the design of the scene makes clear the perceptions and motivations of all the characters, so the viewer can fully appreciate the game of deception being played out.

In the Keystone films little attention is devoted to economic and class distinction. But from the beginning they are an important feature of Chaplin's work. In choosing to come to America and eventually to leave Karno, Chaplin was acutely aware of the class structures that he felt would limit any success he could achieve in his native country. Perhaps that is why in his Keystone films he often imitates wealthy noblemen and uses plots that revolve around the discovery of his imposture (*Caught in a Cabaret, Making a Living, Her Friend the Bandit*). He also does this in two of the Mutuals, *The Rink* and *The Adventurer,* but by that time Chaplin had explored many variations on his character, including a rich man in *One A.M.* Invariably, when he departs from his low-class tramp character, he becomes full of such comic flaws as drunkenness (*One A.M., The Cure, The Idle Class*), absent-mindedness (*The Idle Class*), philandering (as the henpecked

Reisner as a pickpocket. *The Pilgrim.*

construction worker of *Pay Day*). Increased personal power inevitably meant misuse of power. As a head of state he is a maniac in *The Great Dictator;* as a powerless head of state in *A King in New York* (an aristocrat at last for his final starring performance) he is well-intentioned but misused by those in power; as a businessman he is the murderer *Monsieur Verdoux*. Clearly, Chaplin had strong negative feelings toward the rich and powerful, possibly stemming from his early privation.

> *I found poverty neither attractive nor edifying. It taught me nothing but a distortion of values, an overrating of the virtues and graces of the rich and the so-called better classes. . . . Wealth and celebrity, on the contrary, taught me to view the world in proper perspective, to discover that men of eminence, when I came close to them, were as deficient in their way as the rest of us.*[2]

Although Chaplin continued to use his tramp appearance in all his films through *The Great Dictator*, in a number of the films he might just as well have used a different makeup, since he created characters quite unlike the tramp. In some cases this is justified by his playing a double role, with a mistaken-identity theme (in *The Idle Class* and *The Great Dictator*); in other cases he clearly wanted the recognizability of his familiar role, rather than risk confusion for his vast public at a time when silent clowns proliferated. *Pay Day*, in particular, contains many gags and situations that don't blend with the "tramp mythology." The viewer is made aware of Chaplin's body underneath the tramp costume, moving in rather different ways than he usually does—a disconcerting but fascinating effect. The same thing happens in Chaplin's short war bonds commercial, *The Bond,* and at the end of *The Great Dictator* when the Jewish barber, himself a strange, passive new version of the tramp, is transformed into a passionate orator in a sustained and increasingly intense close-up.

The tramp himself is almost invariably powerless in the conventional sense. Increasingly after the Mutual series he loses his "heavy" characteristics, but occupies a world populated by authority figures who are heavies merely by virtue of their disapproval of Charlie or their power over him. Swain and Campbell play Charlie's boss in several of the films, with the expected conflicts and comeuppances. An interesting variation on Charlie's relationship with his employer occurs in *Modern Times*. The boss of the factory sits idly trying to distract himself with a jigsaw puzzle and the funny papers, "communicating" with his employees through closed-circuit television to the point of spying on Charlie in the bathroom when Charlie tries to take a smoke break. Charlie's only direct contact with the man comes after his destructive dance through the factory—a nervous breakdown in dance. He sprays oil into the boss's face. But this is not comically exaggerated villain Eric—this man is only doing his job. Similarly, when Charlie later encounters thieves during his rounds as night watchman in a department store, they turn out to be unemployed factory workers, the victims of strikes and the Depression. Clearly Chaplin was putting the characteristics of the heavy (so stark in his early films) into systems and institutions rather than individual characters. The actions of individuals become much more complex in motivation. The result is that the tramp of the feature films becomes truly an outsider, since he is comfortable neither with individuals nor with the society that spawned them.

Because of their omnipresence, the police are a special class of authority figures in Chaplin's films. At Keystone the police are simply incompetent bunglers, so many bodies for the final chase. By the end of his Essanay year Chaplin had suffused his cops with far more power. At the opening of *Police* he has just been released from jail. Although he wants to go straight, he is disillusioned by a bogus minister who picks his pocket while imploring, "Let me help you go straight." With an old crony he decides to burglarize Edna's house. When she summons the police they are taking their tea—and their time. Casually, they finish their tea and proceed to Edna's house, smoking cigars. Obviously they are not too concerned about doing their jobs.

Although in the Mutuals Charlie leads cops on comic chases, the cops themselves become increasingly humorless and threatening, unlike their ridiculous Keystone predecessors. No longer played by human oddities with comic makeup, they become formidable presences, objects of avoidance in Charlie's world by the time of the First National films.

As always in Chaplin, however, there are exceptions. In *Easy Street* the cops are cowardly, so terrified that a small child is able to startle them all by pointing his finger and saying "Bang." In this one instance Charlie becomes a cop—naturally a heroic cop against the background of the others. Perhaps in tribute, the chief of police is made up to look like Ford Sterling.

But Chaplin's cops, like Sennett's Kops, serve his

filmic needs as anonymous figures of insensitive authority, rarely, as the saying goes, there when you need them. Only in *The Gold Rush* do cops seem more rounded as characters, staying warm in their tent until Black Larson discovers and murders them. Types cannot be killed, but characters can.

In *Modern Times* cops permeate the picture, arresting Charlie several times. They function to prevent the angry strikers from entering the factory, making clear whose interests they protect. They break up a peaceful demonstration by riding through the crowd on horseback. Thus their role becomes ominous as the representatives of the oppressive aspect of society. Jail, ironically, becomes a haven for Charlie in *Modern Times,* an irony that is further stressed by the one cop in the film who emerges as a character. The sheriff is an elderly, kind man who arranges for Charlie to be treated comfortably after Charlie foils a jailbreak attempt, and gives him a letter of recommendation to help him find work. When offered this letter with his pardon, Charlie doesn't want to leave the prison because the real "prison" is the industrial and social world on the outside.

The best expression of this ambivalence about the nature of police is the role of the sheriff in *The Pilgrim.* Even as this sheriff arrests Charlie at the end of the film, he realizes that Charlie is, in fact, a good man, despite being an escaped convict and posing as the town's minister. (Charlie had, after all, recovered and returned Edna's stolen money at the expense of his own freedom). So, taking the law into his own hands, the sheriff boots Charlie over the border into Mexico. In all of Chaplin's films, this lawman comes closest to being an authentic, archetypal hero, both in actions and appearance . . . a man whose honesty and integrity permeate the screen in his scenes, much like that of an early Western hero. A final irony: the actor, Tom Murray, also played Black Larson.

On one occasion Chaplin's ambivalence toward cops led him astray. In *The Great Dictator* the cops take on the specific and ominous role of Nazi storm troopers. These men move with the regimentation of the comic heavies of *Shoulder Arms,* but they are whitewashing the word "Jew" on store windows and bullying everyone within reach, including a sequence in which they throw tomatoes at Paulette Goddard's clean laundry. They speak in whining, sneering tones during this scene with Goddard, and she responds by crying and muttering "Pigs!" As should be apparent from the description, the elements simply don't fit together and cause a serious

confusion in intention. Are these men to be taken seriously, or are they merely ineffectual Keystone Kop types? By their actions and Paulette Goddard's reaction, apparently they are to be taken seriously; yet by their postures and vocal inflections, as well as several comic chases with Charlie, apparently not. Possibly the emotionally charged issues of the time threw Chaplin off in this instance, although in his next film, *Monsieur Verdoux,* his touch is surer and the cops are among the best-drawn characters in the film.

Tom Murray as the good policeman. *The Pilgrim.*

At this time, it may be useful to consider briefly how Chaplin's chief rivals, Keaton and Lloyd, employed the "heavy" roles in their films.

In Keaton's series of short films made in 1920–1923, the main "heavy" is played by Big Joe Roberts, very much in the manner established by Eric Campbell in Chaplin's Mutual series. In his features, however, Keaton's roles and those of his heavies are naturalized in both costume and movement. The Northern military officers in *The General,* the southern gentlemen in *Our Hospitality,* as well as the assorted other villains in Keaton's silent films are quite realistically played and could appear in any serious film of the period, except that they are generally more effectively underplayed than their serious counterparts. Undoubtedly Keaton's love for authenticity in props and settings extended in this way to the other players (though his women are highly stylized). Chaplin, in contrast, never abandoned his clownish costume as did Keaton, and so needed characters who seemed grotesque to humanize his own performances.

Harold Lloyd, though his own character from 1917 on was by far the most ordinary looking of the three, continued to use grotesques as villains. The rural bullies in both *Grandma's Boy* and *The Kid Brother,* though a shade more realistically menacing, are cut from the same cloth as Chuck Reisner's portrayal in *The Kid*. A real giant becomes Harold's ally in *Why Worry*. But by and large Lloyd, like Keaton, preferred his heavies straight and realistic.

This difference in their use of heavies reflects a fundamental difference in the films of these men who so dominated film comedy for fifteen years. Both Keaton's and Lloyd's films are structured around their own character's transformation through necessity, a transformation which enables them to perform the spectacular feats that save the day at the end of each of their films. The real heavy, in a sense, is their own limitations. Chaplin, on the other hand, is complete from the start and transforms the world, rather than himself, in the films. He shares a more intimate relationship with his heavies because they are a projection and exaggeration of an aspect of himself which is never too far below the surface. The psychology of the mask operates here. Paradoxically, the highly stylized roles played by Chaplin and other characters in his films, including the heavies, results in a far greater sense of emotional intimacy and depth in the films, a large factor in explaining his towering popularity over his contemporaries.

Heroines

The Keystone film world Chaplin entered was anything but romantic, despite the presence of many beautiful women. The reigning comic beauty of the period was Mabel Normand. Like so much else about the Keystone films, Miss Normand's performances are puzzling to a modern viewer seeking to verify her reputation as a fine comedienne. It would seem that their chief charm lay in the contrast between her womanly physique and striking prettiness and her tomboyish behavior. Her relationship to Charlie in their films is one of equals, and they match each other kick for kick. While he often abuses and takes advantage of her, she repays him in kind, as by tricking him with the dummy in their apartment in *Mabel's Married Life*. In their 1915 feature *Tillie's Punctured Romance* Mabel is as active in her role as Charlie as in his; the two sweethearts are in fact partners in crime, though he soon deserts her when he sees an opportunity to marry the newly wealthy Tillie (Marie Dressler). At the end both Mabel and Tille renounce Charlie for the scoundrel he is.

Female clowns are rare, and the two chief ones at Keystone came after Chaplin's year. Louise Fazenda played a caricature of a hick country lass. Polly Moran played an even more extreme tomboy than Mabel, without the prettiness to balance it. For a time Moran was the reigning queen of broad slapstick at Keystone.

Character actresses such as Phyllis Allen and Alice Davenport played the roles of battle-ax wives, lowering the boom on errant husbands. Phyllis Allen appears in this role to good effect in Chaplin's last short comedy, *Pay Day*. In *The Kid* she plays the woman in whose baby buggy Charlie tries to put the abandoned infant.

Since Chaplin rarely played a henpecked husband, there are few portrayals of this type in his films until the battle-ax emerges in a blaze of glory—Martha Raye's Annabella in *Monsieur Verdoux*. The bulk and power of the earlier battle-axes are here transmuted into the crassness of the indestructible Annabella, who looks into the water on her fishing expedition with Verdoux and says, "I see one. Ooh, it's a monster. No, it's me." A monster, yes, but the one truly comic performance by a woman in the Chaplin canon. Her nonsequiturs, loudness, and gullibility make a wonderful contrast with the sly and suave Verdoux, and their scenes together are the comic heart of the film.

But the clowns and character actresses at Keystone are outnumbered by the more innocuous ornamental heroines, and it was this role that became most important in Chaplin's later work. Minta Durfee, Cecile Arnold, and other more or less interchangable lovelies are the objects and victims of Charlie's affections in the Keystones, doing little else than standing demurely around to be flirted with, on occasion rejecting his affections, but as often as not, tolerating them. Chaplin found in such women a vein of romantic and comic themes for his character that he would explore thoroughly in the coming years. A poster for Chaplin's eighth Keystone film, *Cruel, Cruel Love,* shows Charlie gazing worshipfully up at Minta Durfee; a label prophetically describes him as "Sentimental Charlie."

When Chaplin himself played a woman, which he did twice at Keystone and once at Essanay, he was lively and, in the language of the period, "saucy." In *A Busy Day* he actually combines various aspects of the female roles. He is a battle-ax when he catches husband Mack Swain with another woman, and, like Mabel, he tries to wring laughter from his "unfeminine" behavior, including repeatedly wiping his nose with his dress. Presumably at this stage Chaplin's fame was not such that he needed to make his identity as a "woman" separate from his tramp character (he plays only the woman role in this film), but in the other films he plays both male and female roles. In *The Masquerader* he in fact begins out of costume, proceeds to put his tramp outfit on, and does his female impersonation only after being fired as an incompetent movie actor. In this film as in *A Woman,* made a year later at Essanay, he becomes a seductive female, establishing many of the demure postures and gestures that his leading ladies employed under his direction.

Immediately after leaving Keystone Chaplin discovered Edna Purviance. Then nineteen years old, Miss Purviance became the leading lady for every film Chaplin made until 1923, with the exception of the solo *One A.M.* Although she plays many different characters in these thirty-five films—naive country girls, chambermaids, women of wealth—there is a consistency about her movements and her relationship to the tramp that makes all these portrayals variations on a single theme. A beautiful blond woman, Edna, slightly fleshy in the style then fashionable, was definitely in the "ornamental heroine" class of actress. Placid in her movements, most of her appearances focus exclusively on Charlie's attentions to her and on her reactions to those attentions. It is remarkable, in fact, how little she actually moves in these furiously paced films. She is demure or mildly annoyed when he flirts with her, but ultimately charmed and amused. In most of their films together she quickly develops concern for his welfare. The reverse is always true as well. Although Charlie often flirts outrageously with Edna, he never kicks her in the pants as he did Mabel. Much of his action in the films centers around saving her from the attentions of lustful villains such as the dope addict in *Easy Street* or the German officer in *Shoulder Arms,* whose lewd glance causes her to turn away and hold the top of her blouse together. In standard silent-film fashion, she turns toward the camera and projects her distress directly to the audience. Many of her gestures, in fact, are conventional, such as this staring wide-eyed at the camera and biting the nail of her forefinger. Chaplin himself used such gestures effectively—in *The Bank* and *Modern Times,* and with devastating impact at the end of *City Lights*—but occasionally he was unable to direct Edna and the other actors so that they rose above "period" in their performances as he usually did.

Edna is the feminine ideal—a vision of beauty in Chaplin's films. She is the romantic center and large portions of the films are devoted to the scenes of their meeting and the ensuing developments—a virtual catalogue of flirtation and budding romance. Chaplin's ease in touching other characters gives these scenes a warm and sensuous ambiance, though Charlie and Edna are seldom seen in anything like a passionate embrace. In some films, notably *The Bank, The Vagabond,* and *The Idle Class,* the romance is only a poignant fantasy on Charlie's part; usually Edna is more accessible. Only once, in *A Day's Pleasure,* do they begin as a married couple. In *Sunnyside* they are already lovers at the beginning, and in an early scene Charlie presents her with a ring. A sequence in which Edna is attracted to another man turns out to be only Charlie's unhappy dream, and they end the film together. But perhaps, in part, because of the lack of meeting and flirting scenes, these two films made successively in 1919 are by far the weakest of Chaplin's late shorts. On the other hand, in one of his finest shorts, *The Immigrant,* the film ends with the two immigrants, Charlie and Edna, getting married on a rainy day. Clearly, Chaplin's off-screen romance with Edna affected the quality of their films together. Late in life he said that *The Immigrant* "touched me more than any other film I made."[3]

Although Edna's performances are derived from the innocuous-pretty role at Keystone, there are important differences. But Chaplin himself was at first doubtful of her acting ability.

I doubted whether she could act or had any humor, she looked so serious. Nevertheless, with these reservations, we engaged her. She would at least be decorative in my comedies.[4]

She was far more than decorative. By contrasting Chaplin in her movements, light coloring, and comfortable, fleshy body, she provided a background that anchored his own performances, physically as well as emotionally. She brought great dignity to her roles, as well as a concentration on Chaplin that helped the audience focus on his more subtle movements, those intimate communications with the audience that from the beginning were the real subject of Chaplin's films.

The combination of Eric Campbell as antagonist and Edna as heroine helps to give the Mutual films their peculiar iconographic quality, for Edna elevated her role to become a symbol of Chaplin's (and many other people's) ideal of womanhood—beautiful, placid, receptive. Although it is not a fashionable ideal today, there is enough integrity in the portrayal, enough human truth to it, that it remains unoffensive to modern viewers, unlike similar portrayals by other women in films of the period. The reason boils down to the relationship between Charlie and Edna, a relationship which seems so genuine

Edna Purviance in *The Immigrant*.

that the films move effortlessly out of the period-
piece look so prominent in Sennett's films. Without
self-consciousness, Chaplin achieved a time-
lessness in the Mutual series that was due in no small
part to Edna's performances.

Among those performances there are two exceptions. In *Behind the Screen* Edna masquerades as a
boy, dressing in overalls to get work at a movie
studio. Unlike Chaplin in his striking female impersonations, Edna is unconvincing. Although basically, like Chaplin, she played variations on a single
character theme, she lacked the range that enabled
Chaplin to be convincing in his far-reaching impersonations. *The Fireman* is also atypical. Here she
plays a rather callous flirt who deceives Charlie to
smooch with Eric, a role similar to that given to Lita
Grey as the flirting angel in *The Kid*. But Edna is
simply not effective or believable out of the ''ideal''
role she played most of the time. Largely because of
this miscasting, *The Fireman* lacks an emotional
center, which all the other Mutuals have; it seems to
be universally recognized as the weakest of the
twelve films in the series, and is seldom discussed or
even shown.

It is clear from Chaplin's *My Autobiography* that
he deeply loved Edna Purviance. He tried, though
unsuccessfully, to launch her into an independent
career after he realized that she was growing too
mature and ''matronly'' to be his romantic leading
lady during the youth-obsessed 1920s. In *A Woman
of Paris,* Chaplin's only venture into sophisticated
drama, Edna portrays a country-girl-gone-wrong,
who becomes the mistress of a Parisian playboy.
This role ended Miss Purviance's career, since the
public found it impossible to accept Edna as a fallen
woman (despite her reformation at the end, when
she devotes her life to helping orphans).

Chaplin kept Edna on his studio payroll until her
death in 1958. Toward the close of his *My Autobiography* he prints two of her last letters to him,
admitting that through all the years he never wrote
to her. He says simply,

Edna in *A Dog's Life.*

> *Shortly after I received this letter she died. And so
> the world grows young. And youth takes over. And
> we who have lived a little longer become a little
> more estranged as we journey on our way.*[5]

Virginia Cherrill in *City Lights*.

Aside from his personal feelings for Edna Purviance even after their off-screen romance ended, in keeping her on his payroll, Chaplin was undoubtedly acknowledging her crucial importance in the films he made during his most fertile and formative period.

Several of Chaplin's heroines after Edna's departure are cast in the same mold: Merna Kennedy in a weak performance in *The Circus,* and Virginia Cherrill in *City Lights,* in a sensitive performance which surpassed the range of Edna Purviance. Both Georgia Hale in *The Gold Rush* and Paulette Goddard in *Modern Times* and *The Great Dictator* are closer to Mabel Normand in appearance and spirit being small, dark, and willful. Miss Hale, more than any other Chaplin heroine, seems bound to that period. With her concave posture and sultry gestures she is very much a flapper type, though her characterization of a dance hall girl (and possibly a prostitute) with low, hard movements is effective, particularly in the light of her later callousness toward Charlie.

Georgia Hale in *The Gold Rush*.

She reflects, in this epic film, the hardness of the cold land from which spring murderers like Black Larson. Love, here, is a commodity secondary to the pursuit of gold, and it is only by fortuitous twists of fate that Charlie finds either.

Paulette Goddard is unique among the heroines of Chaplin's films. She actually seems more like a buddy than a girlfriend. Her quick movements and high energy led Chaplin to characterize her as a "gamine." Like Mabel Normand, she is an active participant in the adventures rather than a vision motivating Charlie's actions. In *Modern Times,* for instance, she first meets Charlie by literally bowling him over in her attempt to escape capture (she has just been caught stealing a loaf of bread). She initiates their escape from a police van and finds jobs and a house for them both. Her dynamism in the film is enhanced by the speeded-up action and Chaplin's movement design for her, seen in her key gesture of jumping in the air and balletically twittering her feet when excited.

The leading ladies of *Monsieur Verdoux* are Martha Raye and an assortment of other variations on the battle-ax type including Lydia, haggard and embittered, rightfully suspicious of Verdoux's intentions and Mme. Grosnay, heavy, vain, and only too willing to fall for Verdoux's flattery. Chaplin originally intended this part for Edna Purviance, but in his *My Autobiography* he states that after a few days it was clear that Edna was unsuitable because of her lack of European sophistication—a pity he didn't realize that twenty-five years earlier when he wrote *A Woman of Paris* for her.

In *Monsieur Verdoux,* however, as in Chaplin's other films, there is a young and pretty heroine, though, in keeping with the film's mood, she is in desperate circumstances, forced into a life of prostitution. Verdoux intends to try a new poison on her, but after hearing about her invalid husband, for whose sake she was imprisoned as a thief (Verdoux murders for his invalid wife), he instead merely feeds her and gives her some money. In a scene

Paulette Goddard in *Modern Times.*

reminiscent of one in *The Immigrant* in which Edna realizes that Charlie has given her his own money to replace money stolen from her mother, the girl (Marilyn Nash) breaks down with tears of unbelieving gratitude. Thirty years earlier, in the eloquence of Chaplin's mime, the scene worked. It is awkward and embarrassing in *Monsieur Verdoux* (Chaplin's problems with this peformance and others in the film are considered in detail in Chapter 13.)

The leading ladies of Chaplin's last three films are all dark-haired beauties. They are Claire Bloom in *Limelight,* Dawn Addams in *A King in New York,* and Sophia Loren in *A Countess from Hong Kong.* In *Limelight* Chaplin returns to the theme he dealt with in *City Lights,* helping the heroine overcome a handicap, in this case paralysis resulting from her "fear of life." As in *City Lights,* he knows that once he has sacrificed to help the woman, their romance must end—in this case because he recognizes the age difference and knows her love is, in a large measure, gratitude. In *A King in New York* Dawn Addams portrays a cynical advertising agent who tricks the King (Chaplin) into appearing on television but soon becomes his advisor and affectionate friend. Sophia Loren voluptuously suggests Mabel Normand, unfortunately in a film with little of the old inspiration. *A Countess from Hong Kong* is a sad charade, a tribute to Chaplin's appreciation of female beauty rather than an example of his gift for creating a world which that beauty illuminated.

Buddies

A role that hardly exists in the amoral world of Keystone is the buddy or sidekick. At Keystone this role translates into *rival.* There is no friendship as such in the Keystones, since "friends" become instand enemies at the first appearance of a woman to fight over. Everything in this world becomes a pretext for the ubiquitous fights and chases.

Chaplin carries this rival role into his first two Essanay films, *His New Job* and *A Night Out.* Ben Turpin as Charlie's "friend" takes an enormous amount of physical abuse—much more than Chaplin gave Fatty Arbuckle in *The Rounders,* a Keystone film with scenes similar to those in *A Night Out.* While some of the routines in the two Turpin films are ingenious, so gratuitous is the cruelty that one is left with the impression that Chaplin genuinely disliked Turpin. He also chose not to include Turpin as a member of the stock company he was beginning to assemble.

At times there is an overlap between the buddy role and the heavy role, as when Charlie must turn against former cellmates in *Police* and *The Pilgrim.* In fact, friendship other than in the Keystone rival sense is very rare for the tramp character. Most often it is provisional, dependent on immediate need, as in Charlie's relationship with Mack Swain in *The Gold Rush*—friendship that evaporates when the men are starving and Swain, in his delirium, tries to eat Charlie. This inconstancy, random at Keystone, becomes pointed and poignant in Charlie's relationship with the millionaire of *City Lights,* who recognizes Charlie as his bosom buddy (Charlie had prevented the man from drowning himself) only when he is roaring drunk.

This attitude toward the scarcity and inconstancy of friendship is echoed in Chaplin's life. On film the tramp is more often rejected than rejecting—a reflection of the shy Chaplin who entered films at age

Another buddy. In *The Kid,* Chaplin created an icon of childhood that made Jackie Coogan into the first child star. Plaster statuette c. 1922.

twenty-four. But with professional success Chaplin found friendship pressed upon him from all sides and from all accounts he never learned to handle this aspect of his life gracefully, stirring up resentments by breaking or "forgetting" appointments without notice. He was unpredictable both in his sudden enthusiasms (for people as well as projects) and in his equally sudden coldness and disinterest. "I like friends as I like music, when I am in the mood. To help a friend in need is easy, but to give him your time is not always opportune."[6]

In the films, the only friendship (in the sense of an affectionate relationship of equals) is with Paulette Goddard in *Modern Times*. She alone shares his adventures, has some of her own which are independent of his, and joins him in the final walk down the road.

Heroes

In dramatic films the action usually centers around the protagonist—the hero—a near superhuman figure in courage, strength, attractiveness, or all three. Although the outlines change, the basic characteristics remain the same, from John Gilbert to Clark Gable to Robert Redford.

At Keystone the conventional hero existed in parody versions, grotesque reversals of the romantic hero by the likes of Ben Turpin. Lloyd could play the hero role, including romantic scenes, with credibility since in appearance and movement he fit the role. Keaton exists in a world of realistic characters who set off his own eccentricity. By his matter-of-fact handling of love relationships he parodies movie conventions and infuses these scenes with humor consistent with his dry, fatalistic view of life.

For Chaplin the hero role is more problematical. As his character in the films becomes more rounded and sympathetic he, more than Lloyd or Keaton, faces the problem of justifying the beautiful heroine's interest. Even Keaton looked handsome and elegant in many of his screen roles, but Chaplin, though a good-looking man offscreen, limited himself by his clownish costume and makeup. In her memoirs Pola Negri recalls his saying to her handsome lover, "Herr Schleber, if I was as tall and handsome as you, there never would have been a tramp. You see, there would have been no need to hide." Certainly the kind of insecurity indicated by this statement is reflected as a major theme in Chaplin's films from the beginning. This theme can be seen in his masquerades as royalty in the Keystones,

the quicksilver adaptations into the jobs and roles expected of him in the Mutuals, and later, in the working out of his relationship with the heroine, central to *The Gold Rush, The Circus, City Lights,* and *Limelight.*

In his own hero role Chaplin substitutes for the conventional qualities his tremendous ingenuity in adversity, his grace of movement and charming mannerisms, a superior moral system to the world around him, and several distinctly Christian virtues; meekness, poverty, and self-sacrifice. Thus, he wins not only his heroine's heart but the audience's as well.

Conventional leading-men types do appear in Chaplin's films, usually in unsympathetic roles. In

Charlie transforms his minister costume to that of a Western hero. *The Pilgrim.*

The Bank Edna's love interest is in Charles, the cashier, the epitome of straight conventionality. Charlie, the janitor, doesn't stand a chance, except in his dreams. In Charlie's dream, the cashier proves to be a coward during a robbery attempt, leaving janitor Charlie to save the day. He wakes up to the rude reality of embracing not Edna, but a mop, and sees Edna embracing the cashier. In this early film Chaplin ensures that the cashier will get none of our sympathy by casting one of the homeliest men ever to appear in movies in that role.

In other films similar roles are played by handsome men, and Chaplin ensures a similar lack of audience sympathy (notably in *The Circus*) by casting "pretty" men, who are so bland and innocuous-looking that little life seems to emanate from them. In *The Vagabond* Edna falls for an artist, and as she drives off at the end with him and her newfound mother, she suddenly demands that they return for

Charlie, too—a rather facile handling of the conflict such men represented for Chaplin. Another handsome artist "does her wrong" in the subplot of *The Kid* and Chaplin's skill at directing underplayed performances does not prevent the Edna-artist scenes in *The Kid* from being cloying. Chaplin removed most of their scenes for the reissue, retaining only an earlier, rather effective scene in which the artist accidentally burns Edna's photograph in his studio, then, realizing it has burned beyond recovery, uses it to light his pipe. Here Chaplin achieves the subtlety and depth of character he sought in the film.

A Woman of Paris is, in a sense, an expansion of the subplot of *The Kid*. Edna is again corrupted, but this time her love is divided between Carl Miller, the simple country-boy artist, and Adolph Menjou, the suave Parisian playboy who takes her as his mistress. The foreword to the film states that people "sin only in blindness," that only the ignorant condemn and judge—thus setting the tone for a film in which Chaplin attempts to depart from the conventional black-and-white portrayal of heroes and villains. In this he succeeds—the motivations of the characters are both subtle and clearly expressed. Carl Miller, however, is a bit bland in his role, as if Chaplin could not bear to have a handsome leading man also be admirable (he commits suicide in the film). Adolph Menjou, closer to the "villain," is by far the most interesting character in the film.

Chaplin was clearly champing at the bit before making *A Woman of Paris*. His increasing sophistication and experience in films was leading him toward explorations outside the possibilities of his tramp films. Indeed, *Pay Day*, made the year before *A Woman of Paris*, is hardly a tramp film at all—more like a Chaplin comedy in tramp's clothing. Yet Chaplin was no "art for art's sake" filmmaker—he wanted the enormous popular success (indeed, needed it when he became his own producer) that his tramp films virtually guaranteed.

But events conspired. The coming of sound made pantomime films no longer a surefire road to popular success, though the compromise measures Chaplin took in *City Lights* and *Modern Times* successfully kept him in the race. In addition, the character was in danger, in Chaplin's words, of becoming "everybody's little ray of sunshine."

When Chaplin finally stepped fully out of his tramp character he explored several variations of the ambiguous hero role, adding his own acting skill and charisma to roles others had played less successfully in his earlier films. The strongest mix of hero and villain characteristics occurs in *Monsieur*

Verdoux. Verdoux is the ultimate bourgeois, dapper and conventionally attractive. The twist is that he earns his living marrying wealthy widows and murdering them for their money, all for the support of his crippled wife and young son during the Depression years. Chaplin clearly takes savage delight in this role, exorcising his contempt for middle-class conventional morality, which allows monstrous atrocities on a global scale while maintaining the proprieties at home. It is also a wry joke on his public image as a "lady-killer," and a stunning reversal of the lovable tramp character.

We can draw a number of conclusions based on this examination of Chaplin's transformation of the world of Keystone characters.

One conclusion is made obvious by the many descriptions of Chaplin at work, all of which stress his particular method of playing all the roles himself. Robert Parrish, who played the pea-shooting newsboy in *City Lights*, describes the method:

> He said he found it best to show people rather than tell them. . . . He became a kind of dervish, playing all the parts, using all the props. . . . Finally, he had it all worked out and reluctantly gave us back our parts. I felt that he would much rather have played all of them himself.[7]

It is in fact possible to trace the development of virtually every role in any later Chaplin film back to a Chaplin performance during the Keystone period.

Ultimately Chaplin's films can be seen as solo performances, not in the sense that he is alone, but because the other actors' performances are molded so directly by Chaplin through repetition and imitation. An appropriate method, since the real subject of a Chaplin film is the Chaplin character. Other characters really exist to illuminate aspects of himself by eliciting his reactions.

On first viewings it is difficult to notice the function of the other actors, since the films so effectively focus on Chaplin. But careful examination shows, within a single film, a startling variety in depth of characterization, from two-dimensional Keystone stereotypes to rounded, realistic characters. *The Kid* is a prime example. The ladies of the slum are hard-boiled characters who seem not to be acting at all; the same is true of most of the bums in the flophouse. But Edna and her artist lover, the orphan officials and doctor, seem to have stepped off the stage of a Victorian melodrama. The bully is a caricature exaggerated beyond Sennett's imagination. Yet all these characters fit smoothly into the fabric of the film.

Herein lies Chaplin's great skill at characterization, his ability to balance these wildly varied types of roles in a film reality that comfortably accommodates them all. Although there is a general movement toward realistic characterization in the films of the late teens through the 1930s, the enormous variety remains. For example, Chester Conklin's performance as the factory mechanic in *Modern Times* is straight Keystone. It must be recognized that these characters illuminate the tramp and the persistence of caricature and stereotype cannot be seen as a flaw or a throwback in the Chaplin films, even when he does not achieve the "universal" look of the Mutuals. They are organic necessities to make the tramp a believable protagonist, serving to ground his broader acrobatic comedy as well as the stylized choreography of the films.

With sound, the film world became necessarily less stylized, complicating Chaplin's balancing act. He falters seriously in sections of both *The Great Dictator* and *Monsieur Verdoux*. But, up to that time, the miracle is that the act is so smooth that the effort doesn't show. The disparate elements are made into a coherent whole by a master juggler of human images.

Notes

[1]Chaplin, cited in Cooke, Alistair, *Six Men* (New York: Berkley Publishing Corp., 1978).

[2]Chaplin, *My Autobiography, op. cit.,* p. 271. Reprinted with permission of The Bodley Head.

[3]Chaplin, *My Life in Pictures, op. cit.,* p. 150.

[4]Chaplin, *My Autobiography, op. cit.,* p. 170. Reprinted with permission of The Bodley Head.

[5]Chaplin, *My Autobiography, op. cit.,* p. 497. Reprinted with permission of The Bodley Head.

[6]Chaplin, *My Autobiography, op. cit.,* p. 269. Reprinted with permission of The Bodley Head.

[7]Parrish, Robert, *Growing Up in Hollywood* (New York: Harcourt, Brace, Jovanovich, 1976), pp. 42–43.

In *A Dog's Life* Chaplin creates a Daumier-like gallery of human caricatures.

7

The Dancer

"Your comedy is balletique, you are a dancer."

Nijinsky to Chaplin, 1917[1]

From the beginning of his screen career Chaplin linked himself closely to dance through his posture. With his splayed feet, tilted-back pelvis, and frequent assumption of elegant attitudes, he presented a virtual parody of a classical ballet dancer.

The crisp precision of his movements also was dancelike. Apparently this was automatic with Chaplin both on screen and off, as noted by many observers. Alistair Cooke comments:

> One of the permanent pleasures of being with him was to watch the grace and deftness with which he performed all physical movements, from pouring syrup to swerving like a matador just out of the line of an oncoming truck.[2]

But the dance aspect of Chaplin's films goes far beyond his posture and personal movement style. An important part of his achievement is that he successfully translates to the screen movement qualities usually seen only on the stage. Chaplin's films have the effect, like good dance, of sweeping the viewer up in their action, infusing him with the impulse to move himself.

The term "dance" in this chapter, then, refers not just to the many dance-floor scenes, but to dance in its broadest sense, as movement which brings awareness and pleasure to viewers because of its formal qualities.

Chaplin's earliest films do not move in this sense. Until the Mutual series of films in 1916–1917, scenes with the distinctive ornate, choreographed look that characterizes all his later work appear only

intermittently. But with the first Mutual, *The Floorwalker*, a dramatic change occurs. Masquerading as the store floorwalker, Charlie helps a lady try on some shoes. The touch of her foot so excites him that, after climbing a wheeled ladder to get her a pair, he pushes the wall with his foot and gracefully sails back to her with one leg balletically outstretched. Although from the beginning his walk and posture suggested ballet, in this film it appears for the first time in a movement both comic and balletic. Later in the film dance emerges even more dramatically. Discovering a satchel full of money, Charlie literally dives into the satchel in his exhilaration. At that moment embezzler Eric Campbell enters and knocks him down, whereupon Charlie springs up and does an elaborate dance, complete with leaps, *entrechats,* and mock toe dancing for the dumbfounded Campbell. He ends the dance in a graceful position with his legs crossed and his arms outstretched, only to have Campbell promptly knock him down again.

This burst of high spirits continues through the Mutual films, and reflects Chaplin's unique career position at this time. Chaplin was by then confident of his popularity, demonstrated tangibly each week by his fabulous $10,000 paycheck. Artistically he felt inspired, backed up by the stock company of players and technicians which he handpicked. The addition of Eric Campbell as his antagonist, by far the best heavy he had worked with, was an additional stimulant. With the anchoring Charlie-Edna-Eric triumvirate of characters, Chaplin could play out his wildest ideas with abandon. He dived into the Mutual series as he dived into that satchel—with

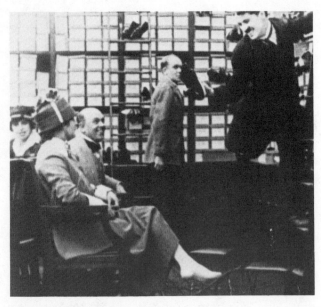 

Arabesque on a ladder . . .   . . . diving into a satchel . . .

. . . and dancing his joy. *The Floorwalker*.

a boldness and confidence that enabled him to make a quantum leap into a new kind of comedy.

The audiences flocked to the new Chaplin films, demonstrating their love affair with the tramp, and Charlie's bold glances and bows at the audience in these films show that he also acknowledged them. Sometimes Chaplin used teasing "in" jokes. *The Vagabond* begins with a shot of Charlie's feet—now an icon—shuffling toward the camera from beneath saloon doors.

Against this background of popular acceptance Chaplin burst into his most fertile creative period, and the twelve Mutual films contain the prototypes for all Chaplin's later work. He also discovered during this time how to press the dance impulse into the very fabric of his films by creating comic ideas based on the natural laws of dance and movement. He learned to devise routines which subtly enhanced the viewer's awareness of, for example, the force of gravity.

A classical ballet dancer plays with the audience's perception of gravity by creating the illusion, through muscular control and strength, that he or she can float. Chaplin, too, manipulates the audience's sense of his own body weight for expressive purposes, and extends this manipulation to his handling of props, as when he adds weight to a fake iron stove he is about to dump onto Eric Campbell (*Easy Street*), or a doughnut in *The Pawnshop*. Chaplin's simple but subtle displacement of his own weight in the doughnut routine shows his respect for film reality (Mack Sennett would probably have shown the doughnut crashing through the floor). Chaplin makes it clear that his movement, not film or prop trickery, creates the illusion.

Another routine Chaplin builds around the sense of weight occurs in *The Pilgrim*. Charlie is helping Edna prepare a pudding. She picks up a breadboard and Charlie rushes to catch a rolling pin which rolls off. He puts the rolling pin on a high shelf which is slightly tilted, and when he turns around it rolls off to hit him on the head. So he puts it back up on the same shelf, this time placing a milk bottle against the pin to hold it. Moments later Edna reaches for the milk and Charlie must make a panicky catch to prevent the pin from hitting her. This delightful sequence is built from the simplest of props and actions, and from respect for the reality of gravity. Chaplin's movement in the scene, rolling the pin to the back of the shelf and turning around just as it rolls off, is exquisitely timed and designed, the pattern deft and ornate. One cannot imagine another comedian doing the routine in this way, with varia-

tion after variation in a single sustained shot. Despite its apparent simplicity it would look too fancy for the more prosaic movement styles of Keaton or Lloyd.

Chaplin creates a startling antigravity image in *The Great Dictator* when his open cockpit plane turns upside down. The film flips so that we share his perception of a topsy-turvy world in which his pocket watch seems to float in front of his face and water from a canteen flows upward.

In all these routines Chaplin's skillful movements direct the viewer's attention to the operation of gravity in his film world.

Inertia, like gravity, is a natural law that is at the root of the appreciation of dance. A moving object keeps moving unless stopped by another object or by force. In ballet, the dancer learns to conceal the effort leading up to the leap as well as the shock of the landing. The flow of energy in the movement is even; the dancer appears to float, or to be transported by some outside force.

Chaplin, however, exaggerates momentum and the force behind it. A kick, a revolving door, or a fall is an excuse for a display of visual and acrobatic fireworks. This emphasizes the viewer's awareness of forces at play, and force is at the heart of most physical comedy. Yet, if Chaplin's falls and spins are compared to Keaton's, it can be seen that Chaplin's are closer to classical dance. When Keaton falls, there seems to be an explosion as he comes to rest, as often as not on his neck. With Chaplin a movement once begun proceeds smoothly, like the elaborate sequence of falls and rolls down the staircases in *One A.M.* In *The Cure* Chaplin is spun by a revolving door into the lobby and up the stairs. He maintains his momentum with balletic smoothness, working in several neat revolutions without breaking his rush toward and up the stairs. The action is so skillfully executed that the door seems to cause the movement, an apparent connection created by exaggeration of the real force of momentum. Because of Chaplin's skill of conception and execution, the viewer is left with the satisfaction of credibility—the reaction seems possible, if not probable.

Occasionally Chaplin plays with forces that cancel each other out to attain a strained equilibrium. In the final chase in *The Floorwalker*, Charlie laboriously reaches the bottom of a moving staircase. Pausing to rest, he is carried up again. The climax of this sequence is a master image of the chase. Campbell chases Chaplin on the escalator, both moving so that they match its speed and remain exactly in place as they run. In the intent attitudes of the pur-

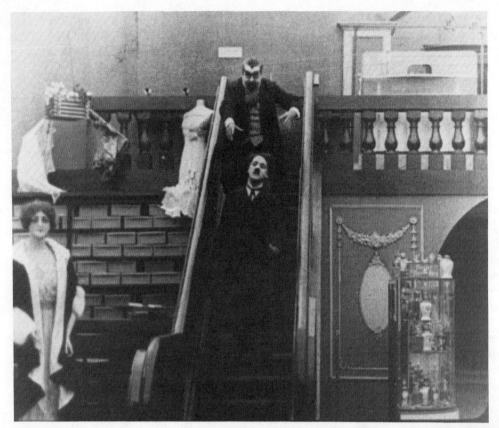

The escalator chase. *The Floor-walker.*

The courtly elegance of the tramp. He offers Edna his cane to help her skate, as he might offer his arm on the street. *The Rink.*

Brinksmanship. The sign reiterates Charlie's peril. *Modern Times.*

suer and the pursued, Campbell vainly reaches for Chaplin. Chaplin attains the same strained equilibrium when he struggles against a wind in *The Gold Rush,* and on roller skates in *The Rink.*

The most delicate expressions of equilibrium are Chaplin's various balancing acts. Perhaps the most splendid is the one that takes place atop a ladder in *The Pawnshop.* Rocking back and forth as he tries to clean the store sign, he finally goes too far and falls, along with the ladder, backward. The viewer's anxiety in watching this sequence is matched by that of a policeman, who draws in his breath each time Charlie tilts backward. As always in such scenes, the payoff is one sustained long shot. The ten-foot ladder topples and Charlie hits the road in a graceful back somersault, hopping up immediately to check his watch and to reassure the audience that he is unharmed.

Generally, though, both Lloyd and Keaton surpass Chaplin in the realm of thrill comedy by their greater willingness to risk life and limb. Chaplin's last ventures of this sort are the tightrope sequence of *The Circus* and the roller-skating scene in *Modern Times.* The latter derives as much interest from Chaplin's graceful patterns of movement as from his precarious skating near the edge of an unfinished floor. Fear of physical harm simply does not play as important a part in his films as it does in those of Keaton and Lloyd.

Chaplin did injure himself several times during his career, including a nasty cut on the nose from a streetlight in *Easy Street* and a broken finger from a slamming gate in *The Great Dictator.* (The latter scene remains in the film—Chaplin simply did not react until after the camera stopped rolling.) However, none of his injuries compares with Keaton's broken neck during the filming of *Sherlock, Jr.*—an injury Keaton himself didn't discover until eleven years later.

A third dance element that Chaplin uses eloquently is rhythm. He had two aids on the set: the loud clicking of the silent camera, imposing a steady beat and also telling him how much the film was being undercranked; and the constant presence of musicians, often a trio, who played to help establish the mood. Virginia Cherrill, costar of *City Lights,* said that the musicians were in constant attendance during the two-year period of filming, playing "whatever Charlie felt like that day."

Chaplin often extracts humor from the tramp's tendency to mechanically repeat actions he begins. Thus, Charlie begins dusting in *The Pawnshop,* maintaining a steady rhythm as he dusts his hat, his cane, a coworker's desk (causing the poor man to sneeze violently as a cloud of dust rises), and the revolving fan on the desk (creating a snowstorm of feathers as the duster is chopped to bits). Later, transforming a fight into a furious floor washing when the boss appears, he grabs a violin and plunges it into the soapy water bucket, scrubbing it vigorously until the boss fires him and orders him out. In these sequences, as in many others like them in the Mutual series, the rhythm itself creates the comedy and somehow makes Charlie's absurd actions seem plausible as he cheerfully mocks common sense and the conventional expectations of the other characters.

The ultimate expression of Chaplin's use of rhythmically repetitive movement for comedy is the lengthy factory sequence that opens *Modern Times.* Charlie's job of tightening nuts on the assembly line finally explodes in a mad dance in which he twists every nut-like object in sight with his wrenches and wreaks choreographed chaos in the factory.

In the early part of the sequence Charlie's movement is imposed by his job; both arms simultaneously twist wrenches, tightening the nuts which speed by on metal plates. When a man relieves Charlie, his body continues to jerk involuntarily in the same rhythm until, with great effort, he "squeezes" it out of himself with a compression-and-release movement.

In the next scene Charlie is strapped into a feeding machine which attempts to rhythmically regulate the act of eating, with predictably disastrous results. Again, rhythm—particularly that of the mouth wiper which slowly does its job after each violation to Charlie—is at the heart of the comedy.

On the assembly line. *Modern Times.*

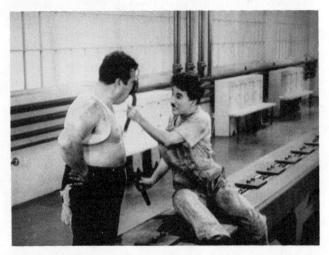

Tightening everything in sight. *Modern Times.*

Charlie flipping out. *Modern Times.*

For the climax Chaplin accelerates the pace of the line until Charlie goes "mad," at his most balletic in form (though his rhythms are staccato). He systematically disrupts the regular rhythm of the factory itself.

That Chaplin attributed a particular significance to repetitive rhythm is indicated by a short story he published shortly after the completion of *Modern Times.* The title is "Rhythm. A Story of Men in Macabre Movement." It deals with an officer who must give the order for a firing squad to shoot a friend. He blanks out and shouts incoherently, which his men interpret as the "present arms" order. Then habit takes over, with disastrous results.

> *The rhythm of their action set his brain in rhythm, and again he shouted. Now the men took aim.*
>
> *But in the pause that followed, there came into the prison yard hurrying footsteps, the nature of which the officer knew meant a reprieve. Instantly, his mind cleared. "Stop!" he screamed frantically at the firing squad. Six men stood poised with rifles. Six men were caught in rhythm. Six men when they heard the scream to stop—fired.*[3]

Possibly Chaplin's most sophisticated film rhythmically is the seldom seen *A Dog's Life.* In his autobiography Chaplin states that it was with *A Dog's Life* in 1918 that he began "to think of comedy in a structural sense, and to become conscious of its architectural form. Each sequence implied the next sequence, all of them relating to the whole."[4] What is, in fact, structural about *A Dog's Life* is the remarkable rhythmic relationship of six major comic sequences.

In the first of these sequences Charlie is sitting coyly on the ground, having just replaced a hot dog he stole from a vendor on the other side of a wooden fence. The cop who inspired Charlie to return the food stands glowering at him from the other side of the fence, and gestures with his head for Charlie to come over to his side. Charlie responds by flirtatiously gesturing with *his* head for the cop to join *him.* The back-and-forth head exchange is a prelude to the larger movement of the ensuing chase, in which the cop runs around the fence while Charlie simply rolls under it. In perfectly matched shots the camera cuts from one side of the fence to the other as Charlie rolls. Back and forth they go in an even, staccato rhythm, broken when Charlie reaches under the fence to untie the cop's shoe, then sticks him with one of the pins which always seem to be conveniently attached to his vest. After a few more repe-

Charlie going balletically crazy in *Modern Times*.

Gloating after avoiding the cop. *A Dog's Life*.

titions of the chase, Charlie rises on the sidewalk to bow gloatingly only to find his outstretched hand touching the badge of a second cop. Rolling under the fence, he runs away and eludes both cops.

Seeking work, Charlie enters an employment office. (A sign proclaiming "Men wanted for work in brewery" attracts a crowd who have been indifferent to another sign saying "Strong men wanted for sewer work.") Just as Charlie reaches the window, one of the other men crosses in front of him. This happens several times, expanding to include a second window. Accelerating his pace, Charlie is soon running from window to window. At one point, Charlie overshoots a window, slamming into a wall while another man steps into place before he can recover. Finally, at full speed, he runs to a window as it closes, to the other as *it* slams shut, and back to the first as one of the clerks emerges from the now-closed office to collide with the skidding Charlie.

Running from window to window in the employment office. *A Dog's Life.*

The third sequence is another of the catch-me-if-you-can scenes of which Chaplin was so fond. Leaning against a lunch wagon counter, he systematically devours a plateful of pastries. Although this sequence was spliced in several places, the rhythm is not disrupted. Tension builds each time the proprietor of the wagon (Sydney Chaplin) whirls in order to catch Charlie in the act of eating the pastries, which are rapidly vanishing from the plate. The cuts allow Chaplin to empty his mouth but never interfere with the comic heart of the routine—Charlie's instant freezes each time Syd whirls on him. In each shot, Syd's whirl and Charlie's freeze can be seen by the viewer, despite the fact that Char-

Filching pastries from Sydney Chaplin. *A Dog's Life.*

lie is not in Syd's line of vision. Although this was probably done using offscreen cuing, it is still impressive in its quicksilver precision, exaggerated as always by undercranking. Once again the rhythm (in this case the rhythmic break of the action into quick freezes) provides the structure and dynamic thrust of the scene.

The fourth sequence emanates from the heaving rhythm of crying. This scene introduces Edna, "A new singer sings an old song." She is preceded on the Green Lantern stage by an exuberant hootchie-kootchie dancer to set off her slow, sad song. It is so sad that it makes everyone in the cafe cry. The bartender returns filched money to the cash register, a fat woman douses Charlie with tears and seltzer water, patrons fall on each other weeping. The comic highlight occurs between Charlie and the band drummer, who seems to be crying under his huge moustache until he looks at the bawling Charlie, which somehow makes him start laughing. Charlie begins laughing too, which inexplicably infuriates the drummer, who turns away and pretends he is crying although he is still laughing. The rhythmic break between laughing and crying is wonderfully worked out, an emotional reversal similar to the strangling-woman scene in *The Kid*. Finally, with a demure bow, Edna exits, and the dancer returns.

The fifth sequence, in which the crooks, Charlie, and the bartender battle for possession of a wallet, is described in detail in Chapter 6. Rhythmically and structurally it is like a burst of machine gun fire. The men, standing in a straight line, rapidly pass the wallet in one direction and then the other until it reaches Chaplin in the end, who grabs it and shoots straight from the line toward the camera and out of sight. Prosaic movements are combined in strikingly effortless choreography.

The strong staccato rhythm leads to the sixth sequence, in which Charlie and Sydney pop up alternately like ducks in a shooting gallery as the crooks fire at the lunch wagon. Then the rhythm changes as Charlie holds up a plate, which is quicky punctured with two bullet holes, and uses it as a "shield" to peer out.

These six sequences give *A Dog's Life* a quality unique in the Chaplin canon. A different rhythm dominates and defines each scene and ultimately provides the comic punch. Even transitions between scenes maintain the rhythmic drive. After he is "bounced" from the Green Lantern cafe, Charlie is angrily about to toss a brick through the entrance when he notices the omnipresent cop. Without breaking rhythm, he throws it offscreen instead, as if

Henry Bergman as a crying patron of The Green Lantern. *A Dog's Life*.

Charlie is doused by Bergman's tears. *A Dog's Life*.

tossing a stick for his dog. As the brick sails off, the scene abruptly cuts to the two thugs walking rapidly away from the camera on their way to a mugging, as if the brick's momentum is continued in the crooks' progress.

The rhythm that percolates through *A Dog's Life* also imposes a playful quality on the film's serious themes, allowing Chaplin to develop explicit dramatic content without succumbing to sentimentality or melodrama.

In most other Chaplin films the rhythm and unity of the best sequences are superior to those of the film as a whole. He approaches the unity of *A Dog's Life* in both *The Gold Rush* and *City Lights*. The former achieved rhythmic unity with the consistent effectiveness of its comic routines, and the latter in its emotional build to the climax and superb blending of serious and comic plots. But no such qualifications need be made of *A Dog's Life*. For once, form and content merge completely. Chaplin achieved in *A Dog's Life* a cumulative rhythmic relationship of the sequences, resulting in a "structural" film in exactly the sense he evidently intended. Judged by its rhythmic unity, it is arguably Chaplin's most perfect film.

In discussing the dynamic qualities of movement in Chaplin's films one may note as many contrasts as similarities with classical ballet. It is Chaplin's design of movement in space that provides his major link with classical dance.

In ballet the major principles of spatial design is the circle. The body is visualized as a series of interlocking circles, and the various positions are intended to approximate the geometric perfection and precision of a series of circles and arcs.

As we have seen, Chaplin at times overtly "quotes" from this repertoire of steps and postures, as when he pushes down the large lever in *Modern Times*, his leg extended in an arabesque, or does entrechats in *The Floorwalker* and *The Cure*. Invariably, these aspirations toward classic beauty, like his love-struck glances, must be balanced by a more gritty reality—the bucket of water in the face, the slap which bowls him over. Romantic as the films are, they are also, unlike ballet, determinedly realistic. Beautiful though the tramp's movements may be, Chaplin doesn't permit him to attain godlike perfection. The audience is always aware of both the flight and the constant downward drag of gravity, just as they are of the character's aspirations and the reality of his circumstances.

Physically, Chaplin contrasts the aspirations implied in his balletic movements with such pedestri-

The lunch wagon becomes a shooting gallery. *A Dog's Life*.

An entrechat in the factory dance. *Modern Times.*

Arabesque on a switch. *Behind the Screen.*

an movements as lighting matches on the seat of his (or other people's) pants, his unique walk, and an entire repertoire of eccentric kicks and falls. Chaplin's film world seethes with this fertile juxtaposition: the legs remaining earthbound while the feet are turned out (as in ballet); the graceful movement in the middle of a frantic chase or fight; the abrupt shift from one way of moving to another; and the formality and politeness toward objects contrasting with the casual cruelty toward people.

In *The Pawnshop,* for example, Chaplin and fellow employee John Rand must decide which one of them should go out of the shop to retrieve their ladder from under the nose of an angry policeman. They decide to toss a coin, as pedestrian an action as exists. But Chaplin transforms the movement into a thing of beauty. He flips the coin into the air and catches it with his right hand, making a complete circle as he does so. At the same time he pretends to catch in his *left* hand, which in turn makes a complete circle perpendicular to the plane of movement described by his right hand. He then slaps his left palm onto the back of his right hand. Lifting his left hand and turning it over, Chaplin feigns surprise at the disappearance of the coin before "finding" it in his right hand. If this is somewhat confusing to read, it is also befuddling to watch, both for Rand and for the audience. The pattern of the double circles, while not exactly a magic trick, is such a convincing illusion that people are usually fooled. As when Chaplin manages to refill his glass of wine by bumping someone else's in *The Adventurer,* the coin trick is one of the innumerable stylizations of pedestrian actions that fill Chaplin's films and give them such richness of detail. As critic William Paul says,

> There is always such an abundance of detail in a Chaplin performance that his acting might well be described as rococo. Yet Chaplin's every gesture, every facial expression is so economical that he always seems to make a necessity of unnecessary movement, transforming his whole body into the expression of one emotion . . . every emotion he feels finds an external expression in his body.[5]

Chaplin's increasing choreographic mastery led him to develop patterns far more sophisticated than his ballet parodies. In *The Kid,* for example, Charlie wants to get rid of an orphan official without leaving the truck with the kid in it. He simply runs in place in a burst of explosive movement whenever the official stops *his* fearful run away from Charlie, until the man is out of sight.

The formal beauty of Chaplin's movement is particularly evident whenever he departs from "ordinary" actions to more presentational scenes. In *The Great Dictator,* the dictator is describing to the assembled throng "der Aryan maiden." He makes a series of circles around his face with one hand, which blend smoothly into a double arc made with both hands to indicate her breasts ("mit der Holsteins") and revolve into a third double arc indicating simultaneously her hips and her hands placed provocatively upon them.

The circles, arcs, and revolutions in Chaplin's personal movements are extended into the movement of all the characters in the film space. If one visualizes the pattern of the characters' movement as seen from above, one sees a graceful series of interlocking arcs, often describing S-curves. The pattern of the drunk's movements across the floor in *One A.M.,* described earlier, is quite ornate. Chaplin achieves equally complex designs in scenes that employ a number of characters.

The cumulative effect of such complex choreography is giving the two-dimensional movie screen a unique sense of depth. The audience becomes conscious of the foreground, middleground, and background as well as the upper and lower spaces. Space in the films is defined by the human movement within the frame rather than by camera movement. In view of this it is understandable that a common critical complaint against Chaplin is the flat and static quality of his camera framing. The irony is that Chaplin's eloquent conceptions of gravity, momentum, rhythm, and space result in films that, like the best stage dance, celebrate the movement of the human body in space.

It is interesting to compare Chaplin's work in this respect with Fred Astaire's. Like Chaplin, Astaire became a master at filming his work so that his skill "translated" to the film medium. His use of sustained long shots (often entire dances are filmed in a single take) forces on the viewer the awareness of Astaire's great skill and stamina, doing much to ground his highly stylized acting performances. Those performances, however, unlike Chaplin's, could effectively take place in a live theatre. The intimacy of Astaire's playing style derives precisely from the illusion that one could be watching a live performance.

Against a background of filmic reality, Chaplin grew increasingly skillful at creating illusions through the manipulation not only of his own movement, but also of the technical capacities of film-making. It has already been mentioned that his use of mime and dance, though theatrically oriented,

could not effectively take place live. The next scene to be examined is a dramatic example of a uniquely filmic conception, since it effectively uses the device of reversing the film's action.

In *Pay Day* Charlie is a construction worker preparing to stack some bricks onto a scaffold. Workers below throw the bricks up to him, which he improbably "catches" with the aid of reverse action— he actually takes the bricks from the stack and drops them, and the shots are reversed in the final film. The routine is extended and elaborate; in a total of seven reverse-action shots, Charlie catches seventy-seven bricks. What makes it remarkable is both the diversity of the variations, and the way the routine is edited into the film so that, until some of the more impossible-looking catches are made, one isn't quite sure that the action *is* reversed. Many people never do recognize the trickery.

The routine begins with a long master shot showing Charlie on his scaffold and the other workers, Sydney Chaplin and Henry Bergman, below. Wiping his hands with his handkerchief in the manner of an aerialist about to do a difficult trapeze feat, Charlie assumes his familiar position, arms spread and feet crossed, and casually drops the handkerchief. Syd catches it and throws it back. This opening gambit is critical, since it establishes in the viewer's mind the action of gravity and the paradigm of Charlie catching an object thrown upward from below. With a balletic flourish of footwork, Charlie then turns his back and bends over, bracing himself in position as Syd readies a brick.

The scene cuts to a tight shot of Syd reaching into his brick pile and rapidly tossing bricks straight upward and out of frame. The third shot shows Charlie alone, intent on his work of stacking. He reaches behind himself without looking and snatches the bricks from the air. The use of reverse action is effectively disguised by Chaplin's design of his own movements to avoid contradicting the appearance of forward motion. In actuality, he picks up bricks from his stack, positions them, pauses a moment, and allows them to drop. The slightest hint of a tossing motion would, of course, destroy the illusion. By pausing he approximates the impact of catching a flying object.

After catching a few bricks in a straightforward manner, Chaplin begins a series of surprise variations. He catches them in the crooks of his knees, at his ankles, and between his legs at the crotch; he catches one and then catches the next one on top of the first. Chaplin skillfully intercuts shots of the workers below tossing the bricks upward. The final

Making a fancy catch. *Pay Day*.

A moment before the woman entered, Charlie had kicked Chuck Reisner across the room. A rhythmic transition from violence to casualness. *The Pilgrim*.

shot shows Charlie catching five bricks—one under each arm, one in each hand, and one between his legs. The foreman blows his whistle and Charlie, in unreversed long shot again, drops the brick from between his legs onto the foreman's head.

It is doubtful that there exists another example in all of cinema of the successful, extended use of reverse action. Cocteau uses it briefly in his surrealistic films to achieve a dreamlike mood. Chaplin himself never again returned to it. But then, the brickthrowing scene would be hard to top, even by Chaplin.

Isolating scenes makes it easy to appreciate Chaplin's formal achievement in spotlighting the various elements of dance. But all of his stylized movement sequences ultimately serve to express the content and tell the stories in the films.

Chaplin's original source for consciously choreographed action was the Sennett chase (or "rally," as Sennett called it). Those weaving lines of men and autos supplied Chaplin with a basic form that he would refine in his own work. While Keaton developed the chase by finding unusual participants (locomotives, rocks, cows) and locations (ocean liners, antebellum Southern mansions, rapids), Chaplin focused on increasingly complex formal designs. What in Sennett's films remains chaotic and one-dimensional becomes, in Chaplin's, something to appreciate on several levels—for the story line, the gags, and the choreographic brilliance of design. For Chaplin, the chase became a functional dance of pursuit.

Most of Chaplin's transformations of one action to another are so stylized that they, like the chases, become dancelike. Often such transformations serve to camouflage Charlie's real intentions, as when he conceals a passionate advance toward dowager Mme. Grosnay in *Monsieur Verdoux* by pretending to chase a bee. Similarly, his rhythmic breaks from action into freezes serve as a camouflage.

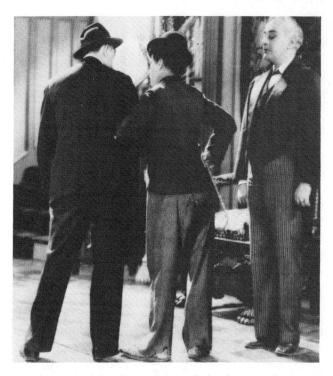

An eloquent physical expression of drunkenness from *City Lights*. L to R: Harry Myers, Chaplin, Allan Garcia.

Chaplin uses stylized movement sequences to portray various altered states of consciousness—madness in *Modern Times,* grogginess from a blow on the head in many films, notably in *The Great Dictator,* and most often drunkenness. To cite just one example of the latter, Charlie rises, drunk, from a chair in *City Lights,* circles around a piano bench, flexes his fingers to play, but staggers backward into his chair. Trying again, he goes in a straight line, walks into the bench, and bends to hit the piano keyboard with his forehead.

The drunken or absent-minded state offered Chaplin some of his richest opportunities for both large- and small-scale choreography. Two of the finest examples occur back-to-back in *The Idle Class.* The absent-minded husband (Chaplin in full dress as a millionaire) stands in front of his dresser mirror and notices, by comparing wife Edna's arrival time from a telegram with his clock, that he is going to be late in picking her up. Picking up his comb and brush, he notices in the mirror that he is wearing his top hat, so he puts down the comb and brush and takes the hat off, unfortunately putting it on top of the brush. He then sprays his forehead with some cologne, picks up his comb but can't find the brush, puts his hat back on his head, picks up the brush and again tries to use comb and brush on his head, but discovers he is wearing his hat, so just puts the comb and brush down.

Edna, meanwhile, has left the station with her maids and chauffeur.

Turning away from the dresser, the husband hooks his cane in the crook of his arm, but patting his breast pockets and noticing that he has forgotten his handkerchief, he turns back, takes a handkerchief from a drawer, sprays it with the cologne and, as he studies himself one last time in the mirror, folds the handkerchief, replaces it in the drawer, pats his breast pockets again, and strides off.

The capper comes in the next shot, showing the man full-figure for the first time as he walks toward the hotel lobby. He is fully dressed except for his pants, and wears, instead, oversized boxer shorts.

In a brilliant extension of the man's self-deception to his totally unwitting deception of a whole group of people, the scene continues as the millionaire walks into the lobby. As Charlie enters the lobby two events occur simultaneously: a lady on a bench turns to look at him, and a workman carrying a rod with drapery hanging to the floor from both ends enters and conveniently covers Charlie with a drape from the waist down. Charlie politely tips his hat. Two other ladies enter, walking diagonally toward

the right of the camera. The younger lady walks out of frame, but the older lady stops, facing the camera. As soon as she is out of the sight line of Charlie, the workman turns around clockwise looking for a place to hang his drapery, revolving the drape so that the opposite side swings *behind* Charlie (exposing him to view) as Charlie takes a step forward. Charlie turns and walks to the other drape (still exposed) and turns his back to the camera. Then *three* events occur simultaneously: Charlie revolves to face the standing lady; she revolves and walks toward him, but before she sees him . . . ; the workman revolves again (completing his circle) bringing the opposite drape in front of Charlie. Finally three more actions complete the sequence. Charlie and the standing lady both turn around again, she walking out of frame and he entering a phone booth, as the workman exits with his drapery.

Millionaire Charlie in the hotel lobby. The workman covers him with the drape each time one of the ladies looks. *The Idle Class.*

The scene lasts less than a minute. Every time one of the ladies turns toward Charlie the workman covers him with a drape. Everytime they turn their eyes away he is uncovered. Repeated viewing reveals the elegance of the conception. Each character's movement seems natural and plausible, yet is clearly the result of painstaking rehearsal.

In this scene, as well as in the brick-catching scene, the viewer's admiration goes not to Chaplin the actor as much as to Chaplin the scenarist and director. This is not usually the case, however; most examples of choreography emanate from Charlie the Tramp. One of the key functions of dancelike movement is to stress the gentlemanly aspect of the tramp, indicating his great suaveness and elegance. Although often comically inappropriate (flicking his

Charlie watches the Apache dancers with mounting concern. The woman at left is Jean Harlow. *City Lights.*

cigarette ash into a lady's hand, a top hat, or someone's open mouth), his movement still communicates courtliness by its form and rhythm. In *The Cure* Charlie efficiently dispatches two drunks who are harassing Edna and, without breaking the rhythm of his actions, doffs his hat and bows to Edna. Escorting her from the scene, he considerately hooks his cane on the arm of one of the men's and rolls him over to make a path for Edna, and, just as considerately rolls the man back when she has passed.

It must be stressed how well these movements are integrated into the films. Only once, in *Sunnyside,* is there a lengthy section of pure ballet unrelated to the rest of the film—probably a result of Chaplin's taking too seriously the many critics who extolled his balletic qualities. Generally, Chaplin's balletic grace is just that—a graceful note lending an undertone of elegance and formal beauty to the whole range of human movement in the films.

At times, however, Charlie actually dances in scenes on cafe floors, in night clubs and saloons, and at society parties. In most cases Charlie, after beginning in a promising way, encounters obstacles that challenge his smoothness such as a slippery floor, gum on his shoe, dogs tied around his waist, or a partner who is unwilling or too fat.

Dancing gives Chaplin a chance to display some of the numerous dance steps he learned on the music hall stage. The charming and poignant dance of the rolls in *The Gold Rush* and the distinctive sliding back step used in *The Count, Modern Times* and *Limelight,* are examples of his expertise.

Unlike the mimic qualities of his work, the dance elements developed gradually and cumulatively. The Mutual films contain the first sustained burst of comedy that is so obviously choreographed that the design *becomes* the gag in many instances. Three in the series (*The Count, The Cure,* and *The Adventur-*

er) contain scenes of social dancing. And most contain passages in which Charlie dances in sheer high spirits, whether or not the situation calls for it.

After the Mutual series dance elements become more tightly woven into the films' fabric. With *A Dog's Life* Chaplin achieved a unique integration of the elements of dance with the progress of the plot. Thereafter, there are choreographic high points in

poetic climaxes of the films. They are Chaplin's unique achievement—no one else so successfully integrated dance, drama, and comedy into single works of art.

Sometimes the seams don't quite fit because the patterns of movement are inadequately designed or seem forced, as in the waiter's attempt to carry a duck across the crowded dance floor in *Modern*

Charlie's pants have fallen down, and he holds them up with a rope, unaware of the dog attached to the other end. The dog is about to lunge for a cat. *The Gold Rush*.

each film—brick catching in *Pay Day*, the dream sequence in *The Kid*, the David-and-Goliath sermon in *The Pilgrim*, the roll dance in *The Gold Rush*, the mirror maze in *The Circus*, the boxing match in *City Lights*, the factory dance and the waiter dance in *Modern Times*, the balloon dance from *The Great Dictator*, and the music hall routine with Buster Keaton in *Limelight*. These are the sequences that burn into the memory and are recalled as the comic and

Times. At one point the duck is "impaled" on a chandelier, but the movement appears planned rather than accidental. In *The Idle Class* the scenes with Charlie the Tramp have a flat and mechanical look in contrast to the scenes with the millionaire.

What is amazing, though, is how often Chaplin hits the mark, successfully blending dance with the content of the films. The choreographic high points remain just that, high points, not mountain peaks isolated from the rest of the film. The silent films, particularly, are spectacularly integrated in this respect. The seams don't show.

Comedian Dick Van Dyke has often publicly stated his preference for Stan Laurel over Chaplin:

> Chaplin is great, a genius—but with Chaplin I can always see the technique showing. Lord knows it's great technique, and I admire it very much—but with Stan the technique never shows. Never. And that to me is proof that he is a better craftsman than Chaplin—an infinitely better craftsman.[6]

Leaving aside the issue of whether invisible technique is the mark of a better craftsman, there is a kind of truth in Van Dyke's statement. Only at rare moments are we aware of the great skillfulness of movement in Laurel's performances. In *Liberty*, he gets a crab down his pants and jumps and freezes in odd positions as the crab bites him. Later in the same film he does an incredible legs-trembling routine on high girders. More often than not, however, his notable movements are silly or impossible, as when he wiggles his ears or "lights" his thumb. Glib, graceful movements simply would not fit the slow-thinking, awkward, childish Stan character.

Charlie the Tramp, on the other hand, is a far more complex creature. Childlike in many ways, he is never childish. Dance and other graceful movement reveals in the films a spirit of play that softens his aggressive and sexual impulses. Certainly Stan's loveable simplicity elicits simpler responses in viewers than Chaplin's multifaceted tramp.

For what, after all, is Charlie the character? Having discussed the many contradictions that Chaplin's brilliant technique allows him, the contrasts of the child-man are clear. He is both tender and cruel, romantic and cynical, courtly and streetwise. Within the skin of the tramp's costume, his creator explores the boundaries of his own vision. A case can be made that Charlie is not really a coherent character at all, but a hollow device that serves a different purpose with each appearance. Then technique—gestures, costume, elaborate movements—is indeed right on the surface. The technique is the glittering shell that expresses its creator, whose ideas could not be contained in his popular character. Chaplin soon felt constrained by the limits that seemed necessary to maintain his vast audience. Ultimately he lost that audience, but not before taking them into areas that no other film artist has ever reached.

Technique, after all, is not simply the skill that one has; rather it is the relationship of skill to the intended communication, of the means to the end, of form to content. In that respect Chaplin's technique is perfect—not merely because of his impressive skills of movement, but because those skills are rarely superfluous to the meaning of the film.

This point is well demonstrated by one of the last great bursts of dance in Chaplin's films; the back-to-back sequences of the dictator's balloon dance and the Jewish barber shaving a customer.

In the balloon dance the movements and postures of ballet and the depiction of the globe as a balloon reveal the true nature of the dictator's wish to dominate the world, his godlike aspiration and power mania. Movements such as batting the balloon upward with his head, the bottom of his foot, and his rear end show childish playfulness of the idea. When the balloon bursts, the dictator sobs uncontrollably like a child having a temper tantrum. What more need be said about the will to absolute power?

The barber sequence is a light lark by comparison. Turning on his radio, he hears the familiar strains of Brahm's Hungarian Dance #5 as he prepares to shave a customer. The simple, pedestrian movements of stropping the razor and shaving are choreographed into a precise and functional dance, which derives its comedy from the barber's adherence to the rhythm of the music at the expense of his customer's comfort. His unpretentious actions contrast with the dictator's pomposity.

At the end of *8 1/2*, Federico Fellini has all the characters join hands around a circus ring, and gravely dance in a symbolic acknowledgment that life is like a circus.

For Chaplin that image is never merely symbolic. It is at the heart of his filmic world. It takes, at various times, a variety of forms. Certainly it goes beyond the playful joy and exuberance of the Mutuals. To view life in all its aspects as dance is more than childish play—it is divine play. To integrate this vision into film is great art.

Notes

[1]Chaplin, *My Autobiography, op. cit.,* p. 203. Reprinted with permission of The Bodley Head.

[2]Cooke, *op. cit.,* pp. 26–27.

[3]Chaplin, Charles, "Rhythm, A Story of Men in Macabre Movement", originally published in SCRIPT (Vol. xviii, No. 445, Jan. 15, 1938), reprinted in Cotes, Peter and Niklaus, Thelma, *The Little Fellow* (New York: The Citadel Press, 1965), pp. 167–168.

[4]Chaplin, *My Autobiography, op. cit.,* p. 209. Reprinted with permission of The Bodley Head.

[5]Paul, William, "The Gold Rush," *Film Comment,* September–October, 1972, p. 17.

[6]Van Dyke, Dick, from Kilgore, Al and McCabe, John, *Laurel and Hardy* (New York: Ballantine Books, 1976), p. 11.

Part Three
The Talking Mime

"Actions speak louder than words."
spoken by "The Mechanical Salesman" in *Modern Times*
and an inventor in *The Great Dictator*.

8

The Sounds of Silents

Although Chaplin's silent films are the most eloquent justification imaginable for the cliché "Actions speak louder than words," words do play an important role in Chaplin's films, and in silent films generally, in the form of subtitles. In the 1920s the writing and illustration of subtitles was considered a sister art to filmmaking, and became more and more elaborate as the decade wore on, particularly in those films that derived from literature or aspired to the significance of serious literature. In retrospect, this tendency is seen as a wrong direction since cinema is, even today, more visual than verbal, and too much dialogue or exposition in silent film subtitles fatally distances a modern viewer from the action.

The better filmmakers, of course, recognized this, though few pushed it to the point of F. W. Murnau, whose film *The Last Laugh* (1924) contains not a single subtitle.

Chaplin and Keaton rightfully prided themselves on their sparing use of subtitles; seldom did either fall into the trap of advancing his stories with words rather than images.

Chaplin, in fact, often went even further, finding reasons to unobtrusively justify the filmic silence. In *The Immigrant,* for example, the language barrier causes comic clashes as immigrant Charlie struggles to order a meal from waiter Eric. In his last starring film, *A King in New York,* Chaplin introduces a sound film variation on the same gag as another immigrant, the deposed king tries to order a meal in a nightclub over the sound of a rock band, forcing him to resort to pantomime. Such excuses for silence permeate a surprising number of scenes in Chaplin's films and greatly help in making the stylized pantomime seem more natural.

Before discussing the content in the subtitles, one must consider an intriguing aspect of watching silent action. As anyone who has ever attended a silent film or stage pantomime show knows, they are not really "silent." The viewer inevitably supplies the sound in his own imagination. An image of someone screaming, for instance, has such strong associations for anyone watching, that they "fill in" the sound quite involuntarily. This fact makes possible a whole class of unique gags which work *only* in a silent-film world. In a brilliant sequence from *The Kid* a cruel doctor is manhandling Jackie Coogan (the kid) as he examines him. He asks Charlie a question (not shown in a subtitle) but has trouble hearing Charlie's reply because of the stethoscope in his ears. Charlie simply picks up the end of the stethoscope and barks his reply into it, causing the doctor to jump in pain.

As a result of his examination the doctor summons the orphan officials to take the child away. The pompous official has no intention of "soiling" himself by dealing with lowlife Charlie, so he directs his flunky to get the needed information. When he finally addresses Charlie directly, Charlie pretends not to be able to hear until the flunky translates.

Both of the sequences described above gain their comic punch from characters not hearing each other. Since the audience can't really hear them either, the gags are much funnier; indeed, the humor would completely evaporate if one could hear the dialogue—the stethoscope gag would seem too painful if Charlie's shout could be heard, and his pretense of not hearing the official would stretch credibility.

Often Chaplin finds visual equivalents to indicate the sounds in the film. When butler Albert Austin pops a champagne cork in *The Adventurer,* escaped convict Charlie automatically puts his hands up, assuming the cops have arrived with guns blazing. The audience can see the cork popping and Charlie reacting in the same instant. Added sound might only stress how the sound of a cork popping is unlike that of a gunshot.`

Reissues of silent films in the sound era often supplied them with sound effects to modernize them, but in sequences such as the one described above, they only distract or contradict the plausibility of the scene. A notable example is the recent reissue of Harold Lloyd's *Why Worry,* in a scene which has Harold simulating cannon fire to fool enemy troops, with a combination of cigar smoke, lobbed coconuts, and drum beats. In silence the gag gets by, but in the sound version (prepared in the 1970s after Lloyd's death) the audience is treated to authentic-sounding cannon and explosion sounds which stretch plausibility to the breaking point. In contrast, Chaplin's reissue soundtracks for his silent films offer an object lesson in proper use of music and effects; sound effects are used very sparingly, Chaplin preferring to let the music provide background and counterpoint for the action. Even the music seldom illustrates the action in the direct way now associated with animated cartoons; rather, it subtly directs the mood of the viewer and stresses the balletic aspects of Chaplin's work through delicate dancelike melodies.

When considering the words in the subtitles, most notable in the early films is Chaplin's fondness for silly, punning names—particularly when impersonating royalty or the rich. In *The Rink* he is Sir Cecil Seltzer, C.O.D. (a waiter in reality), attending a skating party given by Miss Loneleigh (Edna). In other films he is Count de Broko, Count Chloride de Lime, Weakchin (a caveman), Darn Hosiery (Don Jose in "Carmen"), Commodore Slick, and so on to his great explosion of punning names in *The Great Dictator.*

Before going any further, it is necessary to acknowledge the difficulty in establishing authenticity in the subtitles (also known as "titles") of Chaplin's pre-1917 films, which have been repeatedly "modernized" with new ones. In the 1920s particularly, many of Chaplin's Keystones were "joked up" with horrendous editorial commentary and labored-over puns which are wincingly unfunny today. (Chaplin's brother Sydney was one of the offenders.) Authorship of even the authentic titles is questionable, since Chaplin employed assistant directors and writers (the latter of whom ghost-wrote most of the articles he published) whose actual contribution to the

films' subtitles are unknown. The third difficulty is Chaplin's own tendency to alter scenes as well as titles in his reissues of the post-1918 films. For example, in *Shoulder Arms* a joke about being the third person to light a cigarette off the same match, once a superstition of bad luck which has faded with time, was eliminated for 1959 reissue in *The Chaplin Revue.*

Often the subtitles in Chaplin's films serve mainly to humorously or ironically label a scene or character. In *The Immigrant,* after a scene which elaborately deals with the motion of the boat and seasickness of the passengers, the audience is treated to "More rolling" in the form of a crap game. Another title announces "The arrival in the Land of Liberty" followed by a shot of the Statue of Liberty and another of the new arrivals being penned in behind ropes like cattle. In *Shoulder Arms* destitute French girl Edna, living in her bombed-out house, is introduced as "Poor France." The construction workers in *Pay Day* are "Hard Shirking Men." Charlie's termagant wife (Phyllis Allen) is "His wife—and First National Bank" as she paces back and forth outside the construction yard on payday.

If these jokes seem rather tame, it must be said that they seldom get laughs in the viewing. They are midly amusing and serve to set up the usually hilarious visual scenes.

Other titles quote monologue or dialogue of the characters, and occasionally Chaplin scores with a funny line. Capturing thirteen German soldiers by himself in *Shoulder Arms,* he casually describes his success by explaining, "I surrounded them." After Charlie's elaborate dissection of Albert Austin's alarm clock in *The Pawnshop,* Austin leaves the shop and is approached by a bum who asks him for the time. The simple title "What time is it?" brings a laugh, which is increased when Austin angrily pushes the innocent man to the ground. (This concept was reworked later for the brilliant gag in *City Lights* when "millionaire" Charlie shoves a bum aside for a cigar butt.) In *A Dog's Life* Charlie uses Scraps the dog as a pillow but is soon scratching his head, saying via subtitle, "There are strangers in our midst." But Chaplin himself felt that the briefer, the better.

Buster Keaton's subtitles were consistently funnier than Chaplin's. While sitting on the end of a plank he is sawing in two in *One Week,* his first independent film, Buster is called to supper by his wife. "I'll be right down," he answers accurately. Through an intricate series of misunderstandings in *Cops,* Buster believes he has shrewdly bought a wagonload of furniture, but in fact the owners think he is a moving man and wait expectantly at their new address after helping Buster load the wagon. Shots of the family waiting, the father becoming increasingly restless, are intercut with shots of the inevitable disaster which greets their worldly possessions as Buster inadvertently rides into a police parade. First, though, we are treated to the bored Buster asleep on the seat as his horse pulls the cart at a snail's pace. The father, looking at his watch, exclaims, "Maybe he was arrested for speeding." The next title introduces the police parade: "Once a year the citizens of every city know where they can find a policeman." After Buster accidentally throws an anarchist's bomb into the parade, he rides over a fire hydrant which sprays the grandstand dignitaries; next he overturns the cart. In the ensuing melee the police chief accosts the mayor with "Get some cops to protect our policemen." Meanwhile the father, innocent of the fact that his furniture has been utterly demolished, points excitedly toward his wife and says, "Do you suppose anything could've happened to our furniture?"

Chaplin generally didn't put much of the burden of comedy on his subtitles, but effectively used them when necessary for minimal dialogue and labeling. In *The Idle Class* the alcoholic husband and his wife are introduced as "The lonely husband" and "The lonely wife," titles which precede each of their appearances.

Chaplin's last silent film was *The Circus,* and he had great difficulty completing it due both to his unhappy homelife with Lita Grey, his second wife, and the scandalous divorce which threatened to end his career. These personal problems perhaps account for his unusual overdependence on titles toward the middle of the picture, which, though often funny enough in themselves, slow the pace of the film considerably.

But another problem loomed in the background, an esthetic problem which was to change the entire film industry and abruptly end the medium which Chaplin so dominated. Sound films were now a reality.

Facing the Revolution

From the mid-twenties on, Chaplin was vehemently defensive on the subject of sound movies. Visiting William Randolph Hearst's great palace, San Simeon, he furiously stalked out of a room when Hearst dared to suggest that sound films might be a natural and acceptable successor to silents. Chaplin was well aware of the reasons for his attitude:

> . . . if I did make a talking picture, no matter how good I was I could never surpass the artistry of my pantomime. I had thought of possible voices for the Tramp—whether he should speak in monosyllables or just mumble.* But it was no use. If I talked I would become like any other comedian. These were the melancholy problems that confronted me.[1]

Early sound films more than justified Chaplin's contempt. The actors (frequently stage imports with no screen experience) were chained to the limited range of microphones, and tended to stand stiffly and recite their lines. The fluid silent camera became an immobile soundproof room and sound technology was crude, resulting in unintentionally humorous sound effects.

Yet at first the audience overlooked these problems, flocking to the new sensation as they had thirty years earlier flocked to the crude nickelodeons to experience the novelty of pictures that moved. The subject hardly mattered, since the illusion was the attraction. And soon the technology improved and a new breed of performer emerged for the new medium.

For sound films were not merely silent films with sound added. They were an entirely new medium. For Chaplin it was as though the rug he had labored so long to weave was suddenly pulled completely out from under him. He recognized it as both a personal crisis and a crisis for an entire art form. Thus, he vehemently resisted the encroachment of sound by expressing his feelings in interviews. In an article he wrote for the *New York Times* two weeks before the premiere of *City Lights*, he defended his position not only as the master of silent comedy, but as virtually its sole exponent. Despite the fact that silent films had been completely replaced by the three-year-old phenomenon, Chaplin blithely stated:

> Because the silent or nondialogue picture has been temporarily [Kamin's emphasis] pushed aside in the hysteria attending the introduction of speech by no means indicates that it is extinct or that the motion picture screen has seen the last of it. City Lights is evidence of this. . . . I am confident that the future will see a return of interest in nontalking pro-

---

*A solution used to good effect by Jacques Tati much later.

ductions because there is a constant demand for a medium that is universal in its utility. . . . I consider the talking picture a valuable addition to the dramatic art regardless of its limitations, but I regard it only as an addition, not as a substitute. . . . Silent comedy is more satisfactory entertainment for the masses than talking comedy. . . . Pantomime . . . is the prime qualification of a successful screen player.[2]

Modern humor frightens me a little. The Marx brothers are frightening. . . . They say, 'All right, you're insane, we'll appeal to your insanity.' They make insanity the convention. . . . Knocking everything down. Annihilating everything. There's no conduct in their humor. They haven't any attitude. It's up-to-date, of course—a part of the chaos. I think it's transitional.[3]

In fact, Chaplin had halted production midway through *City Lights* to consider the advisability of making another silent film that would (and did) seem anachronistic to an audience which had turned away from that medium. Harold Lloyd virtually remade his completed film *Welcome Danger* in 1929, eagerly embracing the new medium (a move which Chaplin, in one of his rare public acknowledgments of his contemporaries, condemned in another magazine interview entitled "Charlie Chaplin Attacks the Talkies"). Buster Keaton, no longer his own boss at MGM, made two excellent silent films in 1928 and, weary from the creative battles on the job and his personal battle with alcoholism, capitulated to MGM's "guidance" of his career into oblivion in a series of uninspired sound films. He did hold out in the form of a well-done "Dance of the Sea" in which he plays Neptune's daughter in an eccentric dance sequence (*The Hollywood Revue of 1929*).

Only Laurel and Hardy seemed to make the transition to sound without major esthetic fuss, and go on to become even more popular than they had been in the silent era.

But waiting in the wings were the new breed of comedians.

Many of them were of Chaplin's comic generation, but had styles of comedy too dependent on the spoken word to succeed in silent films. Both the Marx Brothers and W. C. Fields virtually exploded onto the screen and into the hearts of a public shocked and jaded by the Depression and the abrupt end of the dreams of prosperity so rife in the 1920s. The cynical content and tongue-in-cheek style of their films exactly matched the mood of the period, and soon Fields was being labeled "the funniest man in the world."

And what of the King of Comedy? Now the statement had to be qualified: The King of Silent Comedy. A king whose kingdom had completely vanished, despite his vigorous protests.

Privately, Chaplin expressed both his fear and his contempt for these "new" comedians.

It wasn't transitional, of course. The kingdom had irreversibly altered, leaving its king to adapt as best he could. On one occasion he met with Fields and outraged him by never referring to Fields' screen work at all. He did express to Groucho his admiration for Groucho's great verbal facility, but otherwise deplored the antiart and antiromantic content of the Marx's and Fields' films, so contrary to his own work at that time.

Against the obviously prevailing trend and the heartfelt advice of his film colleagues, Chaplin elected to continue making *City Lights* as a silent film. It did provide him a chance to develop and demonstrate his talent in a new area of movie making, the film score. There is evidence that Chaplin might not have made even his concession without the insistence of United Artists. But since he had composed music and songs from his early twenties on, this was an exciting new challenge for him, and one which would, in fact, dominate the activities of his last years, as he worked to provide film scores for all of his post-1918 silent films.

The anomaly of releasing a silent film in 1931 hit home forcibly when Chaplin found that distributors—even his own United Artists—were reluctant to take a risk with *City Lights*. Only after he took over the New York premiere himself—rented an out-of-the-way theatre, and personally supervised the ad campaign—and the film proved a smash success and critical triumph, did he secure a proper distribution deal for the picture.

Notes

[1]Chaplin, *My Autobiography, op. cit.*, p. 387. Reprinted with permission of The Bodley Head.

[2]Chaplin, Charlie, "Pantomime and Comedy," *The New York Times* (January 25, 1931), Section 8, p. 6.

[3]Cited in Eastman, Max, *Enjoyment of Laughter* (London: Hamish Hamilton, 1937), p. 108.

9

Pantomime With Music: *City Lights*

City Lights was originally conceived as a silent film, and it can be viewed silently without impairment of its meaning and humor. It begins with a gag dependent on sound, however. A crowd is gathered for the unveiling of a civic monument, and various dignitaries speak, accompanied on the soundtrack with gibbering squawks synchronized to their lip movements (Chaplin made the sounds by speaking through a saxophone mouthpiece). Two later scenes make use of sound effects: At a party Charlie swallows a whistle which blows each time he hiccups, distracting the audience from a pompous classical singer; and in a prizefight scene the bell rope wraps around Charlie's neck so that when he gets knocked down the bell rings, ending the round, and rings again as he trots back to his corner. But most of the film takes place in the charmed silent world of Chaplin pantomime, accompanied for the first time by Chaplin music.

In *The Kid,* his first feature film ten years earlier, Chaplin had opened the film with a subtitle, "A film with a smile and perhaps a tear," to make clear to his audience his dramatic as well as comic intention and to prepare them for the film's long dramatic first scene. Now, addressing an audience that hadn't seen a new Chaplin film in three years and was in addition "hysterical" over what he considered the new fad of talking pictures, he neatly stated what his picture was: "A Comedy Romance in Pantomime." The main title, subtitle, and cast credits are followed by a street scene at night; as if to drive home the main title again, the letters C-I-T-Y-L-I-G-H-T-S

flash on the screen one at a time like an electric-light movie marque. It is a pleasant touch, especially since in *City Lights* Chaplin unquestionably hit upon his most brilliant and resonant film title.

In his earlier dramatic comedy, *The Gold Rush,* Chaplin achieved unity in part by the complex comic-dramatic density of the individual scenes. The cabin scenes such as the struggle for the rifle, the eating of the shoe, and so on have underlying them the very real life-and-death struggles depicted. On the other hand, the romantic scenes with Georgia are lightened by wonderful physical gags, culminating in the dance of the rolls when Charlie is stood up by the dance hall girls for New Year's Eve, a scene so comic and graceful that it both underscores and lightens the pathos of the situation.

But in *City Lights* Chaplin had a greater problem of unity, because the comic and dramatic poles of the film are pushed far apart—the light scenes with the millionaire don't have *The Gold Rush*'s urgent life-and-death undertone. And the dramatic scenes with the blind girl are more romantic than comic, her affliction limiting the kind of humor—invariably at his own expense—that Chaplin can use, as well as making their scenes together "serious" enough that there is no hint of mocking her affliction. The working out of their scenes, full of a delicate humor until the last heavily dramatic encounter, is one of the marvels of the Chaplin canon.

The contrast in tones is clearly stressed by Chaplin's facial makeup. In scenes with the millionaire, particularly in the cafe, it is highly exaggerated—

Charlie, a bit more dapper than usual, in *City Lights*.

Chaplin with Harry Myers as the eccentric millionaire. Note Chaplin's exaggerated facial makeup.

more so than ever before in a Chaplin film. His eyebrows are large half-moons on his chalky-white face, emphasizing his clown aspect; but the make-up is subtle and naturalistic during the scenes with the blind girl.

The musical soundtrack composed by Chaplin helps to unify the disparate elements of the film, providing a gentle background of waltzes and marches to set off the action, and using the Wagnerian leitmotif method of identifying each character with a specific musical theme whenever he appears.*

The final scenes of *City Lights* build emphatically to the film's powerful climax. The fight scene, in which Charlie vainly tries to earn money to prevent the girl's eviction; the final encounter with the millionaire, during which the man's off-again-on-again recognition of Charlie both provides Charlie with the needed money and makes him a criminal in the eyes of the law; the final, furtive good-bye to the blind girl, giving her both enough money for the rent and for an operation to restore her eyesight—an operation that will alter forever her relationship with Charlie, who had assumed the role of a millionaire for her benefit.

The fight scene is particularly important in setting

*In an interview with writer Rob Wagner during the making of *City Lights* Chaplin described an earlier approach to the music of the film. The blind girl's theme (later a borrowed popular tune, "La Violetera") was to be on a record which Charlie plays on a phonograph in the film. The title, shown to the audience on the disc itself, is *Wondrous Eyes*, by *Charles Chaplin*. Later he hears it played by street musicians and in saloons. In the actual film, of course, the music is not nearly so naturalistically welded to the image—even a shot of Chaplin putting a record on the blind girl's phonograph is not coordinated in such a way that the viewer has the illusion of hearing a record being played.

up the mostly dramatic and finally terrifyingly poignant scenes that follow. One reason for this is that some of the earlier comic scenes with the millionaire—the suicide attempt by the embankment and the party at the millionaire's house at which Charlie swallows the whistle—fall considerably below Chaplin's usual comic standard. In the boxing scene, though, working opposite Keystone veteran Hank Mann, Chaplin comes triumphantly into his own again; it is one of the funniest, longest, and most elaborately choreographed scenes he ever did, and leaves the viewer breathless with laughter.

The boxing match itself is preceded by a very funny dressing-room scene which runs about seven minutes, in which it is established that the boxer who had agreed to "go easy" with Charlie must get out of town fast (the police are after him) is replaced by the stolid Mann, who proves himself both a fierce fighter (by knocking out the winner of a previous bout who displeases him) and unwilling to make a deal with Charlie, whose coy overtures he interprets as homosexual. After much other byplay, the match begins, running a full five minutes—a virtual catalogue of boxing gags (Chaplin attended the American Legion prizefights weekly in Hollywood, and in fact met Virginia Cherrill, *City Light*'s blind girl, at one; in the boxing scene his study paid off handsomely).

Chaplin had done boxing scenes twice before, once at Keystone in *The Knockout* and at Essanay in *The Champion*. Even a casual comparison demonstrates Chaplin's growth as a creator of physical comedy in the fifteen years that separates these films from *City Lights*. It is of value to this book's theme to consider the scene, one of the comic highlights of his career, in detail.

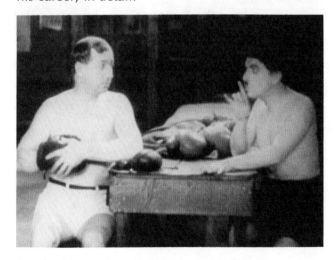

Charlie tries to make a deal with boxer Hank Mann.

Charlie maneuvers the referee between himself and Mann; Charlie and the referee hop one way, Mann the other.

A clinch.

Charlie tries to push Mann down.

Charlie steadies the dazed Hank Mann prior to butting him with a flying leap.

When the bell rings Charlie immediately locks Mann and the referee into a pattern of movement that he will repeat throughout the scene: maneuvering the referee between himself and Mann as all three begin hopping from side to side. Charlie and the referee face each other and hop in the same direction, and Mann, behind the referee, hops in the opposite direction. Circling around the ring they repeat the hypnotic pattern on the other side, then return to their original position and begin it again. But this time Mann breaks the rhythm by stopping, allowing the referee to hop out of the way. Charlie uses this opportunity to punch Mann, whereupon they all resume the pattern of circle, hop-hop-hop, circle back, hop-hop-PUNCH. But this time Mann swings back at Charlie, who ducks and grabs him in a bear-hug clinch.

The referee breaks the clinch, and again the men move into the same pattern of hops, circles, punch-duck-clinch.

A variation is introduced when Mann swings so hard that he spins around and Charlie grabs him in a clinch from behind and Mann tries to "buck" him off. Charlie stays on, even though his legs fly into the air, and he butts Mann in the rear end with his knee. The referee breaks *this* up, giving Charlie another opening for a quick punch to Mann when he moves aside.

The original pattern begins again, but then the participants execute an intricate circling movement; kept within the same rhythm, they switch positions. Now Charlie and Mann face each other, hopping from side to side, as the referee watches and hops behind them. Charlie, ever the master of the situation, gets another punch in, shaking out his hand from the force of it. He runs in a circle around the, by now, thoroughly befuddled Mann and punches him again. Mann begins to sink to the floor but rises, and Charlie helpfully pushes down on his shoulders, but again Mann rises as if powered by an internal spring.

Steadying Mann, Charlie backs off and takes a flying leap (via unseen wire) to butt Mann in the stomach with his head, but Mann gets up. Charlie butts him down again. The referee moves to block Charlie's third butt and gets knocked down by it himself.

After two more futile swings by Mann, and more futile attempts by Charlie to push him down to the canvas, Mann finally connects with his first punch of the fight, causing Charlie to stagger in a semicircle around the ring. In his bewilderment he manages to duck Mann's next few punches and get into

A flying leap. Note wire.

clinches, but he gets into clinches with the corner pole as well as with his own second, who has come into the ring to retrieve him after the bell rings signaling the end of round one.

During the break Charlie imagines his second is Virginia comforting him. He grabs her hand and begins kissing it, but then the image dissolves back to reveal him kissing the hand of the second, who pulls his hand away angrily in a continuation of the homosexual gag motif which permeates the film.

The second round begins exactly as the first, but this time Charlie clinches with the referee, and as the referee pushes Charlie away he receives the punch Mann had aimed at Charlie. Mann catches the staggering referee, and Charlie seizes his opportunity to separate them from their "clinch." The referee, fooled by his latest role change, swings at

Virginia appears to the dazed Charlie.

A role reversal: Charlie becomes the referee.

Out for the count.

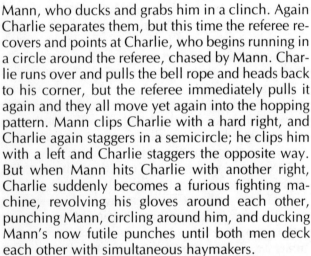

Mann, who ducks and grabs him in a clinch. Again Charlie separates them, but this time the referee recovers and points at Charlie, who begins running in a circle around the referee, chased by Mann. Charlie runs over and pulls the bell rope and heads back to his corner, but the referee immediately pulls it again and they all move yet again into the hopping pattern. Mann clips Charlie with a hard right, and Charlie again staggers in a semicircle; he clips him with a left and Charlie staggers the opposite way. But when Mann hits Charlie with another right, Charlie suddenly becomes a furious fighting machine, revolving his gloves around each other, punching Mann, circling around him, and ducking Mann's now futile punches until both men deck each other with simultaneous haymakers.

The referee counts over Charlie, but he rises before the count of ten so the referee turns to Mann, who also rises before he completes the count. However, by this time Charlie has collapsed again. Charlie again rises before the referee reaches ten, but Mann has dropped. The hapless referee whirls from man to man. Finally they are both standing. Mann swings, Charlie ducks and clinches, and they both stagger against the ropes, where the bell rope wraps around Charlie's neck.

This time when Mann knocks Charlie down, the bell rings. Charlie trots back to his corner, unknowingly ringing the bell again. He rushes into the ring, is knocked down, ringing the bell again, returns to his corner, runs into the ring and the referee removes the rope from his neck.

A final punch by Mann leaves Charlie out for the count.

If the sequence is difficult to follow in print, let it be said that it is so fast-paced it literally sweeps the viewer up in its rhythm and one becomes as hypnotically involved as the referee and Mann in the dazzling display of functional choreography. The key sequence with its hop-hop-hop rhythm is introduced at the start and continues through the routine with ingenious variation; its mechanical nature is recapitulated in the sequences of Mann springing up, Charlie punching like a machine in high gear, and the hilarious business of each man collapsing as the referee counts the other man out.

Underlying the comedy of the dressing-room and boxing scenes is the fact that Charlie had been trying desperately to earn enough money to prevent the blind girl's eviction. In the ensuing scene the drunken millionaire gives Charlie enough money for both the rent and an operation to restore her eyesight, but Charlie becomes a fugitive in the process of taking the money because the millionaire, when sober, does not remember giving Charlie the money. A final, poignant scene in the blind girl's apartment ends with a sad farewell; the dialogue titles are simple and eloquent:

> Girl: "You're not going away?"
> Charlie: "Yes, I must."
> Girl: "You'll come back?"
> Charlie: "Yes, I'll come back."

Giving the girl the money, an act of sacrifice and love, will have grave consequences for Charlie since it makes him a criminal and will inevitably

After prison—his spirits dampened.

destroy the illusion he has so painstakingly fostered of being a millionaire.

Charlie is captured and jailed. With the passage of time, the girl is seen, her sight now restored. Evidently the money Charlie had given her included enough surplus for her to open a flower shop, which seems to be thriving as she eagerly awaits the return of her benefactor.

In *The Gold Rush* Chaplin had ended the film with an ironic subtitle. Posed by a photographer with the dance hall girl he's finally won, they move together for a kiss. The photographer says, "Oh, you've spoilt the picture." It can be read as a sly anticipation of those critics who would argue with the film's happy, fairy-tale ending. Charlie simply waves "Oh, go on" to the photographer and continues his kiss as the scene fades out.

The plot of *The Gold Rush* resolves as fantasy. Charlie becomes a millionaire and, dressed in his tramp clothes for the photographer on board "The good ship success," is discovered by the dance hall girl who now loves him for himself. It is a fantasy which the audience, having lived through Charlie's emotional and physical ordeals in the film, dearly wants to believe.

If anything, the audience watching *City Lights* wants even more to see Charlie succeed. He has, after all, behaved with great nobility throughout the film, and his ordeals are lived through not as much for his own survival as for the survival and comfort of the blind girl. But the plot of *City Lights* inevitably leads to vision, which will shatter illusion. In *The*

Gold Rush the man who looks like a bum is in reality a millionaire, whereas in *City Lights* he is, except for his inner nobility and spirit, truly a bum.

Even that spirit seems dampened when Charlie is released from prison. He is seen as he rounds the old street corner where the girl had sold flowers. His silhouette is a study in downtrodden defeat; the clothes, this once, are not so much a clown outfit as genuinely tattered rags. Chaplin's mime—this time with serious intent—is here seen at its most powerful. His walk, head bowed, is slow and halting as he passes the flower shop. Seeing the girl through the shop window, he breaks into a wide grin—the grin of someone pulling up from the depths of despair or exhaustion—and the girl laughs, saying, "I've made a conquest." This bitter title prepares the audience for the utter seriousness of the final moments as the girl goes out of the shop to give Charlie a flower and a coin. He shuffles away, not wanting to break the illusion in this state. But he cannot resist as she beckons. In another heartrending bit of mime he grins, this time the grin of a child being offered a treat, as he leans and reaches for the flower. Virginia draws him toward her, pressing the coin into his hand, and suddenly her face changes as recognition begins. A close-up of their hands, her touch becoming a caress, makes clear that she is seeing once again the way she saw before—through touch. Haunting close-ups of their faces alternate with the film's final, eloquent dialogue titles. Virginia says simply, "You?" Charlie nods shyly, then, pointing to his own eyes, says, "You can see now," confirming, as

Virginia recognizes the tramp.

if further confirmation were necessary, his own "real" identity. She responds in the final title, as resonant and poignant as any Chaplin wrote, "Yes, I can see now." She is dissolving into tears as the full impact settles upon her, still grasping his hand. The final shot shows Charlie, hopeful, terrified, tremulous. . . . The shot fades to black.

The final half hour of *City Lights*, with its balance of the funniest comedy and the most moving drama, is Chaplin at his best both as performer and scenarist. Even the titles contribute greatly to the final effect, which is utterly disarming. Just as it had in 1931, *City Lights* emerges today as a unique achievement, transcending considerations of sound vs. silent film. Whatever one's feeling about what came before, the boxing scene confirms Chaplin's mastery of his medium. Even repeated viewings do not diminish the impact of the final scenes, so skillfully are they set up and so beautifully are they acted out.

City Lights is Chaplin's triumph of both motion and emotion.

Opposite: The final expression.

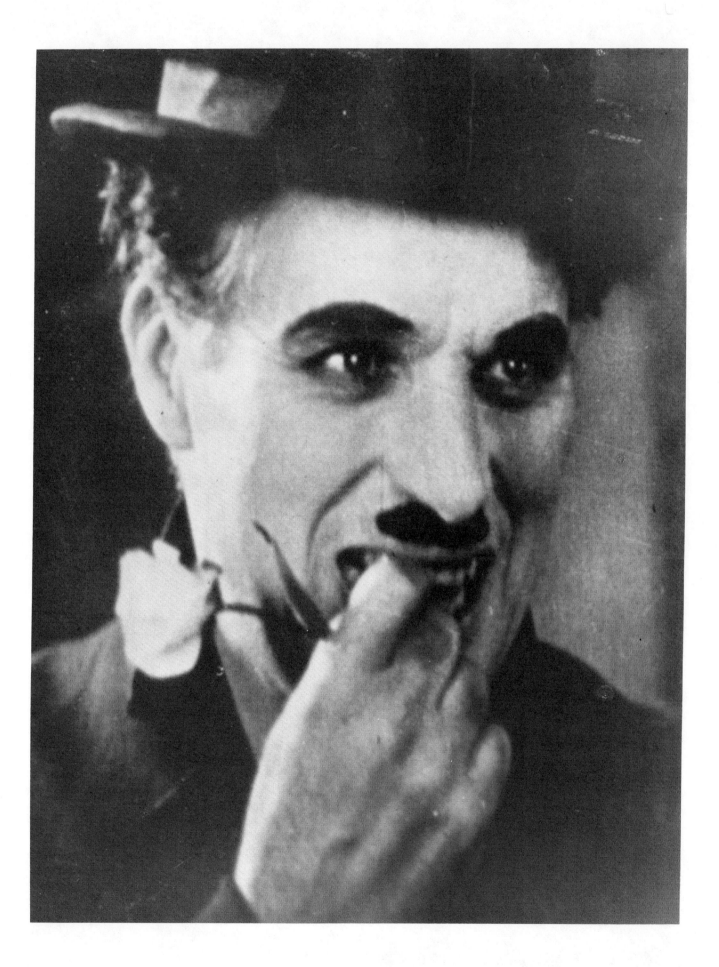

10

The Great Compromise:
Modern Times

As he had with *The Kid* ten years earlier, Chaplin went abroad to generate additional publicity for the European premiere of *City Lights*. The trip stretched to fifteen months, encompassing both Europe and the Orient. Despairing of following the success of *City Lights* with another silent film, he seriously considered retiring and settling in China. He found Oriental customs congenial (his home was staffed by Japanese servants until World War II), and their arts intriguing, particularly the mimelike Kabuki theatre.

Instead he focused his attention on an idea he'd toyed with for many years, a film about Napoleon. In the summer of 1934 he employed Alistair Cooke to do research and collaborate on the script. But by the end of the summer he announced, "By the way, the Napoleon thing. It's a beautiful idea—for somebody else."[1] Cooke also recalls other film ideas Chaplin entertained during that summer, one being a film revue containing several short films. One of these shorts was a nightclub scene in which the floor show is a miming of the Crucifixion; another, a French legend of a tumbler who offers his prayers to God in the form of an elaborate tumbling routine, during which he breaks his back (the Virgin Mary appears and blesses him as he dies—similar to the ending of *Limelight* twenty years later).

But Chaplin lost enthusiasm for this idea, too, telling Cooke pointedly, "They don't pay their shillings and quarters to see Charles Chaplin doing artistic experiments. They come to see *him*."[2]

Yet to make another film with "him" placed Chaplin in the same esthetic dilemma he had faced

in making *City Lights* only now he could no longer harbor the hope that talking films were a passing fad.

Certainly he was still in the public eye. Many of his early (pre-1917) films had been reissued with musical soundtracks, and he had enough income to keep his entire studio staff on the payroll, ready for the moment when inspiration crystallized into production. Had he wanted to, Chaplin probably could have continued making successful silent films with music. He also would have been alone since Lloyd's popularity and productivity in the thirties had declined to a quiet fadeout by the end of the decade and Keaton, by the middle of the decade, had embarked on the depressing series of Educational Films shorts, never to regain his position as a major star.

Alone and old-fashioned. Various of Chaplin's distinguished contemporaries argued that "only Charlie" could still get away with it. Even Winston Churchill, in an article for *Collier's* magazine in 1935, publicly encouraged Chaplin to pursue this course:

> *Pantomime is the true universal tongue. . . . I believe . . . that the future of Charlie Chaplin may be mainly in the portrayal of serious roles in silent, or rather, non-talking films, and in the development of a universal cinema . . . but let him come back— at least occasionally—to the vein of comedy that has been the world's delight for twenty years.*[3]

111

Chaplin doing an early "artistic experiment," in *The Face on the Barroom Floor,* 1914.

But Chaplin dreaded leaving his vast audience behind, either by doing "artistic experiments" or by continuing in a style of film that had become passé.

Finally he hit upon a compromise: a silent film with subtitles, but one in which sound effects and words were wedded in unusual ways with the images—ways that allowed him to vent his feelings about the relationship of sound to image . . . words to movement. Yes, he could give them sounds, give them words, but as always, on his own terms. And who could consider a film entitled *Modern Times* to be old-fashioned?

Chaplin reports that the idea for the film was stimulated by conversation about the mechanization of modern life in general and the assembly line in particular. But in fact, he first had the idea for the feeding machine in 1916. His friend Max Eastman also recalls a scene Chaplin photographed before 1920, in which crowds, moving like automatons,

rush past a beggar seated on the sidewalk. Periodically one of the crowd members turns to hand the beggar a nickel, which he rings up in a cash register. "That's modern life," Chaplin told Eastman at the time, "everything mechanized and regimented—even charity!"[4]

Of course, this tendency to see and visually translate the mechanical aspects of life emanated from Chaplin's own physical technique, and led to some of his major transformation gag variations. *Modern Times'* factory was a natural extension of that thread in his work, a proper final playground for the tramp. Significantly, it also allowed Chaplin to shoot at undercranked speeds, to preserve that crispness of movement so essential to his technique.

But *Modern Times,* as has been pointed out by many critics, is hardly modern at all, for all its up-to-the-minute satire of mechanization. Despite the settings and events—the factory, strikes, strike-breaking police—the real concern of the film is "modern times" in the sense of Charlie's place as a character in the world of sound films, and Chaplin's place as an artist. *City Lights*, strongly contrasting the dissolute and burnt-out life of the millionaire with the gritty poverty of the blind girl, is much more effective in depicting the mood and attitudes of the Depression.

Modern Times begins with a subtitle as misleading as its main title: "'Modern Times.' A story of industry, of individual enterprise—humanity crusading in the pursuit of happiness." The opening titles appear superimposed over a clock, giving a contemporary viewer of the film a peculiar message, since both the typography and the clock now strongly suggest the 1930s. Though the subtitle does not accurately describe the picture as a whole, Chaplin may have wanted to begin the film on a documentary note (the music reinforces this), suggesting the "news on the march" newsreels of the period.

The opening shots further imply that *Modern Times* will be primarily a social satire. An overhead shot of a flock of sheep rushing headlong dissolves into a similar shot of factory workers emerging from a subway. Chaplin's original title for the film was *The Masses;* in light of this, and of Charlie's inability to fit into his various jobs, it is appropriate that one of the sheep, in the center of the flock, is a black sheep. It is the first of several subtle insertions in *Modern Times*.

The president of the Electro Steel Company sits in his office, bored with funny papers and jigsaw puzzles (this actor, Allan Garcia, was Chaplin's utility authority figure). But Chaplin is not saying that the man is living a life of ease, a parasite off the sweat of the sheeplike workers, for the secretary brings the president a pill, indicating that he holds a stressful position.

The president next scans the factory with his closed-circuit video screen (to the sound accompaniment of electronic buzzing—here Chaplin is more generous in his use of sound effects than he was in *City Lights*). Finally he summons Max, the shirtless controller of the generators and assembly belt speeds. As Max stands watching the president's image on his monitor, we hear the first spoken words in Chaplin's cinema: "Section Five. Speed 'er up. Four-one."

As the scene cuts to "Section Five" and slowly pans to reveal Charlie, a voice-over is heard as on a loudspeaker, indicating trouble: "Attention Foreman. Trouble on Base Five. Check on the nut-faces.

A black sheep in the fold.

Nuts coming through from Base Five." Naturally the visual image is reinforcing this background (aural) message, as Charlie is having trouble keeping up the pace due to a large insect hovering around his face.

The president orders the speed up to "Four-seven." Charlie is saved by a passing relief man (indicated on the loudspeaker as the man passes by). Charlie goes to the bathroom and lights up a smoke, but the president suddenly appears on a large TV monitor and says, "Hey! Quit stalling! Get back to work. Go on."

The significance of these utterances sinks in cumulatively, as the viewer realizes that they are all happening through mechanical transmission devices. People rarely speak to each other face to face, when they do their dialogue is translated into subtitles. In addition, sound effects are used so sparingly that the audience has no sense of being in a sound film reality, which allows Chaplin, as always, to undercrank until the last scene of the film.

Another mechanical speech device is introduced as an inventor and his assistants meet with the president. In one of the film's several uneasy moments, they all stand around in silence (no music on the soundtrack) as the inventor cranks up a phonograph which plays the sales pitch on a record as the assistants and inventor rather stiffly present the product:

> *Good morning my friend. This record comes to you through the Sales Talk Transcription Company, Inc. Your speaker, The Mechanical Salesman. May I take the pleasure of introducing Mr. J. Whitticomb Billows, the inventory of the Billows Feeding Machine, a practical device which automatically*

feeds your men while at work. Don't stop for lunch. Be ahead of your competitor. The Billows Feeding Machine will eliminate the lunch hour, increase your production, and decrease your overhead. Allow us to point out some of the features of this wonderful machine. Its beautiful aerodynamic streamlined body. Its smoothness of action made silent by our electro-turret metal ball bearings. Let us acquaint you with our automaton soup plate—its compressed air blower—no breath necessary—no energy required to cool the soup. Notice the revolving plate with the automatic food pusher. Observe our counter shaft double knee action corn-feeder with its synchromesh transmission, which enables you to shift from high to low gear by the mere tip of the tongue. Then there is the hydro-compressed steroid mouth wiper; its factors of control ensure against spots on the shirt front.

These are but a few of the delightful features of the Billows Feeding Machine. Let us demonstrate with one of your workers, for actions speak louder than words.

Remember, if you wish to keep ahead of your competitor, you cannot afford to ignore the importance of the Billows Feeding Machine.

Charlie going through the machine in *Modern Times* makes an image strikingly similar to film going through a projector. This reinforces *Modern Times'* reflexive theme of Chaplin's confrontation with sound movies.

The humor of the sequence depends largely on the presentation of the machine itself, and the viewer's anticipation of the inevitable failure of the device to mechanize the eating process. Note Chaplin's tendency to repeat the key points—he stresses three times that the machine eliminates the lunch hour, for example. In addition, individual phrases are often wordy.

The film's first dialogue subtitle occurs during the test of the machine on Charlie. After the soup is splashed into his face and the corn-feeder goes out of control, the inventor decides that "We'll start with the soup again." After the debacle, the president declares (in another subtitle) that "It's no good—it isn't practical."

The dialogue titles, which henceforth in the film are mixed in freely with the voices coming over mechanical devices, further help to isolate and define the role of speech in the world of *Modern Times.* It is mechanical and artificial—suitable for the orders of bosses to employees, or for glib sales pitches. In this brilliant act of transposition Chaplin has managed to equate his own esthetic problem with and feeling about sound with the problem of the factory worker who is victimized by the powerful forces of technology which dehumanize him, controlling not only his actions on the factory line, but trying to extend that control to every aspect of his nonmechanical (human) self—his need for relief

and breaks (the bathroom) and for food. Chaplin's problem as an artist has been neatly translated into Charlie's problem as a character, in an industrial variant of his usual role; that of the natural man being put upon by the restrictions, roles, and expectations of others.

The feeding-machine sequence introduces a whole series of eating and being-eaten experiences in *Modern Times,* again a culmination of a prominent Chaplin theme (recall the meals and play with food in *The Gold Rush,* and the chicken sequence when Charlie almost becomes a meal for his starving companion). After "time marches on into the late afternoon" (the newsreel sound again) the president orders Max to "give 'er the limit." Charlie cannot keep up the pace and follows one of his plates into the bowels of the machine ("eaten" by the machine). When the belt is reversed the machine "vomits" him out. But this intimacy with the machine is too much for Charlie. He has a "nervous breakdown" (as explained in a later subtitle) in the form of a destructive dance through the factory, managing by the end not only to destroy the factory's routine and possibly some generators, but on a more human scale, to repay the president by squirting machine oil in his face.

Released from a mental hospital, Charlie is told to "Take it easy and avoid excitement." He is quickly mistaken for a Communist leader, however, and jailed.

In previous Chaplin films, jail was a place from which Charlie had just emerged or escaped. Sometimes he is seen inside via brief flashbacks; certainly

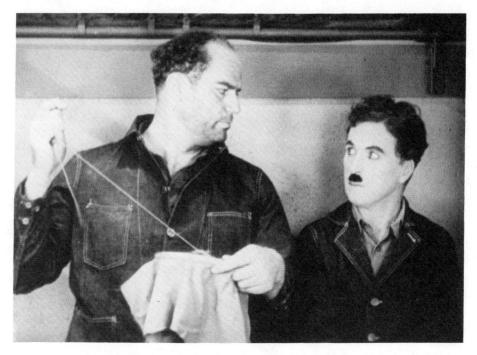

Charlie doesn't quite know how to take his cellmate.

Reacting to the "nose powder" on his moustache.

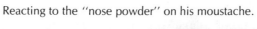

the specter of it hovered over most of his films. But this second major section of *Modern Times* plunges directly into prison life. As he had faced the realistic complexities of the tramp's romantic life in *City Lights,* so in *Modern Times* Chaplin looks unflinchingly at prison life, and manages subtly to insert references to its seamier aspects.

Ushered into his cell Charlie is confronted by his brutelike cellmate, who is busily engaged doing needlepoint. How, after all, does one pass the time in jail? The implication of effeminacy is also there, though not in the brute's manner. In a neatly worked out sequence Charlie manages to infuriate the man by inadvertently preventing him from threading his needle. The lunch call occurs as the brute is throttling Charlie. Hearing the call, he drops Charlie reflexively.

In the lunchroom a rat-faced convict, hilariously identified with a loud chord of music and a rapid iris "down" into his face, is suspected by the authorities of smuggling drugs; before they apprehend him he pours his "nose powder" (cocaine) into the saltshaker. Naturally Charlie uses it liberally on his food. When he wipes his nose with his finger he deposits a large amount onto his moustache and does several very funny wide-eyed comic takes as he inhales.

As the group files out of the lunchroom, Chaplin inserts another sly detail. In front of Charlie and his cellmate in the line is the prison homosexual, unmistakably identified by his "swishy" movements including hands bent upward at the wrist. Because the viewer is riveted upon Charlie during the exit scene (Charlie is revolving in his stoned state) this character goes unnoticed. Such an inclusion certainly would not have passed through the censors in 1936 if they had noticed it, and is a tribute to Chaplin's confidence in his control of audience perceptions, as well as his awareness of the situations that persist to this day in prisons. This aspect of *Modern Times* is many years ahead of its time. In *City Lights* Chaplin introduced a similar "throwaway." As boxer Mann walks through the crowd toward the ring, he pokes a heckler. After the fight he returns by the same route and sees the heckler, who ducks out of sight.

After Charlie, in his hopped-up state, thwarts a jailbreak attempt, he is granted a pardon. Chaplin brings in yet another medium of indirect verbal communication. On a radio in the sheriff's office the audience hears: "Local News. A pardon was granted the prisoner who so recently thwarted the attempted city jailbreak."

The prison homosexual.

Removed from his now-comfortable private cell, Charlie is brought to the sheriff's office and left alone with the minister's wife while the sheriff escorts the minister on his weekly rounds.

As they sit sipping tea together Chaplin introduces the first body sounds in his cinema: The tea gives both of them indigestion (the food theme again), which makes their stomachs gurgle (Chaplin made these sounds by blowing into a bucket of water). To distract attention from these embarrassing sounds, Charlie reaches back to turn on the radio, which blares, "If you are suffering from gastritis, don't forget to try . . . "; Charlie snaps it off.

The routine concludes with a Chaplin transformation gag—this time in sound. Taking out a pill for her indigestion, the minister's wife sprays seltzer into a glass. Charlie reacts to this sound with a startled leap, and looks very relieved and abashed when he sees it was just seltzer. Audiences often miss the full implication of this latest of Chaplin's "obscene" gags. (There were two sound transformation gags in *City Lights.* In the first Charlie mistakes the sound of a piano for a gunshot; in the second his swallowed whistle is mistaken as a summons for dogs and a cabbie.)

But despite its humor and the climactic seltzer gag, the sequence, occurring without background music in another strange silence, drags.

Released from jail Charlie gets a job in a shipyard, and Chaplin confronts another aspect of *Modern Times* in the form of the economical use of rear-screen projection when Charlie accidentally causes a ship under construction to slide into the water. While shooting this sequence in miniature was undoubtedly a necessary economy, the resulting effect—especially by contrast with the realistic treatment of similar scenes in Keaton and Lloyd—impairs the sequence.

It does, however, serve to motivate Charlie to return to his comfortable "home" in jail, prompting him to take the blame for the theft of a loaf of bread by a gamine (Paulette Goddard). She, however, is also apprehended, and the two meet in a moving police van. Rear projection is again used, here much more ingeniously, to show their escape. The viewer's viewpoint is from the inside of the van, the passengers seated along the sides and a cop in the doorway; the road recedes in the distance through the door via rear projection. Suddenly the gamine leaps up and struggles with the cop, and Charlie follows her. All three fall out of sight to the right of the doorway as the van tilts to the side, and appear on the road in the rear-projection shot about a block away, in an exquisitely timed coordination of the movement of the people and the van with the rear image. It all happens so smoothly and quickly that the artifice is undetectable.

The gamine and Charlie steal away, pausing to rest on a curb in a suburban neighborhood. The strain between the silent and sound cinema again surfaces as a housewife bids her husband good-bye and prances back in a ridiculous parody of domestic bliss, made even more ridiculous by being considerably undercranked. Then Charlie makes an even more exaggerated parody of her movements, tearing and throwing pieces of grass in an orgy of simpering glee. But this parody of a parody works only because of Chaplin's skill and charm, and because the scene is in reality only a setup for Charlie's delightful fantasy of himself and Paulette as suburbanites.

This makes Charlie determined to find a home for them. "I'll do it! We'll get a home even if I have to work for it!" But unfortunately for Charlie, his next job, as a department store night watchman, also ends disastrously. And unfortunately for Chaplin, the scene, despite its many pleasures (notably roller-skating), begins to drag when burglars, who are actually Charlie's former associates at the factory, raid the store for food and drink. The next morning Charlie is discovered asleep on a fabric counter and promptly jailed.

Upon his release Paulette greets him with the news that she has found a home. Ecstatic at the door of the decrepit shack, he says, "It's paradise" and shuts the door only to have a piece of wood conk him on the head (accompanied by a sound of wood on wood). Leaning against a wall, he plunges into a

In the next moment Charlie, the gamine, and the cop dive out the door as . . .

. . . the van tips and their images appear on the rear projection.

pond when the wall collapses. After spending the night in a small room next to the shack, Charlie emerges the next morning in a bathing suit, prepared for a dip, but the water is so shallow that when he dives in, he does a somersault as he hits bottom. After dressing, he knocks on Paulette's door (no problem with the censors about their sleeping arrangements), opens the door, and, looking up, closes it—whereupon the piece of wood hits him again.

It should be evident from the above that *Modern Times* contains many not-so-modern gags. A contemporary reviewer stated flatly that "all the old gags are brought out and dusted off for use. But they are such good old standbys that they still earn laughs."[5] Although critical reception of *Modern Times* was more mixed than for any previous Chaplin feature, Chaplin fared far better in this respect than Lloyd, whose *Professor Beware* two years later was labeled by *Time* magazine "an overstocked museum of silent comedy techniques." Chaplin himself defended his use of dated material in a later conversation with his son, Charles, Jr.:

> You can use the unexpected to some extent to get a laugh . . . but the gag that is sure to go over is the one where the audience has been tipped off in advance. That's why I like to use old gags. Like the diving scene—it's been done so many times everyone is already familiar with what is going to happen. All you have to worry about is your interpretation.[6]

But *Modern Times* does run into trouble. It is not just because of the old and familiar gags—after all, they are still funny in their original form in earlier Chaplin films. The main problem is that *Modern Times* has three major sequences in a row which are simply not paced and well-developed enough to keep the film's momentum going. They are the department store scene already discussed, the return to the factory, and the waiter scene.

Eating breakfast in the shack Charlie sees in the morning paper that the factory is reopening. He gets a job as assistant to a mechanic (Chester Conklin). Again, there are delightful passages, notably another eating sequence in which Chester falls into the machine and gets stuck, only his head emerging, upside down. As machine devoured man, now man feeds man, as Charlie feeds Chester his lunch. But the earlier part of the routine, in which Charlie accidentally flattens an oilcan and Chester's heirloom watch in a large press and struggles with the large

toolbox, are not up to Chaplin's usual standard. The ending of the sequence, however, is poignant. A strike is called and the old mechanic and Charlie both turn toward the camera and scratch their heads.

A second problem with the sequence is that Chester is the first highly caricatured character in the film, complete with his 1914 walrus moustache trademark. Perhaps it wouldn't matter if the whole sequence worked better.

Leaving the factory Charlie accidentally steps on a plank which catapults a brick onto the head of a cop. While this is smoothly executed, a third trip to and release from prison begins to wear down the viewer.

Perhaps the slowest of the major scenes is Charlie's waiter job. While the gags—including drilling holes into a wedge of cheese to make it swiss, trying to serve a duck to a frustrated customer, confusion (as in *The Rink*) with the "in" and "out" doors to the kitchen—are enjoyable, they are not enough to pull the film from its slump (the impalement of the duck on a chandelier was discussed in Chapter 7). One subtle touch, however, is the presence of a carpenter sawing wood in the kitchen, presumably to be added to the bread. However, the sequence ends with its strongest gag, when the elusive duck becomes a football for college revelers, and Charlie must "intercept" it to deliver it, in a flying leap, into the hands (literally) of an outraged diner.

Despite the weaknesses in these last major sections of *Modern Times,* what saves the day for the film is the thrust of the plot. For what emerges through the comedy is that Charlie is really struggling, as he had in *City Lights,* to earn money. His failed efforts in the department store, the shipyard, and the factory lead him to the cafe. And the film's various threads come neatly together when Charlie reluctantly agrees to sing. Even without a knowledge of Chaplin's previous career, an audience greets this knowledge with knowing laughter and anticipation, having sat through most of a feature-length film in which Chaplin has "spoken," as usual, in eloquent, silent pantomime. How will he confront the nemesis of sound face-to-face? As he had in *City Lights,* Chaplin focuses the film to a point, in this case the artist's (and his creation's) confrontation with the reality of sound film. And as he had in *City Lights,* Chaplin rises to the occasion brilliantly and surprisingly.

"I hope you can sing!" the cafe boss says after Charlie's clear demonstration that he couldn't wait on tables without chaos resulting. Charlie goes into a room off the stage area to rehearse his song with Paulette. Meanwhile, a chorus of singing waiters files onto the darkened stage, and the audience hears the first directly spoken words in the film:

> *We are honest singing waiters,*
> *we will sing or serve potatoes,*
> *we will try to do our best and*
> *you can leave a modest tip,*
> *and we'll sing the whole night long.*

As the scene shifts back to Charlie and Paulette, the waiters can be heard singing, "In the evening by the moonlight, you can hear those darkies singing." It is unclear whether Chaplin intended this to be yet another negative message about sound (white waiters singing an exploitive song) or whether he thought of it as merely an innocuous folk song. At any rate, the crowd does not receive them well, and is soon booing and demanding the next act.

Charlie, meanwhile, has been having trouble memorizing the lines of his song, so Paulette helpfully writes them on his shirt cuffs. This device allows Chaplin to prepare the viewer by introducing the characters and actions:

> *a pretty girl and a gay old man*
> *flirted on the boulevard*
> *he was a fat old thing*
> *but his diamond ring*
> *caught her eye*

Following his introductory fanfare, Charlie marches out and immediately flings his arms out in one of his dancing movements, and his cuffs go flying. He does a neat backward step, dragging his forward foot, with his hand pulling on the seat of his pants as if that is what is propelling him. Realizing he has lost his cuffs, he goes back into the backward step, looking for them. Seeing his predicament, Paulette says (in subtitle), "Sing!! Never mind the words."

And that is exactly what Charlie does. The crowd is clamoring again. Charlie motions for them to quiet down, and both the tempo of the song ("Titina," a popular song of the early thirties) and the speed of the film slow down as Charlie begins to sing in gibberish as he simultaneously mimes.

Several reviewers and biographers have attempted to phonetically reproduce Chaplin's gibberish and each of their versions, with the excep-

tions of a few key words, is different. A mishmash of romance languages, particularly Spanish and Italian, the sounds are so liquid and sing-song that they defy transcription.*

Pulling himself by the seat of his pants to find the lost cuffs.

English sheet music for "Titina," a French song about a Spanish beauty which Chaplin used for his gibberish song. 1925.

*During the silent era he and Doug Fairbanks were fond of stopping their car to ask pedestrians directions in high falsetto voices and noting their fans' disappointment that their screen idols spoke this way.

The meaning of the gibberish song is made clear by the gestures that accompany it, and close examination reveals that Chaplin has again managed to insert bold material into the film.

The first verse defines the "pretty girl" with elaborate curved movements of Chaplin's eloquent hands, first around the face and then indicating her figure, ending with one hand provocatively on her hip and the other holding a cigarette or cigarette holder. "Se bella" is the one recognizable phrase.

Revolving, as he does at the end of each verse, Charlie becomes the "fat old thing," physically indicating his moustache, cigar, and ample girth ("cigar-etto potto-bello"). The cane is clearly indicated by putting it against the floor, wiggling it from side to side as if gaining purchase, and twirling ("racko spaghaletto").

Turning around for the third verse, the fat man spies the girl, who passes him. He elaborately tips his hat, spits on and polishes his diamond ring and, holding his thumb against his cheek, he looks down at the ring and flutters his fingers to display it, at the same time gesturing with his head for her to approach him. Looking very predatory, he does a comical walk in profile toward the girl, pulls down his waistcoat, twirls his moustache, and again tips his hat. He sings to her and this time the lyrics are more explicit. "Senora," he begins, indicating she is perhaps married, "se la tima" (do you have the time), "voulez-vous la taxi meter" at which point he opens the door to a taxi, admits her and gets in himself, closing the door. "Le jonta su la seata" accompanies her taking her seat and, as he instructs the driver with circles of his hand, "to le tour le tour le wah."

The fourth verse is introduced by Charlie driving, occasionally reaching to honk a horn (which is heard on the soundtrack). Then he moves into the character of the girl, who sits demurely, and then the man (indicated by twirling his moustache), who sits eyeing her sideways and twiddling his thumbs, biding his time. He raises his finger to his lips and kisses the ring, then reaches to pat her knee. Chaplin switches to the indignant girl, who slaps the fat man's hand (the slap sound is heard).

Walking around as the girl for the fifth verse, she points to her right forefinger, then herself. She is asking for the ring (the word "meena" can be distinguished, although Chaplin might not have wanted to make this too explicit an exchange); the final two lines of the verse indicate the man, after a pause, regretfully taking the ring off his finger and giving it to her, after which they embrace for the

"A pretty girl."

The "gay old man" displays his ring.

Embracing.

The girl bids a demure goodbye.

turnaround. With his legs crossed Chaplin rolls back and forth on the outsides of his feet. Reaching behind him, he pulls down a shade, indicating that they are in a room together.

The embrace becomes stylized into a calm position of one forearm lying on top of the other as Chaplin turns to face the camera again. Moving into the posture of the girl for the final verse, she thanks the man, twirls his moustache, pulls him toward her with it and gives him a big kiss, then waves goodbye and goes on her way.

An audience watching this sequence becomes so entranced with the beauty of Chaplin's movements and the humor of some of the attitudes expressed, that it loses sight of the forest for the trees. For the innocent flirtation is in fact a story of prostitution.

The only real precedent for this routine in Chaplin's work is the David-and-Goliath sermon from *The Pilgrim,* in which Charlie as a minister assumes the roles of both David and Goliath. The waiter song-mime, even more stylized, is unique in Chaplin's work. Although the viewer cannot follow the implications of the story, the sheer brilliance of the movements holds him mesmerized. The routine also virtually defines a type of mime performance in which the performer switches from role to role and uses illusionary props, the format popularized by Marcel Marceau nearly twenty years after *Modern Times.*

Aside from making the obvious point that "actions speak louder than words," the routine also gives the tramp the role of self-conscious entertainer. Only in *The Circus,* where for most of the film he is unaware of his role as circus clown, does Chaplin deal with this convoluted theme. He later returned to it, more successfully than in *The Circus,* in *Limelight. Modern Times* leads naturally to his playing this role in the film's final burst of energy.

But the casual viewer can also overlook the fact that the man doing this routine no longer moves with the movements and gestures of the tramp character. Particularly when its meaning is clear, the routine seems too worldly and jaded for the simple romantic vagabond of the streets. The audience is, in fact, treated to the spectacle of Charles Chaplin, mime, the tramp unmasked.

There seem to be three kinds of endings to Chaplin's films: conventional endings which somehow avoid the emotional issues raised in the films, such as the weak endings of *The Kid* and *The Vagabond,* which seem both rushed and forced; endings which confront squarely the issues and find resolutions, albeit temporary ones, such as the run down the border in *The Pilgrim,* the earned happiness of *A Dog's Life, The Immigrant,* and *The Gold Rush,* or its converse, the poetic sadness of *The Tramp, The Circus,* and *City Lights;* and finally, endings in which a different character seems to emerge at the end, as in the waiter-mime of *Modern Times.* This really seems like the same character whose look of experience closes the silent version of *The Gold Rush,** and who will make heartfelt speeches at the ends of both *The Great Dictator* and *Monsieur Verdoux.* Oddly, Chaplin is never criticized for stepping out of character in either *The Gold Rush* or *Modern Times,* perhaps because he did so under the protective umbrella of his mime.

After the brilliant display of mime in the waiter scene, the viewer is once more totally involved with the film. So that when Charlie and the gamine must take to the road again in the film's final scene, the audience rejoices that this time he has a companion, and his road will not be a lonely one, even though the times are hard. For the viewer who knows that this walk down the road is the last the silent tramp would take, the fade-out evokes the sweet sadness of bidding a dear friend good-bye for good.

Notes

[1]Cooke, Alistair, *Six Men, op. cit.,* p. 41.

[2]Cooke, Alistair, *Six Men, op. cit.,* p. 41.

[3]Churchill, Winston, "Everybody's Language," *Collier's* 96 (October 26, 1935). Reprinted in McCaffrey, Donald, ed., *Focus on Chaplin, op. cit.,* pp. 76–78.

[4]Chaplin, cited in Eastman, Max, *Great Companions, op. cit.,* p. 225.

[5]Cited in McDonald, Conway and Ricci, *The Films of Charlie Chaplin, op cit.,* p. 203.

[6]Chaplin, cited in Chaplin, Charles Jr., *My Father, Charlie Chaplin* (New York: Random House, Inc., 1960), p. 113.

*The 1925 ending of *The Gold Rush* is one of Chaplin's most satisfying resolutions to a film, far more complex than the fairy-tale ending of *A Dog's Life.* Newly rich Charlie is first seen in elegant clothing, although he still acts like the tramp. Asked to put on his "prospecting clothes" for a press photo, he indicates a bit more self-satisfaction than usual in his gestures. And finally, after Georgia discovers his "new" identity, he takes the situation completely in command, introducing her as his fiancé, confidently embracing her as the picture ends. Here one sees the dichotomy of rich Charlie in tramp clothes (here without comic flaws) and poor Charlie (in rich man's clothing) neatly merged in the sequence.

11

Through the Sound Barrier:
The Great Dictator

With *The Great Dictator* Chaplin's career entered into a "problem" period, at least as far as critics are concerned. While critical response to *Modern Times* was not as enthusiastic as for previous Chaplin films, *The Great Dictator* was seen by even sympathetic critics as a film with serious flaws, particularly in its six-minute final speech. It was extremely popular with the public, however, and grossed more than any other Chaplin film up to that time.

Today *The Great Dictator* continues to arouse controversy. It remains, along with *Modern Times*, the most often-shown Chaplin film on the museum and university circuit. Yet critical reaction continues to be divided. Some reject the film (and those that follow) as misguided "message" films which do not work as comedy, drama, or propaganda, and others eulogize it as a masterpiece of social satire and a worthy successor to the vein of social criticism in parts of *Modern Times*.

As with all his feature films, Chaplin agonized for years over the conception of *The Great Dictator*. Max Eastman recalls coming upon a distraught Chaplin in a hotel room in New York. Chaplin had just been offered $877,000 to do twenty-five fifteen-minute radio broadcasts.

"I can't do it, you know," he said. And then, with increased mournfulness: "I need the money too! The government just relieved me of a million dollars."

"Why can't you do it?" I said. "You can make a speech!"

"It isn't that," he said. "You know how I love speechmaking. I can't come that close to my public. I have to remain a little remote and mysterious. They have to romanticize me. I would lose more than that at the box office if I made myself real and familiar over the radio."[1]

To keep this distance, Chaplin created the unique treatment of sound in *City Lights* and *Modern Times*. In *The Great Dictator,* which he came to think of as his first "real" sound film, he was able to find another compromise. This compromise allowed him to retain at least the physical tramp image, by capitalizing on Hitler's resemblance to the beloved figure, while at the same time expanding his explorations into sound and dialogue on his own terms.

As Hitler I could harangue the crowds in jargon and talk all I wanted to. And as the tramp I could remain more or less silent. A Hitler story was an opportunity for burlesque and pantomime.[2]

This was a bold decision on many levels. Like *Shoulder Arms* it was an attempt to find humor in the madness of war, before the passage of time provided a "safe" vantage point. But unlike *Shoulder Arms*, which was released just three weeks before the armistice, *The Great Dictator* was begun and released well before America had even entered the war, at a time when popular sentiment was isolationistic.

The earlier film, which both Chaplin and his distributor released with some trepidation, proved to be Chaplin's greatest success up to that time, setting a standard by which Chaplin's films were judged for years to come. Once he had hit upon the idea for *The Great Dictator,* it must have been an irresistible temptation to try to repeat his early triumph and to do for World War II what he had done for World War I. And whatever the criticisms, no one could complain that *this* film wasn't about modern times! Nor could anyone fault the artist's sincerity in his effort to affect those times.

As in *The Idle Class,* Chaplin played two roles, and as in that film most of the vitality of the film is in his performance of the non-tramp role. The scenes with the Jewish barber, in fact, give the film most of its problems of plot and resolution, although as with *Modern Times* Chaplin's premise was brilliant. He indirectly put his finger on the problem when he stated in his autobiography:

> Some people suggested that the tramp might talk. This was unthinkable, for the first word he ever uttered would transform him into another person. Besides, the matrix out of which he was born was as mute as the rags he wore.[3]

War comedy, 1918. Charlie as a doughboy in *Shoulder Arms.*

This is exactly what happened with the more-or-less-silent barber. Although there is some moot critical debate about whether the barber *is* the tramp or only a distant relative, the character is locked into the plot in such a way that, except for certain notable moments, he does not *behave* like the tramp. He is far more passive, and his passivity is emphasized by the fact that, for the first time, Chaplin's movements can be watched at true-life speed.

The film builds, as *Modern Times* had, to the moment when the character is forced to "speak out." But in *Modern Times* the tension of waiting to hear the tramp's song is more than matched by the song itself, Chaplin's great burst of pure mime accompanied by gibberish. *The Great Dictator* lacks both the strong tension leading up to the final scene, and the fully satisfying resolution. Max Eastman pointed out that merely by inserting scenes of the barber making unsuccessful attempts at speechmaking until by the end his intense feeling overflows into eloquence for the final speech, the ending would "connect." But this overlooks the fact that character development and change simply do not play a major part in any Chaplin film until *Limelight.*

Another commonly cited flaw is the film's length (over two hours). It probably could be effectively edited down by at least one-half hour.

Leaving aside what Chaplin did *not* do, the film's accomplishments—its verbal humor as well as its clever ways of subordinating the spoken word to action and images in many scenes—should be examined here.

The Great Dictator opens with two subtitles which introduce the light, even silly vein of parodistic, punning humor which threads through the film. They are:

> *Note: Any resemblance between Hynkel the dictator and the Jewish barber is purely coincidental.*

> *This is a story of the period between two world wars—an interim in which Insanity cut loose, Liberty took a nose dive, and Humanity was kicked around Somewhat.*

As he had punctured the pomposity of German officers in *Shoulder Arms* by picturing them as posturing dwarfs or lecherous swine, so in *The Great Dictator* he reduces them with ridiculous puns on their names. Thus, Adolf Hitler becomes Adenoid Hynkel, Goebbels becomes Garbitsch, and Göring becomes Herring. Benito Mussolini went, in successive scripts, from Mussemup, to Gasolino, to Benzino Napoloni. Germany and Italy are transformed into Tomania and Bacteria, and the swastika becomes the Double Cross.

The vein of light humor continues to the opening scene, a prologue accompanied by a newsreel narrator which introduces the barber as a Tomanian soldier in World War I. In a routine that might have occurred in *Shoulder Arms,* he accidentally lets a hand grenade slide down his sleeve, managing to get it out of his clothing and throw it just before it explodes. Later, lost in gunfire smoke, he calls out "Capitaine! Woo, Woo!" only to discover himself among American soldiers. Politely he exclaims, "Oh, excuse me!" and runs away.

When Schultz, a wounded aviator, asks the barber if he can fly, he replies brightly, "I can *try.*" After the plane flips upside down and Charlie is hanging onto the control stick, he replies to Schultz's demand that he let go of the stick with a terse "Impossible."

Later in the film the barber's utterances continue this kind of gentle, genteel humor. When Schultz, now a storm trooper under Hynkel's regime, en-

Above and next page: Chaplin improvises a series of "ranting dictator" poses for a photo session. Nothing like these appear in the film.

counters the barber in the Jewish ghetto, he says, "Strange, and I always thought of you as an Aryan," the barber replies, "I'm a vegetarian."

The prologue serves to establish the barber's character and his fate—he lives in a hospital, a victim of amnesia from the plane crash—until the emergence of Hynkel into political power.

The audience first meets Hynkel when he is giving a speech to the assembled multitudes, his gibberish and double-talk the direct descendant of the song from *Modern Times* and the gibbering of the city officials at the opening of *City Lights*. "Wiener schnitzel, lager beer und sauerkraut," he shouts,

Chaplin's sunken-chested pose indicates the weak character of the tyrant.

going into a coughing fit after a purse-lipped stream of gutteral sounds. Drinking some water he raises the glass to his ear, taking a *Modern Times* gag one step further by spitting water from his mouth at the same time as he pours some into his ear. Still not cooled down, he pours some down his pants. Now the tramp's idiosyncratic gestures are focused to characterize the political maniac.

A newsreel translator dignifies Hynkel's rantings with his "translation": "Democratia shtunk!" ("Democracy smells"), "Libertad shtunk!" ("Liberty is odious"), "Free Sprachen shtunk!" ("Free speech is objectionable"). Notice that this is a sound version of Chaplin's silent problems with hearing the officials in *The Kid*. Woody Allen uses a similar concept in *Annie Hall* when the characters' thoughts are translated via foreign-film type subtitles as their banal conversation fills the soundtrack.

In the prologue there were sound gags such as the big gun belching out its shell. Now, when Hynkel pauses, the crowd cheers, and when he flips his hand up in a limp parody of the Nazi salute, the sound stops instantly.

Returning to his speech Hynkel refers to his loyal henchmen, the fat Herring and the sinister Garbitsch, and in one of the cleverest wordplays states tearfully that "Herring shouldn't schmelten fine from Garbitsch und Garbitsch shouldn't schmelten fine from Herring."

After rhapsodies to the beauty of "der Aryan maiden" in gestures describing the form of the woman as he had in *Modern Times*, his tirade becomes so violent that the microphones recoil, and the translator explains that "Der Phooey has just referred to the Jewish people." Concluding with a plea for austerity, "tighten der belten," the scene becomes broadly physical as Herring, bowing to a lady, butts Hynkel down the platform steps.

Going to his car Hynkel poses for a picture holding a baby, smiling in a tight grimace. This time there is no transformation gag as he wipes off his hand after returning the child.

Driving along, they pass statues of "The Venus of Today" and "The Thinker of Tomorrow," both with arms upraised in the Hynkel salute. When Garbitsch tells Hynkel his tirade against the Jews was too mild, he responds in an incredulous "Whaat?" This introduces a problematical element into the film as Chaplin must balance his moments of spluttering double-talk with normal dialogue which presents him as not only arrogant and stupid, but also as something of a dupe to Garbitsch, a theme which is inadequately developed in the film.

The scene now shifts to the ironically picturesque Jewish ghetto (which has a wooden sign introducing it as such). The first serious problem in the film's tone occurs as the storm troopers, an uneasy mix of Keystone Kop and Nazi, with Bronx accents to boot, brutalize the residents. When they throw tomatoes at Hannah (Paulette Goddard), she mutters "Pigs."

Meanwhile the barber has regained his memory, but thinks only a few weeks have passed. He escapes from the hospital and returns to his shop in the ghetto, to find it full of cats and cobwebs. Chaplin's portrayal of the barber's bewilderment is one of several fine dramatic moments in the film.

Emerging from the shop, he finds that the troopers have painted the word "Jew" on his shop window, and begins washing it off. An encounter with the men results in skillfully worked out business with paintbrushes and buckets. Hannah gets into the fray, conking the troopers with a frying pan. When she accidentally conks the barber he does an inspired little dance backward and forward along the sidewalk, not stopping his momentum as he steps on and off the curb. This and many other action scenes are undercranked.

In *The Bank*, a quarter-century earlier, Chaplin had used a subterfuge to get a man to lick a stamp for him. Back at the palace Hynkel merely extends his envelope toward a flunkey for the licking. In a parody of the tight schedule of public figures, Hynkel strides into a studio room to pose for an artist and sculptor. "Enough," he commands after about three seconds, a gag which is repeated several times during the film. He examines unsuccessful military inventions (a bulletproof material and a hat-parachute), intently plays a few notes at the piano, and makes snorting advances toward his secretary, dropping her when the phone rings.

When Garbitsch enters, the tone changes. Concentration camp prisoners, he claims, are complaining of the quality of the sawdust in the bread. "It's from the finest lumber our mills can supply," exclaims Hynkel. As the conversation continues, Hynkel opens a three-way mirror, beetling his brows and looking stern as he addresses his images, saying "We must do something more dramatic, like invading Austerlich." This illustrates Chaplin's method of finding physical business to underscore his statements in the film, which occasionally, like the sawdust comment above, are awkwardly worded.

In his restored barbershop the barber strops a comb on the razor strop, opens the cash drawer but deposits the money in his breast pocket. These absent-minded gags continue in a pleasant scene as Hannah sits in the chair and he prepares her for a shave, lathering up her face as she jabbers in rapid-fire patter which doesn't allow him to get a word in edgewise. She is hopeful that the persecution is letting up, since the troopers, owing to Hynkel's desire to appease the Jewish banker Epstein, have been instructed to ease up.

At the palace, Hynkel dictates a long letter which his secretary transcribes with a few pecks at the typewriter. When he says "der punkt" (period) she unleases a machine-gun volley of rapid typing. When he is unable to find a working pen with which to sign the letter, Hynkel petulantly decides not to mail it, and rips it up.

Garbitsch fills Hynkel with dreams of world conquest and Hynkel scampers up a drapery. "Leave me, I want to be alone," he says in one of Chaplin's rare references to any film other than his own. The ensuing balloon dance fulfills Chaplin's vision of the character as a combination of Napoleon and Nijinsky.

Back in the barbershop, the barber shaves a customer in time to music from the radio, Brahms' Hungarian Dance #5. This lovely sequence contrasts with the dictator's dance of world domination in several respects: in its lively, functional and pedestrian movements; in the fact that the music comes over the radio instead of from nowhere; and in the nature of the music, Brahms' folklike music vs. Wagner's ponderous, mystical, syrupy prelude to *Lohengrin*. There could be no greater contrast between the maniacal dictator and the simple people he victimizes. These back-to-back scenes provide the core of the film.

But Epstein refuses to deal with a man he characterizes as "a medieval maniac." In another clever verbal bit, Hynkel spits out, "He'll deal with a medieval maniac more than he *thinks*." Because Schultz objects to the renewed persecution of the Jews, Hynkel exiles him to a concentration camp. Hynkel's shoulders droop as he says, "Schultz, why have you forsaken me." Underscoring the pomposity and posturing, an aide drops a cape onto the dictator's shoulders, startling him out of his studied attitude.

The barber and Hannah are about to buy Hynkel buttons when the dictator's voice over loudspeakers reverses the policy of goodwill. After preliminary altercations with the troopers, they escape to a rooftop and sit watching his barbershop burn. Hannah speaks optimistically about starting over in Austerlich as the barber sits immobile, watching his

Face-off. Garbitsch (Henry Daniell) tries to calm down Hynkel (Chaplin) and Napoloni (Jack Oakie).

shop go up in smoke. It is a beautifully understated and moving moment. As he had when he entered the dance hall in *The Gold Rush,* Chaplin plays the scene with his back to the camera. The audience is left to imagine his facial expression.

Schultz escapes to the ghetto, a revolutionary now, and tries to convince the men to join him in an assassination attempt. They try to select the assassin by eating small cakes, one of which has a coin hidden in it, but Hannah sabotages the attempt by putting coins in all the cakes. The men prove to be all too human as each in turn slips his coin onto the barber's plate, and he swallows them in turn. But the next morning he and Schultz are captured and sent to a concentration camp, while Hannah escapes into Austerlich.

If Chaplin had brought the film to its resolution now, it would have been much shorter, but he would have eliminated the Napoloni subplot which provides some of the funniest scenes in the film. An additional change is that Jack Oakie, in the role of Napoloni, is the first comic actor in a Chaplin film to get a significant amount of laughter from his own performance, a sharing Chaplin would continue with Martha Raye in *Monsieur Verdoux* and Buster Keaton in *Limelight.*

"Napoloni! That grosse peanut, that cheesie ravioli!" screams Hynkel in a rage when he learns that the Bacterian dictator plans to invade Austerlich before Tomania does. He invites Napoloni to confer with him, intending to intimidate his rival with a show of Tomanian might and his own domineering personality.

Napoloni's train and the Tomanian red carpet seem to keep missing each other, but he finally disembarks and approaches Hynkel. Hynkel gives his salute as Napoloni extends his hand, then they reverse, going back and forth several times until

Napoloni, now and later the master of the situation, grabs Hynkel's hand. This gag was used in Buster Keaton's last silent film, *Spite Marriage,* throughout which Buster encounters a man and tips his hat as the other extends his hand, and so on.

Prompted by Garbitsch, Hynkel plans to physically intimidate Napoloni by making him walk a long way to Hynkel's desk and sit in a low chair with a bust of Hynkel staring down at him. Prepared, Hynkel sits posturing with a flower. But the exuberant Napoloni enters from the back door, slaps Hynkel cheerfully off the chair, chooses the desk instead of the chair to sit on, and casually strikes a match on the bust. Sitting in barber chairs for a shave together, both elevate their chairs until, near the ceiling, they crash down.

A military parade is efficiently depicted in the same "stagey" manner as Chaplin had indicated doughboy Charlie shooting down a plane in *Shoulder Arms*—by focusing on the reactions on the faces of the spectators as they follow the action. Chaplin introduces several sound jokes into this sequence, including crashing planes, silence when the "light artillery" passes, and Hynkel's mistaking Napoloni's peanut-chewing motion for talking.

Verbal and physical humor combine as Garbitsch suggests that Hynkel dance with Mme. Napoloni at the ball that evening. "It will carry weight," he says. "You mean *I* will carry, weight," says Hynkel, laughing maniacally at his witticism. Chaplin skillfully exaggerates Mme. Napoloni's weight as he tries to pull her out of her chair toward him, and he

Jack Oakie as the pompous Napoloni.

falls over backwards trying to maneuver her on the dance floor. Reversing his compliments, he tells her that her dancing was "superb . . . excellent . . . very good . . . good."

Hynkel and Napoloni meet in a buffet room to discuss the invasion. Mixing food with politics, Hynkel "bombs" fruit into a punchbowl and tries to tear some strands of rubbery spaghetti to demonstrate his might. Both men ladle hot mustard onto their food and continue their argument in "heated" gibberish as their mouths burn. They finally agree to sign a treaty before the meeting degenerates into a food-throwing free-for-all.

The scenes with Napoloni are the most effective in the film for highlighting the dictator's pompous yet stupid manner, as the extravagant Italian continually knocks him physically and mentally off balance. The physical contrast between the boisterous, strutting Napoloni and the posturing Hynkel provides a background for the film's cleverest verbal humor, in contrast to some of the more forced palace scenes earlier, which are complicated by the more naturalistic portrayal of Garbitsch by Henry Daniell.

The barber and the dictator now neatly switch identities, as the dictator, duck hunting to avert publicity during the invasion of Austerlich, is arrested as the Jewish barber, who has since escaped with Schultz from the concentration camp. The barber, mistaken for Hynkel by the troops, is escorted to a platform to address the assembled troops following the successful invasion of Austerlich. As in *Modern Times* he must reluctantly speak.

His eyes downcast, his manner diffident, the barber begins. "I'm sorry, but I don't want to be emperor. I don't want to rule or conquer anyone. I should like to help everyone, if possible—Jew, Gentile—black men—white." As he continues his look becomes more intense as he speaks against greed and technology that makes people cynical and hard, thinkers rather than feelers, that creates systems in which men lose their humanity. He pleads for soldiers to switch their allegiance from dictators, who are unloved and unnatural men, to the forces which would eliminate them, along with greed, hate, and intolerance, from the world; for a world in which technology is dedicated to human happiness and the elimination of national barriers results in universal brotherhood. As he ends with a message to Hannah, the camera shot of the impassioned barber, which had moved steadily closer during the six-minute oration, dissolves into an image of Hannah as the soldiers cheer this message:

Look up, Hannah! The soul of man has been given wings and at last he is beginning to fly. He is flying into the rainbow—into the light of hope. Look up, Hannah! Look up!

Rising as she hears these words broadcast on the radio, her profile outlined against the cloudy night sky, Hannah begins to smile as the film ends.

As the balloon dance became one of Chaplin's most celebrated scenes, so his final speech became his most vilified. The writing style was called poor and the ideas, muddled. Perhaps this is inevitable since the speech, addressed to soldiers, is enmeshed in the inevitable paradox of war: that soldiers are fighting for peace, regimented in the name of freedom, killing for life and liberty.

The scene was universally criticized for being a stylistic disruption of the film and out of character with the barber. The only thing about it that escaped criticism was the power of Chaplin's acting. He was offered the award for best actor of 1940 by the New York Film Critics' Circle. Chaplin refused, insulted to be considered a mere actor.

Even at this distance from the political climate of the time, *The Great Dictator* remains a movie of parts. For once, the juggling act of theme and character, comedy, drama, and farce, falls apart. The reason is not so easy to pin down, since other Chaplin films contain equally disparate elements. *City Lights* is the prime example, a film of utterly different parts bound seamlessly together.

A large part of the problem must be ascribed to Chaplin's old nemesis—sound. As in *Modern Times,* he found a number of brilliant ways to deal with it on his own terms. But despite many clever verbal gags and dialogue scenes, particularly with Jack Oakie, the dictator's opening speech and the balloon and shaving scenes stand out in stark contrast to the rest of the film. If Chaplin could have rivaled his skill at visual conception with his verbal facility apart from the gibberish scenes, *The Great Dictator* would have been the major artistic triumph he had hoped for.

Even with some of the less successful scenes, the film probably could have been structured to leave the best for last, as he had in both *City Lights* and *Modern Times.* Chaplin was well aware of the importance of strong openings and closings for his films.

For the problem is not simply that the speech is out of character—it is no more out of character than the waiter pantomime that ends *Modern Times* or the knowing look that ends *The Gold Rush.* But without his great gift, his mime, as the focus, Chaplin's verbal virtuosity as both writer and actor cannot lift the film to the level of the endings of the earlier films. The mistaken-identity plot, so painstakingly worked out, does not lead to a strong enough payoff, as it had in the delicate romantic exchange between Edna and the tramp in *The Idle Class*.

Chaplin himself remained stubbornly proud of the final speech, reprinting it in its entirety in his 1964 autobiography. A master of mime in an era of sound, he was determined to bring the elusive element under the umbrella of his filmmaking genius.

But through the decade of the 1940s that goal eluded him.

Notes

[1]Eastman, *Great Companions, op. cit.,* pp. 235–236.

[2]Chaplin, *My Autobiography, op. cit.,* p. 392. Reprinted with permission of The Bodley Head.

[3]Chaplin, *My Autobiography, op. cit.,* p. 366. Reprinted with permission of The Bodley Head.

12
Rewriting the Past: *The Gold Rush* (1942)

Charlie's dream of Georgia.

The "undaunted lone prospector."

In his biography of his father, Charles, Jr. recalls private screenings Chaplin ran for him, his brother, and their friends. Beginning as a spectator, Chaplin would soon be standing studying the reactions of his youthful audience:

> Dad, however, couldn't stay quietly watching for long. Presently he was providing a running commentary for us.
>
> "There he is now, there comes the Little Fellow," he would say, rubbing his hands together gleefully.
>
> "Yes, there he is, with the big fellow with the bandaged foot. That means trouble. Watch it, boys."
>
> Our father's eager monologue seemed quite natural to us. We never thought once, then, that we were the only children in the world to enjoy the privilege of Chaplin dialogue with silent Chaplin films.[1]

In 1942 the rest of the world got the opportunity, when Chaplin reissued *The Gold Rush* and replaced the subtitles with his own spoken narrative and musical soundtrack.

Comparison of the 1925 and 1942 versions of the film reveal that Chaplin removed more than the subtitles. He also reduced the epic, almost mythic power of the film to the level of a childlike fairy tale.

Subtitles in the 1925 version are terse, introducing the tramp simply as "a lone prospector," and Big Jim as "another lone prospector." Repetition of short phrases continues as Black Larson is introduced as "a lone man" in "a lone cabin." The names of the latter characters are shown on Big Jim's claim stake and a wanted poster Black Larson casually tosses aside.

In his narration, spoken briskly and with mock-dramatic inflection, Chaplin introduces the tramp as "an undaunted lone prospector." Later he refers to him as "our little Columbus," "our hero," and most often as "the little fellow."

Chaplin indulges his verbal humor in increasingly extravagant phrases, introducing Big Jim by saying, "Somewhere in that Nowhere, another lone prospector," and Black Larson as "an unmitigated predatory scoundrel."

When Jim and Black Larson glare at each other prior to their struggle over the rifle, the drama of the scene (which sets up the comedy of Charlie having to avoid the pointing gun during their fight) is hardly embellished by Chaplin's statement that "Big Jim looked deep into the eyes of Black Larson and saw there the soul of a skunk." Nor does this do much to enhance the sense of raw villainy and power of the Larson character.

Chaplin continues his editorial comments throughout the film, often offering more information than is needed or wanted in his thumbnail character sketches:

> Jack was a ladies' man. Georgia was quick and impulsive, proud and independent. Jack had lots of appeal for Georgia—perhaps that's why she resented him.

Or this, intruding into the delicate scene when Georgia comes upon the abashed Charlie in his borrowed cabin:

> There she stood, her loveliness lighting the room, filling his heart with romance for which he was so ill-suited. And as she introduced her friends his heart began to sing. . . . In the world of the Dance Hall it wasn't wise to reveal their hearts . . . and so she fooled and flirted and stroked his hair. He knew she was fooling but he was happy.

Such interpretations take from the viewer the privilege of coming to their own conclusions. By defining motivation, they limit the power of the performances in the film.

Another disturbing element occurs when Chaplin mouths dialogue, often lip-synching the characters' words. This creates a strange dislocation between the sound and silent film worlds, especially since, as in his previous silent film soundtracks, Chaplin is very sparing with his use of naturalistic sound effects. When the tramp "speaks" in this way he becomes more specific as a "real" character. "What are you doing here?" asks Larson when he discovers Charlie in his cabin hungrily munching a chicken leg. "Eating, obviously." (In 1925 this exchange occurred entirely in pantomime.) Leaving Georgia to find the lost cabin with Big Jim, he exclaims, "I'm going away. But when I return I shall come back!"

In the cabin-teetering scene Charlie's hangover is compounded by the movement of the cabin, indicated silently in 1925. But in 1942 Chaplin supplies his thoughts: "This is the worst liver attack I've ever had."

As both men struggle for the door in the now precariously tilted cabin, only two silent subtitles accompany the exciting action, as Big Jim looks at Charlie to caution him to "Take it easy!" and later

"Don't move . . . Don't breathe!" The exchange is amplified in 1942 into a comic speech:

> "Now," said Big Jim, "don't get excited. Take it easy. Don't move, don't breathe! I said don't breathe, stupid. You can be most annoying at times.
>
> "See what I mean," said Big Jim. "Your mind is keyed up, you have no psychology. You have no control."

At times, as in this example, the narration introduces verbal humor which runs parallel to but does not support the visual humor. Occasionally it contradicts it, distracting the viewer from the subtle pantomime, as in the scene in the borrowed cabin when the girls leave and Charlie ecstatically dances his joy, swinging on a ceiling beam, and causing a "snowstorm" by punching a feather pillow. He sits on the floor exhausted when Georgia suddenly reappears in the doorway. But when Chaplin says, "And of course at that moment Georgia would forget her gloves," the attention wanders just enough that the impact of Charlie's embarrassed little foot-twitch is lost—the gag often fails to get a laugh.

Chaplin also does some reediting for the sound version, cutting two important scenes. In the original, after Georgia disappoints Charlie by forgetting to come to his New Year's Eve dinner, she remembers only after coming to the now empty cabin with her friends to play a joke on the tramp. Jack tells her to forget it and asks for a kiss. When he insists, she slaps him.

The next night, in the dance hall, Georgia sends Jack a note:

> I'm sorry for what I did last night. Please forgive me—I love you, Georgia.

Georgia watches Jack from the balcony as he gets the note. He laughs and shrugs. She turns away.

When Charlie enters, Jack has a waiter deliver the note to him. Of course, Charlie thinks that Georgia finally returns his love.

But in 1942 Chaplin removed the scene of Jack receiving the note, so it really becomes a note from Georgia to Charlie—a rather abrupt change of character for her. In addition, Georgia's note in the 1942 version reads:

> Please forgive me for not coming to dinner. I'd like to see you and explain. Georgia

So it is likely that Chaplin considered both versions of this scene (and shot both) in 1925.

The change removes some of the cynical quality of the love story. But both versions reveal a slight plot hole. Since Charlie believes the note is from Georgia, he would undoubtedly seek here out before leaving Alaska, rather than meeting her by accident on the boat. It's probable, in fact, that Chaplin shot the scene then removed it after the film's premiere, at which time he edited approximately a reel from the film.

A second and even more critical change is Chaplin's mysteriously lopping off the final "tintype" scene in which Charlie and Georgia, posed by a photographer, slowly move together for a kiss. Instead Chaplin ends the film with the preceding—and innocuous—shot of the two of them heading for a shipboard ladder to the upper deck, saying, "And so it was. A happy ending." Perhaps Chaplin felt the note of cynicism—the photographer saying, "Oh, you've spoilt the picture!"—was not fitting for his "modern" version. But the original is one of Chaplin's magic moments.*

With all its flaws, the reissue of *The Gold Rush* makes a fascinating companion piece to the 1925 version. The music, as always, effectively underscores the action. A theme similar to "The Flight of the Bumblebee" is used for the more violent scenes, and the tramp's dance with Georgia, complete with dog attached to the rope around Charlie's waist, is effectively counterpointed by the famous theme from Tchaikovsky's *Sleeping Beauty*. It must be admitted that Chaplin's narration is well presented and often witty.

Unfortunately Chaplin's representatives failed to renew his copyright to the original version of *The Gold Rush,* so it passed out of his control (although his estate still owns the original negative). So the 1942 version is the one most commonly seen now—a diminished version of a masterpiece. If only he had scored the 1925 version. . . .

Chaplin never repeated the error of narrating a silent film. In subsequent reissues he simply provided musical soundtracks. Fortunately, he managed to score all of his films made after 1918, including *A Woman of Paris.*

---

*Film scholar Timothy Lyons suggested that this and other changes in Chaplin's reissues might have been necessitated by deterioration of the original negative.

The tintype embrace. Original ending for *The Gold Rush*.

His next reissue was *The Chaplin Revue,* in 1959. It is a compilation of *A Dog's Life, Shoulder Arms,* and *The Pilgrim,* preceded by documentary footage showing his studio being built, a mock rehearsal scene, and Chaplin applying his makeup. Chaplin's narration over the documentary footage is entirely appropriate, both witty and fascinating. He refers to the films as "comic ballets," explains that they will be accompanied by music but not intrusive sound effects such as "footsteps on the gravel path." Chaplin invites the viewer to return to the "good old days of silent films," retiring behind his "curtain of silence."

However, Chaplin ran into another problem with *The Chaplin Revue,* Presumably to make it more accessible to modern viewers, he had the film "stretch printed," a process of repeat-printing certain frames at even intervals to slow the action down to normal speed.

Unfortunately this process also gives the movement a peculiar hesitant quality, particularly marring the rhythmic scenes of *A Dog's Life.*

For the rest of his reissues Chaplin avoided both narrations and stretch printing. (An exception is *The Idle Class.*) He adds a song, sung by himself, at the opening of *The Circus,* and one at the beginning and end of *The Pilgrim* with the incredible lines:

> *Bound for Texas-land,*
> *To hear the moo and rattle*
> *Of snakes and cattle,*
> *Bound for Texas-land.*

Another change that occurs in the reissues, which will be difficult to most viewers to recognize, is that they differ from the original versions in varying degrees. Before scoring them Chaplin had the opportunity to reedit according to any second thoughts he might have had in a lifetime of viewing the films. Happily, most of these changes are minor, such as the rewording of titles and elimination of dated references such as the "three-on-a-match" gag in *Shoulder Arms.* In *My Life in Pictures* Chaplin publishes the production sheets for *A Day's Pleasure.*

Comparison of these with the current release version reveals that Chaplin restructured the film. In the original the action occurs in three major scenes: starting the car; being stuck in traffic; and the boat ride. For the reissue, Chaplin places the traffic scene last, which is not as neat for plot flow but better for the film, as the traffic scene is the comic highlight.

The only way a viewer can be aware of such changes is by a careful reading of detailed descriptions of the films in early biographies (Theodore Huff's *Charlie Chaplin* is the standard reference) or by comparing the current reissues with pirated prints in private collections—a chancey business since pirated prints are often mutilated, and titles are frequently translated from foreign versions. However, the comparison can be fascinating. In *A Dog's Life,* for example, Chaplin substitutes several "takes" within certain scenes. In one of these he looks through the dog's back legs as it is digging for the wallet and gets dirt in his face (original version); but in *The Chaplin Revue* he looks, winces, and puts the dog's tail down with his hand—perhaps a gag Chaplin deemed a little *too* explicitly earthy in 1918. The shooting-gallery-lunch-wagon scene in the same film is also shortened, eliminating the heads popping up alternately, and the shot of Sydney emerging after the fracas, reaching behind his collar for a broken cup, is replaced by a more neutral shot.

One hopes that the Chaplin estate will make the original silent versions available, at least to major archives or museum collections, so that film scholars and interested individuals can see the films as Chaplin originally released them. One can be grateful, though, that despite his tendency to rewrite his filmic past, he preserved even those aspects of it he rejected (the outtakes) and in addition provided perfect musical settings for his entire post-1918 output.

Note

1Chaplin, cited in Chaplin, Charles Jr., *My Father, Charlie Chaplin, op. cit.,* pp. 92–93.

13

Locking Horns with the Monster: *Monsieur Verdoux*

As the serious subplot of *The Kid* begat *A Woman of Paris,* so the serious concluding speech of *The Great Dictator* begat *Monsieur Verdoux.*

Many observers have noted (and usually condemned) Chaplin's desire to hold his own among intellectuals. Virginia Cherrill commented on his tendency to assume for a time the personality of those who impressed him, noting that at one point during the making of *City Lights,* "overnight Charlie became Waldo Frank and it was a terrible bore until he got it out of his system."[1] Two other major factors made *Monsieur Verdoux* an attractive project to Chaplin: his public image during the 1940s, and his stubbornness.

For the second time in his career, he was the subject of tabloid headlines. As in 1927, when Lita Grey's lurid divorce complaint made Chaplin's sex life the subject of public interest and (among certain elements) outrage, so now the Joan Barry paternity suit did the same.

Public fascination with and ambivalence toward the sex lives of the stars had earlier resulted in the ending of Fatty Arbuckle's career despite his acquittal in court on a rape charge. As his own producer, Chaplin could not be blacklisted in the same way, except by the critics and the public itself. Compounding his unpopularity were his outspoken political speeches, prematurely advocating the opening of a second front to defend Russia, and his consistent refusal to become an American citizen, to the annoyance of the superpatriots and to many in Congress.

The paternity trials, occurring during the height of anti-Chaplin sentiment, were a farce, a travesty which was unfunny to Chaplin who was at the receiving end. Despite blood tests which proved medically that he was not the parent, he was nevertheless ordered to support the child.

Underscoring the public humiliation which included problems with the I.R.S. and, ultimately, harassment into exile (and in some respects causing it) was Chaplin's stubbornness. Charlie, Jr. comments on his father's unwillingness to retract statements or *ever* to admit error to outsiders. The reception of the last speech of *The Great Dictator,* which was also a blast at Chaplin the "thinker," must have angered him considerably. It has already been noted that he defended it vehemently in his 1964 autobiography. If the critics didn't approve of his prescription for a better world, then he would show them just how rotten this one was.

So it must have given Chaplin sardonic satisfaction to create *Monsieur Verdoux,* a black comedy in which he gleefully transforms his notorious "ladykiller" image into a literal profession, and boldly defends it with "speeches" that blithely explain the insignificance of personal murder in a world of mass-murdering nations.

While Verdoux, at first glance, seems like a stunning reversal of the tramp character, he was, in fact, present in Chaplin's work from the beginning—as the cruel-though-suave Charlie of the early films and as the drunken rich men, how sober and no longer absent-minded, desperately trapped in the middle class as Charlie was always trapped in the lower. Thematically, of course, the film was a return to making a living—survival in the world of modern times.

The original inspiration for the character was the real-life murderer Landru. Had Chaplin made the film as a drama it might well have been called *A Gentleman of Paris,* since he once again sets his film in that land of urbane sophistication.

But the times had changed, and Chaplin created his story as a comedy, "A comedy of murders," as the opening subtitle informs. Although it is usually classed as a film ahead of its time, it was in fact released only three years before the British *Kind Hearts and Coronets,* another murder comedy—no doubt influenced by *Verdoux*—which failed to cause the furor aroused by the Chaplin film. Later films such as *Bluebeard's Ten Honeymoons* (1960) also failed to arouse the blast of anger and indignation which was the critical reaction to *Monsieur Verdoux,* until *Verdoux*'s revival in 1964, when critical opinion reversed.

If *The Great Dictator* is Chaplin's first "real" sound film, *Monsieur Verdoux* is his first "real" talkie. Although in the previous film he found numerous excuses to throw the emphasis onto expressive movement, in *Monsieur Verdoux* Chaplin integrated most of its visual gags with the text. It is, in fact, the first Chaplin film one can imagine being performed by another company of actors.

In a sense, Chaplin returned to the basic appeal of his early Keystones. Judgments on its controversial content aside, his own performance is as magnetic and engrossing as ever. His delivery of his own lines is expert and deft, and aptly reinforces his physical portrayal of the suave murderer.

The same, unfortunately, cannot be said of the other characters in the film. Although in earlier films Chaplin's conceptions of the other characters presented a problem of balance for him as scenarist, at least the quality of performances was professional. In *Monsieur Verdoux* several of the players seem embarassingly amateurish.

Monsieur Verdoux has the weakest opening of any mature Chaplin film, because of the actors' delivery of their lines and the awkwardness of the movement patterns, made particularly obvious by a bungled physical gag in which a tray is overturned. This illustrates Chaplin's complaint in his autobiography that the actors after the silent era had trouble doing pantomime. Yet there is really no excuse for this scene, since the rest of the film is infused with Chaplin's characteristic elegant choreog-

raphy. Perhaps the scene served as a "warm-up" for Chaplin after a seven-year absence from the cameras.

Even worse is the performance by Marilyn Nash as the prostitute whom Verdoux picks up to test poison on, for she embodies the film's positive philosophy. In *My Life in Pictures* Chaplin sums it up by saying she was pretty but, "to put it politely—a little naive."[2]

The awkward opening scene shows the Couvais family rightfully worried about the fate of Thelma Couvais, who has not been heard from since she married a mysterious stranger named Varnay. The film's first well-done gag is a frozen moment, as they hold up a picture of Verdoux—his expression is silly, his lips pursed in Verdoux's eternal efficient fussiness.

In this first visual departure from the tramp, Chaplin—in the guise of Verdoux—plays a variety of roles. The audience first meets him as Varnay, working placidly in his garden as ominous clouds of black smoke emerge from the chimney. When a mailman comes with a package for Thelma, he adroitly informs the man she is bathing, goes upstairs and signs for the package while keeping up a conversation with his now-defunct wife. This is, in effect, a dialogue version of the classic Chaplin visual gag of wiping the mouth of a baby (*The Circus*) or an unconscious crook (*A Dog's Life*) after filching their food.

When Varnay opens the package containing Thelma's money, he counts through it with incredible speed and dexterity, thanks to an undercranked camera. Holding his body immobile except for his flying fingers, the ex-bank teller quickly disposes of the large stack in Chaplin's typically skillful fashion. This bit, perhaps the best visual material in the film, becomes a running gag as Verdoux similarly flips not only through his victims' money but also through ledgers and telephone directories.

Meanwhile the Couvais family learns from the police that twelve other widows have mysteriously disappeared recently.

The ample and vain Mme. Grosnay now calls with a real estate agent, and Verdoux quickly identifies her as his next victim. When the agent comes into a room as Verdoux is making extravagant love to the unwilling dowager, Chaplin launches into one of the few visual flights in the film, as he pretends to have been merely trying to catch a bee, and takes a backward tumble out the window. (His vocal inflection and movement recall similar episodes with the Jewish barber.)

Verdoux with Lydia (Margaret Hoffman).

In *The Great Dictator* Chaplin had a field day with puns. In *Verdoux* the few puns are sardonic rather than silly. "You must have made a killing," says a former bank colleague upon seeing Verdoux's latest bankroll. "Yes," he replies after a pause and a sinister smile.

Verdoux's deadly game must continue, as he needs cash to protect his stock market investments. So he becomes M. Floray and visits another wife, the cronelike Lydia. After he tricks her into withdrawing her money from the bank, they retire (in a scene which gave Chaplin trouble with censors). From the balcony, Verdoux poetically extols the beauty of the moon. He exits into the bedroom, but the camera remains fixed on the balcony shot. Time is compressed in a theatrical way when the lighting changes to that of daylight and Verdoux briskly emerges after another job well done. The conception of both wife murders shows Chaplin the filmmaker at his best, since he skillfully leaves to the viewer's imagination the acts themselves (in that

way also insuring their sympathy for the main character). Lest the audience be in any doubt of what has happened, he assures them by setting the breakfast table for two, and, realizing his "silly" mistake, removes one setting. As he had in *A Woman of Paris*, Chaplin conveys the essential information swiftly, subtly, yet with unmistakable clarity.

Having established the murderer's profession the film now delves deeper into his character as he visits his refuge—his country home—complete with crippled wife and bright-eyed son. The goal of his work is shown as he presents his wife with the deed to their house. "*That* they'll never take away from us," he says heartfully. Ironically he upbraids his son for pulling the cat's tail. "Violence begets violence, remember." Chaplin wants to stack the deck in every way possible to insure sympathy. Verdoux was a bank employee for many years before the Depression resulted in his layoff and he found this desperate way to continue to support his family. The only wife the audience actually meets before her death is

Lydia—and she is such an embittered old crone that Chaplin ensures that she receives no audience sympathy. Of Verdoux's three other intended victims, wife Annabella proves indestructible; he spares the prostitute because her philosophy touches him; and he never quite manages to marry Mme. Grosnay.

As Captain Bonheur, Verdoux makes the first of three unsuccessful attempts on the life and fortune of Annabella. These three scenes are by far the funniest in the film, although Chaplin later admitted (in *My Life in Pictures*) that Martha Raye's performance was "out of key" with the rest. In fact, she would have fit right into the spirit of the farcical *Great Dictator*. Like Jack Oakie in that film, Martha Raye as Annabella boisterously counterpoints the pinpoint fussiness and precision of Chaplin's character.

There is amusing verbal business as Verdoux contemptuously exposes phoney business schemes the gullible Annabella falls for, including The Pacific Ocean Power Company and The Salt Water Fuel Company (which claims to transform salt water into gasoline).

Returning home, Verdoux learns the formula for an undetectable poison from a druggist friend, in a scene which may have been suggested by a similar exchange in Hitchcock's *Shadow of a Doubt,* which was released in 1943 when Chaplin was beginning work on *Verdoux.*

Although he ends up sparing the prostitute, who was to be his test case, by an adroit manipulation of the poisoned wine, he is given the opportunity to test it when he is visited by a detective. Once again Verdoux, like the tramp, proves himself the master of the situation.

The hardness of the character is revealed in his second encounter with the prostitute, whom he brushes off, and in a pursed-lip nod he tips his hat to a pretty girl in a cafe, who is herself greeting someone behind him. This is the same gag that is so touching in the dance hall of *The Gold Rush,* but in

Verdoux with the indestructible Annabella (Martha Raye).

this incarnation the romance has withered.

Trying to poison Annabella, Verdoux is unaware of a mix-up of bottles. The maid uses his poison, thinking it is peroxide on her hair; Annabella drinks wine spiked with peroxide (and likes it); and Verdoux thinks that he has accidentally downed the poisoned wine. His hilarious imagined death throes are topped by the arrival of the maid—what hair remains on her head stands up like a fright wig.

His final attempt on Annabella, in a rowboat, contains the film's best vocal and visual humor. Verdoux explains his murder weapons—a rope and a rock to drown her—as fishing tools. He will "lasso" the fish, he tells her. As he tries to work his way toward her with a handkerchief soaked in chloroform, the audience is treated to a Chaplin "peek-a-boo" scene complete with winsome looks, like the ones in the dressing room in City Lights. Naturally Verdoux ends up chloroforming himself instead of Annabella, and gets a dunking as well.

Through all this Verdoux has persistently bombarded Mme. Grosnay with flowers, and she has finally succumbed to his entreaties and agreed to marry him. The threads of the film neatly come together at the wedding party, for Annabella is one of the guests. Verdoux and Annabella bump into each other backward, but turn alternately to apologize, so they don't recognize each other. When Verdoux hears Annabella's loud laugh he crawls into the greenhouse. He explains his doubled-over posture to guest William Frawley as the cramps—another verbal amplification of a visual gag motif, the transformation of one posture (hiding) to another (sickness). Verdoux escapes.

Time passes, as the audience learns in a montage of newspaper headlines spotlighting the social unrest and turmoil of the thirties. The montage includes brief shots showing Verdoux's financial wipeout in the stock market crash of 1929.

As he had in City Lights, Chaplin makes an eloquent physical transformation to show his character after the passage of time—a time during which he has lost both his fortune and his family (they die of unspecified causes). Verdoux is bent, deflated, walking with a limp. The characterization is also vocal, as Verdoux now speaks in a breathy, raspy tone. Chaplin the actor was never better.

Verdoux encounters the prostitute—now a "success" as the mistress of a munitions manufacturer—giving Verdoux opportunity to begin the explicit connecting of his lifestyle with the fabric of contemporary society. Despite his ability to elude the police, he elects, when discovered by the Couvias

family in a cafe, to "fulfill his destiny" by permitting himself to be captured.

That destiny is fulfilled in the courtroom and his prison cell, giving Verdoux the chance to elaborate on the film's premise—that he is only an "amateur" in a world that encourages mass killing, and a villain rather than a hero because he was self-employed as opposed to working for the state. In an encounter with a priest Verdoux makes it clear that society is to blame whereas he is at peace with God. "May God have mercy on your soul," says the priest. "Why not? After all, it belongs to Him," replies Verdoux.

Offered rum before his walk to the guillotine, he refuses, then decides, "Just a minute. I've never tasted rum." Chaplin, the master actor, stiffens slightly as he drinks, subtly suggesting that Verdoux is not a hedonist; his suave chatter is, to some extent, a front and he feels the need for a stiff belt to face the end.

Stepping outside, he takes a deep breath, then walks slowly away from the camera toward the guillotine. For those who have not been alienated by the film up to this point, the ending is powerful and moving—the ultimate, ironic walk down the road.

The film is a triumph for Chaplin as an actor, so much so that it almost compensates for the absence of a single sustained flight of magical Chaplin pantomime (the only major Chaplin film without one).

Monsieur Verdoux continues to be a controversial film. One prevailing view is that:

> Everyone recognizes Charlie Chaplin's genius as a pantomime actor; everyone equally recognizes that his skill evaporates when he turns to dialogue.[3]

In his autobiography Chaplin vigorously defends the film, quoting pages of script and stating that he thinks it is "the cleverest and most brilliant film I have yet made." In My Life in Pictures, though, while stating that he still liked the ending, he goes on to say:

> There was some clever dialogue in Monsieur Verdoux but now I think it was too cerebral and should have had more business. If you have a bit of a message it's better to put it over through business than through words—better for me, anyhow.[4]

Yet, later in the same book he defends its philosophy, stating that "The film was disliked in America where its message of antimaterialism was mistaken for immoral cynicism."

The fact is that Chaplin had finally made the "artistic experiment" he had resisted for so long, with the dubious result that the film tends to be too lowbrow for highbrows and too highbrow for lowbrows.

But whatever its faults, Chaplin was right to feel proud of his accomplishment in cerebral cinema. That it does not reach the level of his great silent films does not negate the artist's integrity and courage in pressing into unknown territory. Like all Chaplin's films, it is a chapter in the emotional life of its creator, and as such will continue to excite interest and arouse controversy.

Notes

[1]Cherrill, Virginia, Kamin interview, September 24, 1978.

[2]Chaplin, *My Life in Pictures, op. cit.,* p. 290.

[3]Nicoll, Allardyce, *The World of Harlequin* (London: Cambridge University Press, 1963), p. 18.

[4]Chaplin, *My Life in Pictures, op. cit.,* p. 34.

14

Divide and Conquer: *Limelight*

It is striking how in a number of films, minor sub-plots and unresolved scenes led Chaplin into the heart of his next film. Thus, *The Kid* led to *A Woman of Paris,* the gibberish ending of *Modern Times* to the principle of characterization for the dictator character, and that film's final speech into the thesis treatment in *Monsieur Verdoux.*

By any reckoning, the prostitute scene in *Monsieur Verdoux* is the film's weakest major scene. The prostitute's positive philosophy as well as her definition of love as sacrifice (her husband, like Verdoux's wife, was an invalid), stand in opposition to Verdoux's cynical capitulation to life in society's jungle.

And so in *Limelight* Chaplin creates Calvero, a has-been comedian and another of life's losers. But he recovers his own positive zest for life when he elects to psychologically nurse a young dancer back to health.

Even a brief plot outline of *Limelight* reveals how central a work it is in Chaplin's career. While such films as *The Kid* accurately re-create the emotional world of Chaplin's childhood, *Limelight* is alone in reflecting his attitudes toward his adult life as a performer. Although on some level all of Chaplin's films are thinly disguised autobiography, in *Limelight* the disguise is virtually transparent. Every line and every situation in the film is full of self-reflection. The character of Calvero was inspired partly by Frank Tinney, a Broadway comedian who became self-conscious in his art and lost touch with his audience. But Calvero is an emotional portrait of Chaplin at that point in his life. His only film in the previous twelve years, *Monsieur Verdoux,* was a critical and public failure. One of the reviews said

Chaplin as a comedy tramp in *Limelight.*

145

that it was "a pity to see so gifted a motion picture craftsman taking leave of his audience."[1] The only real difference between the men was that Calvero, after his failure, lived in obscurity while Chaplin was still in the limelight he earned during his years of public acclaim.

Limelight is often likened to *City Lights*. Both films center on Chaplin's efforts to help an afflicted woman, at great personal sacrifice, including ultimately the sacrifice of the possibility of the conventional "happily-ever-after" ending. It is also the first film since *City Lights* to center on the formation and development of a love relationship. Like the earlier film, which is built around the Chaplin character's feeling of unworthiness in the eyes of his beloved (and which followed a decade of romantic disasters in Chaplin's offscreen life), *Limelight* is built around obstacles to love. Calvero feels Terry's love for him is too mingled with pity and gratitude so that he nobly won't permit her to "sacrifice" herself to him. This is an ironic reversal of the real domestic happiness Chaplin had found with his wife Oona during the decade preceding *Limelight*.

Limelight can also be seen as an extension of the ending of *Modern Times*, in which Chaplin presents himself as an entertainer.

But *City Lights* and *Modern Times* are films complete unto themselves—fully realized works. The film that is closest to *Limelight* is the film generally considered Chaplin's least "finished" feature, *The Circus*. All the same elements appear: the hopeless love; the self-consciousness of portraying a performer (an opening subtitle of *Limelight* introduces it as "The story of a ballerina and a clown"); even the similarity of the costumes worn by the equestrian and the dancer.

But in *The Circus* the elements don't cohere. Except for Charlie, the characters don't come to life, the opportunity for reflexive comments about performing passes unused, and the love story is perfunctory and unanchored. Even the film's comedy sequences are uneven.

Limelight, however, is a triumphant working-out of the themes and ideas that plague *The Circus*. Chaplin's nemesis, the film with dialogue, is finally brought under control with a dazzling display of the full range of his verbal and physical skills. He is, by turns, wry and witty, wise, silly, self-indulgent; he acts, he sings, he dances, and, best of all, he does pantomime. In his autobiography Chaplin explains that he was certain of his achievement. "I had fewer qualms about its success than any picture I had ever made."[2]

The keys to the triumph of *Limelight* are the role Chaplin plays—a music hall entertainer—and the milieu—the world of the theatre. His previous two films cast him in roles that fall into the "imposter" category of his early work, roles that were alien to his personal experience. Charlie, Jr. describes Chaplin tortuously pacing the house, pondering the motivation of such a character as Monsieur Verdoux.

But in *Limelight* Chaplin is on firm ground. It is unique among Chaplin's films in that he could abandon the juggling act of characterization which was a serious problem in his other sound films. For in *Limelight* all the characters seem well-founded and realistic, drawn as they are from Chaplin's vast professional and personal experiences. For once, he includes notable actors in his cast, and their professionalism shines through and grounds the film. Claire Bloom, arguably the most sensitive dramatic actress he ever worked with, is well-supported by his son Sydney Chaplin, Nigel Bruce (of Dr. Watson fame) and, in a casting decision both brilliant and moving, Buster Keaton to share his final moments of triumph on stage.

The achievement of *Limelight* stems from Chaplin's separation of the stylized, presentational performance of the onstage acts from the offstage "real" life of his character. In doing this it was as if Chaplin relaxed into the roles both on and off the stage, with the result that each becomes more luminous. Without the sometimes forced bursts of physical business in *The Great Dictator* and *Monsieur Verdoux*, he could devote his energy to simply acting the heartfelt lines of Calvero, and allow a much more subtle visual humor to enter the scenes; and onstage he could indulge his most ornate and stylized impulses to sing, dance, pantomime, and even do a bit of rapid patter. Divide and conquer.

Backstage films have always fascinated moviegoers, but few go beyond superficial, distorted biographies which sentimentalize their subjects. One exception is the French film *Children of Paradise*, a biography of Deburau, the celebrated nineteenth-century French mime. Its opening contrasts life with art as the dreamy Deburau becomes alert to reenact a scene which the audience has just witnessed. A thief picks a fat man's pocket as the man ogles a pretty girl, whom he grabs when he discovers the theft. Depicting these three characters for a policeman, and to the great amusement of the crowd, Deburau (played by the great French mime Jean-Louis Barrault) leaps from character to character as Chaplin had in the song-mime of *Modern Times*; his characterization of the girl is taken directly from Chaplin's similar movements in both *Modern Times* and *The Great Dictator*. To show the act itself, he plays the fat man as the arm of the thief creeps around to lift the watch, creating the illusion of being two people simultaneously in an ingenious variation on Chaplin's body-part transformation format.

far more subtle than the stage scenes of *Children of Paradise,* in which offstage and onstage life become literally mingled together. Because the elements of *Limelight* work independently, Chaplin can afford this subtlety.

The theme of public success appears in the film's title and its opening subtitle: "The glamor of Limelight, from which age must fade as youth enters."

Fish and philosophy. Calvero with Terry (Claire Bloom).

Children of Paradise continues to contrast the "real-life" actions of the characters with the onstage performances as Deburau becomes a theatrical success. The mime sequences (which total about fifteen minutes of this three-and-one-quarter-hour film) are seen on two levels: as beautiful, stylized mime; and as artistic translations of what is known to be the real-life relationships among the characters. By this device the film succeeds in presenting stage performances in a way that is totally engrossing. Chaplin had seen and admired this film in the 1940's.

Two of *Limelight*'s four music hall acts reflect directly on the content of the rest of the film. One is an act Calvero does (in a dream) with dancer Terry, with much of the snappy sexual patter which is muted in their actual relationship. The other act is a song that comments on the film's preoccupation with age moving aside for youth entitled "The Sardine Song," which deals with reincarnation. But these connections, though thematically direct, are

The next subtitle introduces the time and place, London, 1914, neatly joining Chaplin's two actual "beginnings," his birthplace and the year he entered the movies—his beginnings as a person and as an artist.

Calvero, neatly dressed, comes stumbling gracefully down the street. As in *One A.M.* he struggles to open the front door with his key. But the comedy is toned down—this man is no amusingly tipsy millionaire, but a drunk coming home to his modest rooming house.

Inside, Calvero smells gas coming from Terry's room. In yet another Chaplin transformation, he first suspects his cigar, then checks the bottom of his shoe for the source of the offending odor.

Efficiently, Chaplin establishes the basic characters and situation as Calvero struggles against his inebriated state to rescue the girl, find a doctor, and begin taking responsibility for her rehabilitation. Terry, a former dancer, is a hysterical paralytic.

Faced with a task outside his failed professional and personal life (five ex-wives), Calvero stops drinking and begins probing to find the source of Terry's self-defeat, and in the process rediscovers his own fierce enthusiasm for life.

The verbal exchanges between Bloom (Terry) and Chaplin in their scenes together were vilified by many critics as extensions of Chaplin's presumptuous desire to be known as a sage. But away from the political and philosophical complexities of his two previous films, the talk in *Limelight,* with all its aphorisms, does contain both wit and wisdom. It is also dramatically grounded by the story Chaplin created in which Calvero must inspire the despairing Terry. Further, it is lightened by subtle physical business most critics seemed to have missed. During the entire dramatic scene in which Terry reveals to Calvero that she cannot walk, for example, he stands holding two large kippers. Later, discoursing about not wasting youth, he stands next to a framed photo of himself as a young man. This sort of expressive use of properties is echoed in Woody Allen's *Manhattan,* when characters earnestly talk with the skull of a primitive man looming in the background.

Calvero's intense and sometimes cosmic pronouncements to Terry are also balanced by his humorous encounters with the landlady, a direct descendant of Mme. Grosnay, and also possibly influenced by a similar landlady in *Children of Paradise.* ''You have a leaking gas pipe,'' he excitedly tells her. ''I mean . . . your room has a leaking gas pipe.'' When she later confronts him with a demand for the rent money she exclaims, ''Just the man I want to see.'' With his most ingratiating grin he replies, ''How thrilling!'' Then he proceeds to turn all of Verdoux's charm on her, deflecting her demand.

It is in his many comments about Calvero's life in the theatre that Chaplin's heartfelt opinions are best expressed:

> Terry: But you're not the great comedian?
> Calvero: I was
>   (later)
> Terry: To hear you talk no one would ever think
>   you were a comedian.
> Calvero: I'm beginning to realize that. I can't get a
>   job.
> Terry: What a sad business, being funny.
> Calvero: Very sad if they won't laugh.

And so on, telling of his love of his craft, his ambivalence toward his audience, and his despair over

his failure. Chaplin puts Calvero in a neat double bind. Losing his touch, he begins to drink to be funny, but this soon becomes a dead end, since he becomes too incapacitated to perform.

Like *The Great Dictator, Limelight* is built on the structural principle of a checkerboard. As barber and dictator alternated scenes in the earlier film, so in *Limelight* the offstage scenes alternate with onstage sequences.

The first two of these onstage acts occur in Calvero's dreams. Each begins with Calvero in bed. Outside, three street musicians play a haunting melody (one of these is Keystone comic Snub Pollard, one of Chaplin's few remaining colleagues from the early days. These musicians, incidentally, are clearly the inspiration for many such characters in Fellini's films, notably in *La Strada* and *Amarcord*).

Calvero dreams of the days of his glory. Striding onto the stage in the first of several costumes he wears in the film, he is dressed as a lion tamer, complete with top hat, tails, checkered vest,

Chaplin's roles in *Limelight.* A variation on the tramp costume for the sardine song (top left), the flea trainer (top right), the musical act (center), and the despairing Calvero (lower left). A montage from an exhibitor's press book.

The Flea Trainer.

jodhpurs, and boots which extend to his thighs. He snaps his whip smartly and sings "The Animal Trainer," describing his discovery of fleas on his person which he has trained to perform. A table behind him is labeled "Phyllis and Henry/Performing Fleas." Finishing his song, he brings the table around to begin the act. Looking down into his hat Calvero says, in broad double entendre:

> Phyllis! Henry! What do you think you're doing? Stop that! You ought to be ashamed of yourself— fighting like that.

The act proceeds as Calvero tries to get the fleas to hop from the back of one hand to another (indicated in mime, of course). Predictably, he has obedience problems. Phyllis jumps onto his eye and despite his threats ("Do you want me to *squeeze*?") gets into his clothing. "Come out at once! You go too far! Crazy little creature you!" When he finally fishes her out, he exclaims, "That's not Phyllis!" But Phyllis makes herself known, biting him in the rear end and "forcing" him to make his exit.

As Calvero returns for his bow, the camera closes in on his shocked face, and the viewer sees that the auditorium is empty. Dissolve to Calvero sitting up in bed with the same shocked expression.

The next night, Calvero, having discovered Terry was a dancer, dreams up a new routine which includes her. He begins again with a music hall song, "Spring is Here," which, like the flea patter, deals with sex. It describes the various creatures, from birds to whales to worms, who are all "wagging their tails for love." Dressed in a straw hat and comedic tramp clothes, Calvero executes some fancy dance steps, including the backward glide from *Modern Times* and a fan kick which Buster Keaton had done in *The Playhouse*. He goes into a rapid series of kicks while singing, "Oh it's love-lovelovelovelovelovelovelovelove," whereupon he is interrupted by Terry, with parasol and ballet costume.

What follows is a delightful quick-patter routine. Calvero begins his "Ode to a Worm," but is stopped short by the realistic Terry, who explains that a worm, contrary to his poem, cannot smile. "How do you know?" he asks her, "Have you ever appealed to its sense of humor?" "Gesundheit," she says when he sneezes. "Certainly does," says he. "I beg your pardon." "The dress—it certainly goes on tight."

Making light of the more ponderous sections of the film, Calvero puts his arm around her waist and says, "I'm beginning to grasp the meaning of life." "You're sensitive, you feel things," she says, which prompts him to hop backward, slapping his leg with his cane. "Now, don't encourage me!" "So few people have the capacity to feel," she informs him, "Or the opportunity!" he quips.

Calvero escorts her out in grand style, stepping high with each leg as they exit. This exit is rather reminiscent of Astaire's exit with Rogers at the end of their "Let's Face the Music and Dance" number in *Follow the Fleet*. It gives the viewer a similar chills-up-the-spine feeling with its bold theatricality.

Encouraged by his own pep talks, Calvero responds to a summons by his agent, mustering his battered dignity to deal with a man who is determined that Calvero "must be made to realize the facts" that he is a has-been, should be grateful to get any work at all, and should even perform under a different name ("You're succeeding splendidly," Calvero informs the agent). Chaplin, for the first time on film, exhibits an expression captured only in news photos of his offstage self: an expression of tense, arrogant hardness.

For the first time the viewer sees Calvero before an audience in the film, and his appearance is a disaster. Halfheartedly singing his "Sardine Song," he falters in his patter. Finally he just gives up and leaves the stage, as the audience itself begins leaving. A performer's nightmare. Removing his makeup as the other performers leave the dressing room, he can barely mutter his good-byes. As the makeup towel reveals his face, the viewer sees that he wears the same expression of shock he wore at the end of his dream of the flea act.

Lest the reader think that the fear of failing at performing was outside the experience of the eminently successful comedian, we quote again from Charlie, Jr.'s biography:

> For my father, who was at his best among a circle of close friends, to come out cold before a strange audience and be funny was excruciating torture, with the dread of almost certain failure.
>
> He tried it once at the request of the head of the personnel division of one of the big aircraft corporations near Los Angeles. One noon in the company's open-air theatre where all the workers were gathered with their lunches, he laid, I think, the biggest egg of his career. No one laughed, no one clapped, apparently no one was even watching him. Everyone was too busy eating. My father came out of the experience unnerved and shaking.

"I'll never do it again, never,'' he said. "I can't. It's not my kind of entertainment."[3]

Returning to the apartment, he breaks down when he tells Terry. "They walked out on me. They haven't done that since I was a beginner. The cycle is complete . . . I'm finished, through."

The camera moves off Calvero, hunched defeated over the table, as the roles abruptly reverse and Terry rises, unable to bear him in this state. Suddenly she realizes what she has done and cries, "Calvero . . . look . . . I'm walking . . . I'm walking." She keeps repeating this as the camera moves closer to her, a strange moment in the film since she is not walking at all, but standing. However, it is well-played by Bloom.

Part of Terry's psychological problem, learned earlier in the film, was her discovery that her sister supported her at the cost of a life of prostitution. Now, visiting the ballet where Terry has gotten a job in the corps de ballet, there is a shot (in another understated moment) of a prostitute circulating among the well-dressed gentlemen.

Calvero accompanies Terry to an audition for a major role. The role switch is completed as she reveals herself to be a brilliant dancer. Calvero sits alone in the wings as everyone leaves. The lights are turned out, leaving him in deep shadow. While the lighting in *Limelight* received some criticism for its "artiness," it is in fact entirely appropriate to its theatrical setting and characters.

Terry arranges for Calvero to have a job as a clown in her new ballet. Before the performance she suddenly panics, and, in his final bit of professional counseling, he slaps her hard and practically pushes

After his disastrous performance.

her onstage. "Whoever you are, whatever it is," he prays, "just keep her going—that's all." She is a triumph.

But Calvero suffers a double humiliation. His performance as a clown (the part requires him to amuse Terry on her deathbed) is deemed inadequate. Calvero discovers this outside the theatre the next day as he meets an old colleague who has come to audition for his part. And, sitting drunk behind a door, he hears Terry talking with Neville (Sydney Chaplin) on the other side. He is the young composer of the ballet, and they love each other. But Terry refuses Neville because of her loyalty to Calvero, explaining that she loves his soul, "his sweetness, his sadness—nothing will ever separate me from that."

Nothing, that is, except Calvero himself, who is convinced that Terry and Neville belong together. He simply disappears, and is next seen as a street musician, dressed in multicolored patchwork jacket and large top hat, strumming a banjo and singing his "lovelovelove" song with the three street musicians who serenaded him earlier. He tells Neville:

> All the world's a stage, and this one's the most legitimate. . . . There's something about working the streets I like. It's the tramp in me, I suppose.

Terry finds Calvero and for the second time he breaks down, as she implores him to come back to her. "I can't—I've got to go forward. That's progress." But he is interested when she explains that a benefit performance has been arranged for him. This intrigues him because "I would like the chance just to show them I'm not through yet." He tells her about "a comedy act for myself and my friend. It's a sort of musical satire . . . it's very funny, got a lot of funny business."

And so it is. But before that, the audience is treated to the most intense of backstage scenes, as the friend (Keaton) and Calvero, is one of the magical moments of all cinema, sit sharing a tawdry dressing room. Keaton says:

> I never thought we'd come to this. Here we have the star dressing room without a dresser. I guess we can put up with it for one night. . . . If anyone else says it's like the old times I'll jump out the window.

At which point Nigel Bruce, as Postant the impresario, enters and says just that. Buster just walks out, leaving the old impresario and the old comedian to talk. Calvero wants a success this night. "Not that I care for success—but I don't want another failure." They converse about old times:

> Postant: In those days you were drunk instead of
>   sober.
> Calvero: I'm supposed to be funnier that way.
> Postant: You were killing yourself.
> Calvero: Anything for a laugh.

When Postant leaves, Calvero seals his fate by taking a drink. Terry enters and the wry comments continue with some of the romantic sadness of the ending of *City Lights.* Responding to her statement that they'll soon have a home in the country together, he says:

> Calvero: This is my home . . . I don't like it. Every-
>   one's so kind to me. It makes me feel
>   isolated. Even you make me feel isolated.
> Terry: Why do you say that?
> Calvero: I don't know. I really don't know.
> Terry: Remember, I love you.
> Calvero: (with cynical expression and voice tone)
>   Really?
> Terry: Really! With all my heart.

But *City Lights,* out of necessity, ended with the confrontation of the misfit lovers, whereas in *Limelight* Chaplin is able to end the film with more finality, while still preserving the bittersweet hopeless romance.

Calvero strides onstage for his flea act. The viewer sees it begin and end, and it is a great success—but the viewer also learns that the audience has been "padded" to ensure a good response.

Calvero returns in his tramp clown outfit for a proper rendition of "The Sardine Song." This ends with an undercranked and reverse-action shot of Calvero somersaulting into a split, "squeezing" himself up to standing position, and trotting off.

Another filmic device introduces the final act, as Calvero and Buster retire behind a screen and instantly emerge with Calvero in his final costume.

This last costume is the most ingenious in the film. A form encircles Chaplin's waist, giving him a huge, buoyant, potbelly. This functions to keep his wide, black trousers away from his knees to preserve the short-leg illusion in the piece (when Chaplin draws his leg upward, there is no visible telltale bend at the knee). Striped socks also contribute to the effect.

Buster wears a large moustache and thick spectacles. As the men enter for their act, Buster bumps into the piano. Calvero guides him around to the stool, where he puts a huge sheaf of music on the stand. It promptly cascades down whenever he strikes the keys.

Meanwhile Calvero is also having troubles. His collar is so high that the lower half of his head vanishes as he positions his violin. Finally he pulls the collar off.

Unlike the other acts at the performance, the musical act is not accompanied by audience reactions, for reasons which will be discussed shortly. Instead, very soft background music is heard.

Calvero turns and walks toward the piano to see if his friend is ready. He taps the piano with his bow. But when he returns he trips over his own foot, which mysteriously causes one leg to shorten, resulting in a hilarious lopsided walk. He shakes the leg out to its proper length, but it happens again. The many variations of this brilliant gag include the leg drawing up by itself, Calvero extending it by stepping on it with the other foot and "pulling" it out, and another trip which results in *both* legs shortening—at which point Calvero passes the bow between his legs and pulls himself up by the crotch (a movement he performed in the audition scene of *The Circus*).

Finally ready to tune up, Buster hits an "A," which rises in pitch (another filmic gag). Calvero breaks his violin strings as he tries to match the rising note. Putting his violin down on the piano, he lifts the lid to examine it, and the violin falls to the floor only to be stepped on by the oblivious Buster. It remains attached to his shoe.

After Buster cuts the tangled piano wires with a large wirecutter, Calvero is able to play a perfect glissando on the "repaired" piano.

But now Calvero can't find his violin, until Buster sits down and crosses his legs. Calvero pulls it off by jerking with his hands and pushing against Buster's chest with his foot—but it is ruined, so he discards it and reaches behind himself for a new one!

The men play, and Calvero is transported. "You darling," he murmurs to the violin, kissing it as Buster watches patiently. A sad tune makes both men fall sobbing on the piano. A bright one, which Calvero plays with demonic glee, ends with Buster spinning himself off his stool (but without missing a note) and Calvero falling off the stage into a bass drum. He continues fiddling furiously as three men carry him offstage in the drum.

By keeping the soundtrack free of audience sounds during this scene, Chaplin brilliantly makes

Chaplin and Keaton.

it clear that the audience he is really playing to is not the audience within the film, but rather the audience *watching* the film. He does this at his (and Calvero's) moment of comic triumph. With any sizable audience there is virtually continuous laughter throughout the long (eight-minute) routine. The movie viewer is his audience, and provides the film's true soundtrack with hearty laughter.

Calvero has suffered a heart attack during his fall. Carried back out in the drum, summoning his strength, he says, "On behalf of my partner and myself I'd like to continue—but I'm stuck." Backstage, Terry rushes to him, and he bravely assures her that they will be together, touring the world with her ballet and his comedy. He insists she go on with her act.

"I believe I'm dying, doctor," he says in the film's last theatrical reference. "But I don't know. I've died so many times."

Watching Terry take the stage, his great colleague Keaton behind him, he finally dies as the spotlight—

the Limelight—follows the new dancer in her journey across the stage.

Limelight is Chaplin's last great gift to the world. Pulling away from his attempts to integrate mime into a sound film world, perhaps tiring of the kind of conceptual mime exemplified in the balloon dance of *The Great Dictator,* Chaplin returned to the simplicity of the music hall which spawned him, and which he brought to the highest expression in his joyful comedy of movement.

Notes

[1]Cited in McDonald, Conway and Ricci, *The Films of Charlie Chaplin, op. cit.,* p. 215.

[2]Chaplin, Charles, *My Autobiography, op. cit.,* p. 459. Reprinted with permission of The Bodley Head.

[3]Chaplin, Charles, Jr., *My Father, Charlie Chaplin, op. cit.,* p. 347.

Death in the wings.

Fade Out: Afterword

"I suppose I shall always be a bit of film."[1]

Chaplin began working on *Limelight* fully expecting it to be his last picture. Certainly it would have been a respectable film with which to end his remarkable career. But he could not resist making two more films, though many of his admirers wish he hadn't.

Why didn't Chaplin quit? Long after his fortune would have permitted him, like Harold Lloyd, to retire at the height of an unparalleled career; long after the technical revolution of sound movies ended the era of "pure" mime in movies and popular entertainment; long after his own preoccupations and choices of subject matter ceased coinciding with popular taste; long after increasing age decreased the vitality and resiliency which were so much a part of his performances; long after reviews went from unanimous raves to cautious appreciations and outright pans; long after the public which idolized him in the United States turned against him; long after the government of the United States selected him as a political and moral enemy of the people and ultimately harassed him into exile—long after all these inducements to quit, Chaplin kept making films.

The answer is, he just couldn't stop. Call it love of work or call it ego—Chaplin himself expressed it eloquently when interviewed by *Life* magazine during the making of his last film, *A Countess from Hong Kong:*

> What has always sustained me—the place where I have really existed—has been my work. . . . I care about my work. It's the best thing I do.[2]

As stated at the outset, this book is not intended to be a biographical study of Chaplin. However, the temptation to draw parallels between his work and his life is irresistible because of the extraordinary crossover of one into another with this artist.

One example of this crossover is Chaplin's attitude toward money. Money meant two things to Chaplin; freedom from the poverty and discomfort of his childhood and independence. Obviously, themes of freedom and independence are thems that permeate Chaplin's films. Until Chaplin began working as his own producer, he was essentially an employee, a kind of bondage which rankled him just as it always rankled his fictional creation. This attitude is reflected in his final films for each of his sponsoring companies until he achieved independence in 1923. Each of these films deals explicitly with escape. In *His Prehistoric Past* (Keystone 1914) Charlie "escapes" to the past via a dream, to have an adventure as a caveman; in *Police* (Essanay 1916) he is a released convict who burglarizes a home, escaping capture only through the good graces of Edna; in *The Adventurer* (Mutual 1917) he is an escaped convict who is still on the run at the end of the film; and in *The Pilgrim* (First National 1923) he is again an escaped convict who, at the end, is prodded over the Mexican border by the "good" sheriff. He makes the same "free at last" gesture which ends *Police* and also occurs in *The Adventurer*, and then goes further. Mexican bandits begin gunfights. Torn between the risk of returning to the U.S. (the law) and the dangers of Mexico (lawlessness), Charlie walks uncertainly down the border, in one of his finest film endings, which is also a virtual presentiment of his own personal and professional difficulties in the years to come.

On the other hand, Chaplin's first films for each new sponsoring company reflect his enormous jump in both artistic freedom and salary. In effect,

Chaplin made an artistic leap with each "job" change. This leap is particularly obvious in his first Mutual, *The Floorwalker,* and first First National, *A Dog's Life,* both of which were discussed in some detail in this book. This is a delight for biographers, since the character of films Chaplin made for each company is so strikingly different, falling neatly into categories of beginner, apprentice, craftsman, and master.

Chaplin's personal life is certainly as fantastic as any of his film adventures—a classic rags-to-riches story. But the economic and artistic freedom his money gave Chaplin was matched by consistent invasions of his privacy by a world eager to know the "real" Chaplin. This meant, as many celebrities find, particular difficulty in finding real friends. Anyone in contact with Chaplin, however casually, had a guaranteed income if he chose to write about him, and many did. One gets the rather sad impression that Chaplin expected, and to some degree even encouraged, these Boswell-Johnson relationships, while at the same time he felt caged by the inescapable publicity he generated.

A celebrity *among* celebrities, Chaplin quickly sought and was ushered into a unique society of people who, by virtue of royal birth, genius, political power, or simply wealth, constituted the world's elite. "We all despise ourselves, the best of us," he says in *Limelight,* but the elite company did much to assuage his own insecurities, as his autobiography reveals.

Although in his early films he is rich or royal only as an imposter, the world of wealth becomes an important part of his film world in that most moving of Chaplin pictures, *City Lights.* There, it is neatly externalized from his tramp character in the form of the millionaire. For his final films Chaplin returns to the world of the rich and powerful, with some important variations.

In his last starring role Chaplin plays King Shahdov, a deposed monarch who hopes to bring his message of peace to America. It requires little imagination to transpose Shahdov into Shadow (Chaplin, King of Moving Shadows) and to relate the king's situation to the plight of Chaplin, both in his exile and in the refusal of his "adopted" country to heed his humane messages.

A King in New York is another sound-mime experiment for Chaplin, somewhat along the lines of *Monsieur Verdoux* in its integration of physical business into the script, but with some of *The Great Dictator's* sense of the ridiculous. It is a film that seems to have pleased almost no one. Chaplin, per-

haps smarting from the disastrous reviews, doesn't even mention the film in his autobiography. In *My Life in Pictures* he writes its epitaph:

> *I was disappointed in the picture. I meant it to be so up-to-date and modern but perhaps I didn't quite understand it. It started out to be very good and then it got complicated and I'm not sure about the end. There are funny gags in it . . . yet even these seem too elaborate to me now, and I feel a little uneasy about the whole film.*[3]

One of the peculiarities of the film is that Chaplin chose, after a lifetime of "classic" films, to do comedy material that might appear on *The Carol Burnett Show* or *Saturday Night Live*—topical parodies of TV commercials, depressing 1950s movies, rock-and-roll music, plastic surgery, and wide-screen movies.

As he had done selectively in all of his sound films, Chaplin includes several sequences of under-cranked action—a man tripping over a fire hose, and a pantomime nightclub act reminiscent of the clowns' shaving cream act in *The Circus.* Neither, unfortunately, is well-conceived nor well-executed. Chaplin's own physical bits in the film include a brief miming of his order in a noisy restaurant, and an equally brief scene in which, excited by the touch of Dawn Addams' foot, he takes a fully clothed leap into a bathtub, suggesting memories of both *The Floorwalker* and *Pay Day.* But times have changed. Forgetting his old editing principles, he divides the leap into several shots—Shahdov jumping balletically into his bathroom, an awkward medium shot as he whirls around and throws his bathrobe away, and another full-figure shot showing him taking the plunge. However, it *is* impressive to see the sixty-eight-year-old comedian still so spry—obviously the shot's intention.

Unfortunately, though, Chaplin's choreography, if not his body, seems to have stiffened. The movement of actors within the frame lacks the fluid patterns that characterize his previous work.

In *Limelight* Chaplin avoids the sexual theme by putting it into the music hall numbers. In his offstage portrayal of Calvero he acts strictly like a father to Terry, flirting only with the substantial landlady. But in *A King in New York* Chaplin is comically eager for sex, so he introduces a kind of heroine new to Chaplin films: a sexpot, á la 1950. While the heroines in Chaplin films certainly were beautiful women, they were costumed modestly and acted in ways that didn't distract from Chaplin. Dawn Addams, in the new film, is introduced in her bathtub while Shahdov and his aide take turns at the keyhole. Throughout the film they flirt and make advances at each other. But Chaplin is one step ahead of his audience. He is old, and looks his age. He knows the sight of such May-December sex play will be offensive to some. So he includes a scene in which he boldly draws attention to his aging face: he gets a face-lift which raises his nose and makes him look something like a pig. It is both grotesque and funny.

There are more visual pleasures in *A King in New York,* including bathroom-wall TV screens (shades of *Modern Times*) complete with windshield wipers, and the hose sequence in which Shahdov—in a scene that must have given Chaplin great pleasure—douses the House Un-American Activities Committee. As in *Monsieur Verdoux,* Chaplin was ahead of his time; moviegoers had to wait until the early 1970s for films like *Bananas* and *The Front* to poke similar fun at such governmental sacred cows.

The soundtrack contains subtleties as well. When Shahdov walks down Broadway, a voice in the background (Chaplin's voice) croons: "when I think of a million dollars tears come to my eyes." The whole character of Dawn Addams, of course, is Chaplin's view of America, with its virtues of youth, beauty, and vitality, and its vices of opportunism via capitalism. In her bathtub scene she is singing a song about selling her soul, indicating her willingness to "commit any sin" to get what she wants.

There are several well-executed visual-verbal gags. When Shahdov arrives in America, he is interviewed by reporters and says:

> I am deeply moved by your warm words, friendship, and hospitality. This bighearted nation has already demonstrated its noble generosity to those who come to seek a refuge from tyranny.

All this while he is being fingerprinted.

At a party, Shahdov is asked to recite Hamlet's soliloquy. During it he puts his hand in a food dish, shakes some off into his hostess's eye, and never misses a word as he wipes his hand with a napkin, saying, "There's the rub!"

Some of the dialogue is witty. Earlier in the party scene, the gaucheness of the hosts is well established when Shahdov asks about a painting on the wall. But his host thinks he is referring to the servant:

> Shahdov: Oh, by the by, is that an El Greco?
> Host: Oh, no sir. He's a Filipino.

> Shahdov: I meant the picture opposite.
> Host: Oh. I'm not sure. My wife bought it at an auction sale.

Thematically at least, the plot of *A King in New York* is very much in the mainstream of Chaplin's films. It contains many echoes of previous films, such as *The Kid* when Chaplin befriends a young boy. And it introduces new autobiographical elements, such as a scene in which the king is being mobbed by autograph hunters, as Chaplin was throughout his life.

But *A King in New York,* unlike the airplanes on which Shahdov arrives in and departs from America, never gets off the ground. Like *The Great Dictator,* its best material occurs too soon, and somehow fails to build in momentum.

Yet, if it doesn't fly, it doesn't quite crash either. The cast, as in *Limelight,* is uniformly good, though the British actors rely too much on Southern dialects, occasionally letting British inflections slip in. Chaplin himself performs with characteristic polish.

Perhaps the main fault of *A King in New York* is the problem that plagues all of Chaplin's sound films after *Modern Times:* his decreasing use of his comic trademark—transformation gags. The comedy that replaced those gags is often good. It just isn't great.

Finally, *A King in New York* hearkens back to *The Kid* in the rushed, innocuous tone of its ending—Shahdov simply sits reading a paper as his plane flies out of New York. Perhaps Chaplin's stubbornness is at work again, and he simply won't allow his real emotions about leaving the U.S. to show. Certainly, none do.

In his final film, *A Countess from Hong Kong,* the Chaplin figure is played by Sophia Loren as a stowaway countess. For the second time Chaplin created a film that did not feature him as the star. Like *A King in New York, Countess* is a sex comedy. But without the Chaplin presence, it lacks the basic appeal of movement that was central to every Chaplin film except *A Woman of Paris,* a film that pleased the critics but not the general public. *A Countess from Hong Kong* pleased neither.

In Chaplin's feeling that his writing and directing skills could stand as independent entities apart from his acting, perhaps his lifelong megalomania finally exceeded his artistic powers. But *King* and *Countess,* for all the satire of the former, are very gentle films. They look light, as if their creator enjoyed himself immensely in making them.

Who would deny him that?

Notes

[1]Chaplin, Charles, "Does the Public Know What it Wants?" *The Adelphi*, January 1924.

[2]Chaplin, cited in Meryman, Richard, "Chaplin," *Life*, March 10, 1967.

[3]Chaplin, *My Life in Pictures, op. cit.,* p. 306.

Free at last—at least temporarily. *The Pilgrim.*

Appendix 1: Chaplin's Influence

In successfully transferring a stage skill such as pantomime to the silent screen, then to the sound screen, Chaplin was part of a select company of artists who made similar transfers. These artists include Buster Keaton, whose acrobatic stage comedy was magnified into his epic, fatalistic struggles against colossal odds; W. C. Fields, whose Dickensian misanthrope incorporates the timing and movements of the great comedy juggler; the Marx Brothers, whose broad burlesque of everything in sight perfectly suited the desperate mood of the Depression; and Fred Astaire, who, like Chaplin, found ways of translating and expanding his unique stage style.

In a sense Chaplin, like the others, has had no direct influence at all. For his achievement was closed, completed. No one can use the gags or acting principles Chaplin discovered for himself without appearing to be merely a Chaplin imitator.

But as well as being a public and critical idol (at least through the mid-1930s), Chaplin is a direct inspiration—an ideal, as it were—to virtually everyone who does any form of pantomime or comedy. Thus, Harpo Marx, Red Skelton, and Marcel Marceau extol his work, just as the stars of the present world of dance all seem to name Fred Astaire as their favorite . . . their inspiration. In this sense, Chaplin's work exerts profound influence.

The one artist who seems to have derived much of his style directly from Chaplin is French filmmaker Jacques Tati. Tati has been virtually alone as a sound filmmaker who de-emphasizes dialogue. A music hall pantomimist, Tati began making feature films in 1949 with *Jour de Fete*. Like Chaplin, Tati spent years conceiving his films—he made only six features in a thirty-year period. Each one features the Tati character embroiled in situations that unfold visually. Sound, as in *Modern Times,* often merely creates confusion and barriers between the characters. Tati's character, Mr. Hulot, is closer to Keaton's passive silent hero than to the dynamic, aggressive tramp, but the elaborate visual gags—often transformation gags—owe much to Chaplin.

To many, Tati's films are too "precious" and elaborate to be enjoyable. Certainly he has never enjoyed a wide popularity in America. For this viewer, however, they work wonderfully well. Like Chaplin and Keaton, Tati is a shrewd observer of absurdities. His films transform the world. Leaving the theatre after a showing of *Traffic* (1971) or *Playtime* (1967), the patterns of traffic waiting at lights, moving in ritualistic ways, seem hilariously funny.*

Early television witnessed the popularity of performers who prided themselves on their mime ability. Clown-comedians such as Red Skelton, Sid Caesar, Jackie Gleason, and Milton Berle dominated television comedy throughout the 1950s, and featured their mime abilities in silent sequences such as Caesar's pantomimes with Imogene Coca, Skelton's Silent Spot, and so on. They introduced a new audience to a broad style of pantomime reminiscent of the short Keystone films, but ironically with stage restrictions.

During the 1960s situation comedy wiped this form off the slate. But some of the writers and behind-the-scene creators waited in the wings and, by the end of the decade, Woody Allen and Mel Brooks emerged as major forces in American comedy films. Both have attempted, with varying success, to use physical material in their films, with Woody Allen's *Sleeper* the most successful example.

Since the early 1970s there has been an explosion of interest in stage pantomime. Marcel Marceau, with more than three decades of world touring, has created a major theatrical audience for himself in a

*I refer interested readers to *The Films of Jacques Tati* by Brent Maddock (Metuchen, N.J.: The Scarecrow Press, 1977), an excellent, and to date the only, work on Tati in English.

161

style which, as indicated, owes much to the kind of compressed mime Chaplin did in his "onstage" numbers in *Modern Times* and *Limelight*. With an influx of performers and demand from audiences, the form has expanded, resulting in a fertile array of experiments out of which the next generation of entertainers will be born.

The situation is healthy, for the achievements of artists like Keaton, Astaire, and Chaplin are squarely based on their onstage training and on their having learned their craft in front of audiences. With the demise of music hall and vaudeville, it has been impossible to produce artists of the caliber of these performers. If the present interest in live theatre continues to grow and results in new institutions of entertainment being formed, audiences may enter another era in which some artists, at least, will do nondisposable work.

Until then, they can be happy with Chaplin's work—a treasure from the past and a legacy for the future.

Appendix 2: Word Portraits

It is safe to say that Chaplin has been written about more than any other figure in cinema. Since the beginning of his film career writers have produced millions of words for an eagerly waiting public. Much of this has been fan-magazine exploration of the "real" Chaplin—the man behind the screen image. With the scandals in his life, this soon took, particularly in the United States, a sordid turn. But as far back as 1916 serious writers were beginning to search beyond pop biography to study the phenomenon of the art and the artist, trying to account for the mysterious power that the Chaplin films cast over the entire world.

Interpretive works on Chaplin often reveal more about the author than about Chaplin. As happens with Shakespeare, different cultures and different eras have ascribed varied meanings to the films. Film criticism, the development of which Chaplin's art certainly stimulated, evolved in several distinct directions in respect to Chaplin and is well-charted by Timothy Lyons in *Chaplin: A Guide to References and Resources* (Boston: G. K. Hall & Co., 1979). Lyons points out that the two primary schools of Chaplin criticism derive from French and English traditions. The French tend to see moral, spiritual and esthetic meaning in Chaplin's work and treat his films as isolated phenomena. English and American critics, on the other hand, emphasize biographical and sociological contexts of the films.

Fortunately, there have been a number of excellent straight biographical studies. The basic work remains Theodore Huff's *Charlie Chaplin* (New York: Arno Press, 1972). This book, originally printed in 1951, has recently been joined by John McCabe's *Charlie Chaplin* (New York: Doubleday, 1978). McCabe, a meticulous researcher and skillful writer, contributes fascinating new data, including comments by Stan Laurel. Both McCabe and Huff blend biographical discussion with film de-

scription and commentary. There are a number of less ambitious volumes along the same lines, including Roger Manvell's *Chaplin* (Boston: Little, Brown, 1974), and *The Little Fellow* (New York: The Citadel Press, 1965) by Cotes and Niklaus. Denis Gifford's *Chaplin* (Garden City, N.Y.: Doubleday, 1974) is well-illustrated, and has the pleasant conceit of chapter headings drawn from the names of Chaplin's Keystone films, e.g., "His Prehistoric Past" for the chapter on Chaplin's prefilm life. Less effective are works by Edwin Hoyt (*Sir Charlie*, London, Robert Hale, 1977) and Robert Moss (*Charlie Chaplin*, New York: Pyramid, 1975).

A number of Chaplin's relatives wrote books about him, and of these the best is *My Father, Charlie Chaplin* (New York: Random House, 1960). Charles Chaplin, Jr. gives a warm and rounded picture of life with father, and is particularly effective at sketching Chaplin's life in the 1930's and 40's.

Of course, any survey of film in general, and comedy film in particular, will deal with Chaplin. In these shorter works the author's frame of reference is usually immediately apparent, from the idolatrous chapters on Chaplin in Gerald Mast's *The Comic Mind* (Indianapolis: Bobbs-Merrill, 1973) (considered in detail later) to the more "sober" attempt to strike a balance between positive and negative attributes in Donald McCaffrey's *Four Great Comedians* (New York: Barnes, 1968).

Many works have the advantage of being compelling just because of their illustrations from the films, including Isabel Quigley's *Charlie Chaplin: Early Comedies* (London: Studio Vista Limited, 1968). Some are simply scrapbooks, including Chaplin's own coffee-table volume, *My Life in Pictures* (London: Bodley Head, 1974). *The Films of Charlie Chaplin* (New York: Citadel, 1965) by McDonald, Conway and Ricci is notable in this regard. It offers excellent introductory chapters, pictures, plot synopses, and contemporary reviews of the films.

In his Introduction to *The Films of Charlie Chaplin* McDonald makes a point that many authors should have heeded. "To see a Chaplin comedy, then to try to tell what you have seen, is a difficult thing to do" (p. 16). This point is, unfortunately, borne out by the many inaccuracies of description in works about Chaplin. Two major works, considered later, Gerald Mast's *The Comic Mind* and Walter Kerr's *The Silent Clowns* (New York: Knopf, 1975) both contain a number of such errors. To give one example, both Kerr and Mast refer to the metal bolts pushed into Charlie's mouth by the feeding machine in *Modern Times.* Nuts, gentlemen, nuts. Perhaps this is nitpicking, but in ambitious studies such errors are annoying and misleading.

Although this book will not consider the vast body of periodical literature on Chaplin (Donald McCaffrey's *Focus on Chaplin* [Englewood Cliffs, N.J.: Prentice-Hall, 1971] offers a good selection), it will examine five critical works which have been widely read. Two, Robert Payne's *The Great God Pan* (New York: Hermitage House, 1952) and Parker Tyler's *Chaplin: Last of the Clowns* (New York: Vanguard, 147), are in the French tradition; Gerald Mast and Walter Kerr steer a middle course between French and British traditions; and Sobel and Francis' *Chaplin: Genesis of a Clown* (London: Quartet Books Ltd., 1977) offers a neo-Marxist approach. Finally, it will include some comments about Chaplin on Chaplin.

While this author obviously believes the approach of this book to be a valid way of discussing Chaplin's films, he has a healthy respect for the unique problems of writing about Chaplin. Having derived enjoyment as well as insight from the work of others, this author hopes his comments will stimulate others to delve further into both the films themselves and the literature on those films.

The Silent Clowns
by Walter Kerr

The Silent Clowns is impressive before one even begins reading it. The book is not only beautifully designed and illustrated, but it is written by a famous critic as well. Further, Kerr writes in a graceful, forceful style which makes his ideas persuasive. Almost a third of the book is devoted to Chaplin.

New studies on Chaplin are citing Kerr's work as an authoritative interpretation. John McCabe, in his recent Chaplin biography, says the book "must be read to appreciate Chaplin's art fully" (p. 76 fn.).

Kerr builds his vision of Chaplin on what are, to this author, unjustifiable assumptions. For Kerr, the combination of Chaplin's glances at camera, his ease in imposture, and his outsider status add up to a character who is "no one," who in fact wants to be one of the audience. He suffers from "the hopeless limitation of having no limitations." While this is a nicely turned phrase, and Kerr's interpretation is seductively neat, it ignores both realistic and unrealistic aspects of Charlie the character. As a "real" character Charlie, quite apart from his skillful masquerades, has a consistent and evolving value system. He *feels* real, albeit idiosyncratic. On the other hand, Chaplin's presentation of Charlie has so many highly stylized elements that he seems to some degree unreal or schematic. The care with which Chaplin creates Charlie's physical and social environment demonstrates his awareness not only of the difficulty of logically justifying love interest in the films, as he states in his autobiography, but of maintaining his own consistency and realness as a character. This is an esthetic problem Chaplin wrestles with, not necessarily an attempt to communicate a philosophy of instability.

Further, Chaplin shares his audience addresses and self-consciousness with a majority of filmic clowns, as is well-documented by Steve Seidman in *Comedian Comedy: A Tradition in Hollywood Film* (Ann Arbor, Michigan: UMI Research Press, 1979). This work effectively demonstrates that most clown comedians hearken back, as did Chaplin, to live performance traditions of style which acknowledge the audience and playfully "contradict" the filmic reality.

At any rate, Charlie is a character whose adventures move the audience because his films touch on emotions the audience shares with him, not because they are aware of such philosophical subtleties as Kerr posits—any more than they enjoy the films because they, like Robert Payne, see Chaplin as Pan reincarnate. Both positions are thoughtful and stimulating, but can hardly be considered the last word.

Kerr goes further, concluding that Chaplin's detachment "taught him to dance." This is at best an arguable version of the genesis of this aspect of the films. The book is filled with such premises and conclusions. Kerr states, for example, that the audiences of Chaplin's Keystone films sensed "a promise of things to come." Maybe, but such an opinion cuts short examination of what the 1914 audience did see that so rocketed Chaplin to stardom.

After effective discussion of Chaplin's integration

of serious and comic material, Kerr largely ignores his basic premises to discuss *The Gold Rush,* seeing Chaplin as "a whole man, this one time." Overall, however, the discussion is sound. Not so with his chapter on *The Circus.* Even the title of that chapter is confusing: "The Transition, After and Just Before: A Self-conscious Chaplin." Here Kerr's desire to cut to the philosophic heart may have hindered perception. The premise of *The Circus,* he states, is that "comedy is created by accident, not intention." This is hardly the premise of this film. *The Circus* is about Charlie's relationship to the circus people and their audience, and Chaplin runs into serious problems with both—he was not yet ready to fully articulate his internal conflicts about being a performer. But Kerr writes as though he had never seen the film with an audience, searching for complexities which are simply not there. For example, Kerr believes Chaplin gives himself an insoluble problem when he has Charlie unsuccessfully audition for the circus owner—how can he be funny and not funny at the same time? And further, how can he fail as a clown when he is so good at everything else? But does Kerr not remember all the things Charlie spectacularly fails at, which are juxtaposed with his comically inappropriate skills? And there is no contradiction about being unfunny to the characters within the film while being hilarious to the film audience. Perhaps significantly, Kerr also had little sympathy for *Limelight.* In his well-known essay "The Lineage of Limelight," he thoroughly panned the film at the time of its first release.

More perceptive are Kerr's discussions of *City Lights* and *Modern Times.* In dealing with the central themes of appearance vs. reality and rootlessness as exemplified by these films, he effectively presents his vision of the power and poignance of Chaplin's art.

The Comic Mind
by Gerald Mast

Gerald Mast begins *The Comic Mind,* a book now widely used in college film classes, by deploring the refusal of literary critics to deal with comedy films. He reveals his own desire for such respectibility by writing the bulk of his book from a literary standpoint.

Such an approach has both advantages and disadvantages in Mast's chapters on Chaplin, to whom he devotes the largest section of his book. He begins with the ultimate literary parallel. Chaplin, he states, "is to movies what Shakespeare is to the drama." Then, in the manner of literary critics, he proceeds to detail the objections other critics have to Chaplin's work, and to rebut those objections. He makes a fairly good defense of Chaplin as scenarist and technical filmmaker.

As Mast goes on to summarize Chaplin's film career, his chief strength is his ability to isolate themes. These include major motifs such as Chaplin's transformation gags, definition of love as sacrifice, and moral dimension of the character as Chaplin's tool for social comment. Mast also considers minor motifs such as Charlie's identification with flowers and his tendency to experience "human happiness" (Mast overuses the word "human") vicariously. Particularly persuasive is the way Mast relates his thematic discussions to the films' endings. Significantly, dance is not treated as a motif by Mast.

To analyze structure, Mast borrows major plot classifications from literature and drama and applies these to the films, which is informative, although he uses the term "structure" rather loosely. But the literary approach leads Mast to misjudgements and nonjudgements of individual films. Isolating plot and theme, which are only parts of the films, he loses sight of the tree for the forest, to reverse the cliché. Mast's "evaluations" often become little more than summary because he is delineating only what applies to his own study. For example, he gives no clue that *The Circus* is a weaker film than *The Gold Rush* or *City Lights.* His most serious misjudgement is his eulogization of *Sunnyside,* which this author accepted until he actually saw the film. Not surprisingly, Mast's only negative criticisms deal with literary flaws (the talky endings of *The Great Dictator* and *Monsieur Verdoux*), not comic flaws.

Overall, though, as with Kerr, Mast's own emotional involvement leads him to effective celebration of the films (this is characteristic of most interpretive works on Chaplin). His discussion of *Limelight* (which, continuing his comparison of Chaplin to Shakespeare, he likens to *The Tempest*), takes on some of the moving quality of the film itself.

The Great God Pan
by Robert Payne

Almost everyone who writes about Chaplin tries to find keys to share the beauty of his art, perhaps a hopeless task. Most settle for conventional biographical or critical approaches.

In this unusual book Robert Payne conveys a strong sense of the excitement and significance of Chaplin's films by bringing them into historical, mythical and literary contexts. After discussing Pan, tribal clowns, marionettes, and English and French comic traditions, he evaluates the films according to his unique point of view: that Chaplin is Pan reincarnate. This leads him to certain arguable opinions, such as that Charlie's performing heroic acts while "hopped up" on drugs in *Easy Street* and *Modern Times* is "out of character."

Yet, Payne's study is hardly less objective than others cited, for once one departs from straight biography or plot description, the field is wide open.

This is one of this author's favorite works on Chaplin. It provides fascinating historical data at the same time as it presents a most personal view of the films. Many consider that it goes too far in its comparisons of Charlie with Pan and Sir Galahad, and Chaplin with Dickens and other literary lights, but Payne writes with impressive sincerity and authority.

Payne also had the good fortune to have known and spoken with Chaplin in the early 1950's, and includes fascinating descriptive and interview material.

Chaplin: Last of the Clowns
by Parker Tyler

If Robert Payne's book is rhapsodic, Parker Tyler's is a meditation. Some of the author's premises are based on dubious biographical sources, primarily Gerith von Ulm's *Charlie Chaplin, King of Tragedy* (Caldwell, Idaho: Caxton Printers Ltd., 1940), which was based largely on interviews with a disenchanted Chaplin employee. However, this does not deter Tyler, who blithely states:

> I hardly pause here—as hardly elsewhere—to consider if this incident be a "true" one. It is enough that it is consistent both with a profound and my conception of Chaplin."[1]

"My" (Tyler's) conception is a peculiar hodgepodge of Freudian symbol analysis applied simultaneously to both artist and film character. Tyler follows tortuous paths of reasoning to reach such conclusions as:

- Charlie's shoes are symbols of his father;
- Chaplin considered his early professionalism responsible for his short stature;
- A single revolution of the cane is "cosmic";

- Charlie's falls symbolize "falling" for the fatal woman, indeed suggest the fall of Lucifer.

In an expanded version of the book written in 1972 Tyler coyly implies that Chaplin read and agrees with his premises—then goes on to attack Chaplin for not "owning up" in his autobiography. Although Tyler reveals a more sober view in the updated section, and his analysis of Chaplin's later films is sounder, the book as a whole is disappointing, or worse. Though hardly less "far out" than Payne's book, the author's mystical-manifesto tone is, for this reader, offensive. It should also be noted that the book says nothing about the interesting premise to its title. The reader is given no clues as to why Chaplin is the "last of the clowns."

Chaplin: Genesis of a Clown
by Raoul Sobel & David Francis

This fascinating little volume traces Chaplin's historical antecedents and influences. There is much interesting data on the Victorian milieu from which Chaplin sprung, as well as detailed examinations of Italian *commedia dell'arte*, music hall and burlesque theatre as they relate to Chaplin. The authors are able to convincingly establish Chaplin's "borrowings" from his theatrical past, and particularly from the Karno troupe.

Sobel and Francis refer to Robert Payne's book, which similarly discusses Chaplin's antecedents, as "elaborately effusive." This attitude becomes understandable given that their own book maintains a most acid tone throughout when discussing Chaplin, this despite the fact that Sobel is described as having been "obsessed since his childhood" with the comedian. As both man and artist, Chaplin is portrayed in the most unsympathetic light possible. For example, the authors assert that the film character "inherited" some of Chaplin's personality problems. Unfortunately, this makes their often valid arguments seem like attempts to discredit Chaplin.

The final chapter of the book, however, is excellent. After reiterating the influences of Karno, Max Linder, and Sennett on Chaplin, and tracing his typical gag subjects, the authors go on to a brilliant, if brief, discussion of transformation gags as Chaplin's unique contribution to silent film comedy. Their position is that Chaplin's fluid world as created by transformation gags was, in effect, his given—his technical equipment—and that this informed the film character and made him elusive, not vice versa, as Kerr maintains.

Chaplin on Chaplin

Chaplin's tendency to misrepresent and even lie in print has seemed alternately puzzling, frustrating and annoying to those who want the details of his life and art from the prime source. Many theories have been put forward to explain this, and this author will add his own.

Chaplin was drawn to writing about himself for three reasons: first, because he knew he could make money doing so (*My Trip Abroad* was commissioned by a magazine and earned him $25,000.00—more than paying for that 1921 journey). Second, it must have been irresistible to have the last word about himself, given the proliferation of Chaplin "experts," many of them from the ranks of his friends, employees and acquaintances, whose interviews, articles and books guaranteed them their own moments in the public eye.

Finally, the self-educated, culturally insecure Chaplin must have found it very satisfying to be an author—never mind that many articles were ghost-written by his own staff. Contrasting views of Chaplin the writer were given by Jim Tully, a member of that staff in the 1920's, who described Chaplin's unsuccessful struggle to articulate the written word; and Charles, Jr., whose description of Chaplin at home in the 1930's makes it clear that he wrote voluminously to develop his film stories.

This author believes that Chaplin bowed to economic and egotistic pressure to write, but that something deep within this fundamentally shy man recoiled at the "exposure" of himself in words. Given the vast fascination with personal revelation about Chaplin, his desire to set the record straight may have been modified by his feeling that it really was none of the public's business. The torture Chaplin went through during his periods of public immolation is amply documented (though not by him). What resulted was Chaplin's deciding that he didn't *owe* the public the truth. His autobiographical fictions and evasions can be seen as an avoidance of unpleasant facts about himself, but they can also be read as a hostile playfulness, much as Charlie exhibits towards his foes in the early films.

For Chaplin fans, of course, his writings, and most particularly his 1964 *My Autobiography*, will continue to compel interest and comment. Although it is usually deplored for its fictions, the lack of data about Chaplin as filmmaker, and the lack of self-exploration or insight, there exists a thread in this book that relates it strongly to the films in that the reader (viewer) is always made clearly aware of Chaplin's feelings and reactions to events. That there are many feelings and events he does not explore is a matter for regret, but does not negate the rest.

Note

[1]Tyler, Parker, *Chaplin: Last of the Clowns* (New York: Vanguard Press, Inc., 1947), p. 58.

Index

Boldface page references indicate illustrations

About the Author

A childhood interest in sleight-of-hand magic began Dan Kamin on the path to becoming a professional mime artist. Along the way he found strong inspiration in the work of Charlie Chaplin.

Since 1970 Kamin has toured his one-man shows throughout the world, contributing to the growth in popularity of this latest manifestation of man's oldest art form. Kamin has created four specials on mime for PBS, and been honored in his home state of Pennsylvania with invitations to perform for the inauguration of Governor Richard Thornburgh, for the state's Art Council and Theatre Association.

Dan Kamin with Virginia Cherrill, Santa Barbara 1978.